Beyond Diversity

Beyond Diversity

Queer Politics, Activism, and Representation in
Contemporary Japan

Edited by
Kazuyoshi Kawasaka and Stefan Würrer

d|u|p
düsseldorf university press

ISBN 978-3-11-076582-3
e-ISBN (PDF) 978-3-11-076799-5
e-ISBN (EPUB) 978-3-11-076803-9
DOI https://doi.org/10.1515/9783110767995

Library of Congress Control Number: 2023946624

Bibliographic information published by the Deutsche Nationalbibliothek
The Deutsche Nationalbibliothek lists this publication in the Deutsche Nationalbibliografie;
detailed bibliographic data are available on the Internet at http://dnb.dnb.de.

© 2024 with the authors, editing © 2024 Kazuyoshi Kawasaka and Stefan Würrer, published by
Walter de Gruyter GmbH, Berlin/Boston.
The book is published with open access at www.degruyter.com.
d|u|p düsseldorf university press is an imprint of Walter de Gruyter GmbH.

Cover image: lokomotif / DigitalVision Vectors / Getty Images
Printing and binding: CPI books GmbH, Leck

dup.degruyter.com

Acknowledgments

This book would not have been published without the emotional, intellectual, and financial support of so many people, especially during the COVID-19 pandemic, which was a trying time for all involved in this project. A big thank you goes out to our contributors. Despite heavy teaching loads and numerous other academic duties, you managed to meet the deadlines, always responded carefully to our requests for revisions, and provided us with invaluable insights.

We are extremely grateful to Andrea Germer and her team at the Institute for Modern Japan at Düsseldorf University and Vera Mackie of the University of Wollongong for providing us with the academic resources to develop and finish this project. We would also like to thank Shimizu Akiko and the Komaba Safer Space at Tokyo University, as well as Tanaka Kazuko, Ikoma Natsumi, and the Center for Gender Studies at International Christian University for years of personal and intellectual support, and for teaching us how to fight the heterosexist norms within and outside of academia.

We would like to express our appreciation to our copyeditor Sara Kitaoji whose intricate knowledge of the English and Japanese languages and constructive criticism ensured that each of our contributors found the right words to express their thoughts. We also owe our deepest gratitude to Anne Sokoll and Jessica Bartz from De Gruyter for believing in this project and patiently guiding us through the publication process.

This project was supported by the German Research Foundation (DFG) as part of the individual research project Sexual Diversity and Human Rights in 21st Century Japan: LGBTIQ Activisms and Resistance from a Transnational Perspective (Project no. 446477950). We are also thankful to Heinrich Heine University Düsseldorf's Open Access Fund, which has enabled us to publish this volume with open access and make it available to a wider readership.

Finally, we would like to express our gratitude toward our partners, friends, and families. Each in their own way provided support, critical feedback, and safe spaces to rest. It is thanks to you that this book is now out in the wider world.

Notes on translation and transliteration

We present all names following the standard romanization rules in each language: the modified Hepburn system for Japanese names; Hanyu Pinyin for mainland Chinese names; and Gwoyeu Romatzyh (or other preferred spellings) for Taiwanese names.

All Chinese and Japanese names are presented in traditional order – family name first, followed by the given name – with the exception of scholars publishing in English.

Terms from languages other than English are presented in italics if they are not listed in English-language dictionaries or not widely known in English.

Table of Contents

List of Abbreviations

API	application programming interface
BL	boys' love
CCP	Chinese Communist Party
CEDAW	Committee on the Elimination of Discrimination against Women
CESCR	Committee on Economic, Social and Cultural Rights
CRC	Committee on the Rights of the Child
CRPD	Committee on the Rights of Persons with Disabilities
DPP	Democratic Progressive Party
DRRM	disaster risk reduction and management
EMA Japan	Equal Marriage Alliance Japan
GID	gender identity disorder
GRA	Gender Recognition Act
HRC	Human Rights Council
ICCPR	International Covenant on Civil and Political Rights
ILGA	International Lesbian and Gay Association
IOC	International Olympic Committee
JCP	Japanese Communist Party
JOC	Japanese Olympic Committee
LDP	Liberal Democratic Party
LGBT	lesbian, gay, bisexual, trans
LGBTQ	lesbian, gay, bisexual, trans, queer or questioning
LGBTQ+	lesbian, gay, bisexual, trans, queer/questioning, plus (others)
NHRI	National Human Rights Institutions
NHK	Nippon Hōsō Kyōkai (Japan Broadcasting Corporation; Japan)
NLP	natural language processing
PACS	*pacte civil de solidarité* (civil solidarity pact; France)
SAR	special administrative regions
SOGI	sexual orientation and gender identity
TERF	trans-exclusionary radical feminists
TOC	Tokyo Organising Committee
TPP	Tokyo Pride Parade
TRP	Tokyo Rainbow Pride
UN	United Nations
UPR	Universal Periodic Review
VOD	video-on-demand
WHO	World Health Organization

Kazuyoshi Kawasaka and Stefan Würrer

Introduction: A new age of visibility? LGBTQ+ issues in contemporary Japan

The 2010s was an epoch-making decade for LGBTQ+ people in Japan. The cultural and political representation of sexual minorities became mainstream in many areas of Japanese society in ways that were reminiscent of, but considerably different from, earlier periods. While LGBTQ+ issues in Japan have received scholarly attention since the 1990s[1], there is little scholarship in English that focuses on developments after 2000, let alone the 2010s. With this volume, we aim to bridge this gap by shedding light on political and cultural representations of and by sexual minorities in Japan from the 2010s, making available in English novel perspectives on LGBTQ+ issues in Japan. In the following sections, we outline the major sociopolitical developments in the Japanese LGBTQ+ context during the decades leading up to the 2010s, to provide the necessary context for a more nuanced understanding of the issues discussed in the papers included in this volume.

Early activism: Challenging the heterosexist status quo

Japan never criminalized sexual activities between same-sex partners, nor did it outlaw cross-dressing, except for a short period between 1872 and 1880. In addition, Japanese law provides the option of adult adoption, a system sometimes used by same-sex couples to circumvent property, inheritance, and other family-related issues such as hospital visitation rights or legal guardianship of one's partner. Since the authorities do not prosecute sexual minorities and adult adoption of one's same-sex partner is possible, Japan might be considered "tolerant" toward LGBTQ+ people. But tolerance implies prejudice. Moreover, modern Japanese society has been shaped by male-centered, heterosexist, and cis-genderist norms based on the ideal of the heterosexual family and tends to stigmatize non-normative expressions of gender, sexuality, and kinship (Lunsing, 2001). The social acceptance of sexual minorities is also often unfairly distributed by gender, as well as by class, race, ethnicity, and nation-

---

1 Baudinette, 2021; Chalmers, 2002; Frühstück, 2022; Lunsing, 2001; Mackintosh, 2010; Maree, 2020; Martin et al., 2008; McLelland, 2000, 2005; McLelland et al., 2007, 2015; McLelland & Dasgupta, 2005; McLelland & Mackie, 2015; Pflugfelder, 1999; Reichert, 2006; Roberson & Suzuki, 2003; Suganuma, 2012; Summerhawk et al., 1998; Vincent, 2012; Welker 2019, 2022.

ality (Khor, 2010). For this reason, LGBTQ+ activism developed in response to "common sense" (*jōshiki*) and social stigmatization, rather than legal issues.

Tōgō Ken (1932–2012) was one of the earliest openly gay activists to publicly tackle Japan's heteronormative status quo. He ran for office in numerous national elections since 1971 as "Tōgō Ken, the faggot (*okama*)," not so much in order to establish himself as a serious political candidate and to improve the social position of gay people through legal and social reforms, but rather to provoke society (McLelland, 2012; see also Oikawa, 2007). During electoral campaigns, wearing a kimono and light makeup instead of the more conventional suit and tie, he spoke uninhibitedly about the need for sexual liberation in Japan (Tōgō, 1979). In addition to proposing the abolishment of the emperor system, he sexualized the emperor to strip him of his authority and remind the public that the emperor is but another human being with sexual desires. This intentional conflation of the "public" realm of politics and the "private" sphere of sexuality can be most clearly seen in a satirical cartoon that Tōgō published in the monthly magazine *Shinzasshi X* in August 1984, which showed the emperor being penetrated by Douglas MacArthur, the commander of the Allied Occupation between 1945 and 1951. Its publication led to an attack on Tōgō by a far-right activist (Oikawa, 2007).

Early lesbian activism took a different path. It centered around community-building and a critical engagement with Japanese feminism. While the *ūman ribu* (women's liberation) movement of Japan in the late 1960s to mid-1970s addressed issues of sexual liberation and women's social independence, lesbian women and voices tended to be excluded (Chalmers, 2002, p. 34; Iino, 2008, pp. 67–81; Welker, 2018, pp. 50–55). Wakakusa no Kai (Young Grass Club, 1971–1985) was the first organization that provided a space for lesbian women to meet and share their experiences. Between 1975 and 1976, the initiative Subarashī Onnatachi (Wonderful Women) shed light on the situation of lesbian women within the women's liberation movement through surveys and roundtables (Welker, 2018, p. 56). Some of the women involved in this initiative went on to form the lesbian feminist groups Mainichi Daiku (Everyday Carpenter/Dyke) and Hikari Guruma (Shining Wheel) in the late 1970s and early 1980s (Iino, 2008, pp. 81–88), which positioned themselves within the broader struggle for women's liberation and its fight against the patriarchal gender norms of Japanese society, while addressing the homophobia both in and outside the *ūman ribu* movement.

The 1980s and 1990s: The AIDS crisis, the gay boom, and new queer approaches

During the AIDS epidemic of the 1980s, homophobia and more generally the stigmatization of non-normative forms of sexuality became an issue on a national scale. While the AIDS epidemic in Japan was initially caused by the government's lack of safety measures concerning unsterilized blood products from the US, which mainly affected patients with hemophilia, it did fuel homophobic sentiments. Gay men were singled out by the Ministry of Health and Welfare – despite its own responsibility in disseminating contaminated blood products – as one of the fundamental sources of HIV infection, based on their sexual orientation, that is, as an identity group, rather than their sexual behavior (Kazama & Kawaguchi, 2003, p. 181). In addition, sexually transmitted HIV infections were represented as the result of a questionable lifestyle and juxtaposed with the innocent victims of tainted blood products, leading to intensified discrimination against, and social exclusion of, gay men and female sex workers in particular (Itō, 2006, p. 127).

As Mark McLelland and Katsuhiko Suganuma (2009) noted, "it was this social milieu that prompted many gay activists … to challenge such negative stereotypes through public campaigns that drew upon previous successful strategies developed by gay activists during the AIDS panic in Western countries" (p. 337; see also Kazama, 2009; Kazama & Kawaguchi, 2003; Shingae, 2013; Treat, 1999). One prominent example of this new wave of activism was the AIDS-related symposia and art performances of the artist collective Dumb Type (founded in 1984), one of whose core members, Furuhashi Teiji (1960–1995), came out as HIV-positive in 1992 (Pendleton, 2021).

Further, in 1984, Minami Teishirō founded the Japan chapter of the International Lesbian and Gay Association (ILGA), which organized the first Tokyo Lesbian and Gay Parade in 1994. This was followed by the foundation of Ugoku Gei to Rezubian no Kai (Organization for Moving Gay and Lesbians), also known as Akā (OCCUR), in 1986, which between 1991 and 1997 successfully fought the Tokyo Metropolitan Board of Education in court for discriminating against their gay members at the Fuchu Youth Hostel (Fuchū Seinen no Ie), a publicly run conference and recreation facility, in one of the first trials in Japanese legal history to recognize discrimination based on sexual orientation (Kazama & Kawaguchi, 2010; Lunsing, 2001; see also Hiroyuki Taniguchi's paper in this volume).

Public visibility of sexual minorities also increased in the realm of popular culture in the early 1990s, when movies, television, and print media started to show an interest in gay culture, mostly featuring a variety of discussions and portrayals of gay men and their lifestyle during what was later termed the "gay boom"

(McLelland, 2000; Ogawa 2017). Prominent examples include movies portraying gay men and their relationships with heterosexual women, such as *Okoge* (*Fag Hag*, 1992), the movie adaptation of Ekuni Kaori's 1991 gay novel *Kira kira hikaru* (*Twinkle*, 1992), and the drama series *Dōsokai* (*Class Reunion*, 1993), as well as the movie adaptation of Matsu'ura Rieko's 1987 lesbian-themed novel *Nachuraru ūman* (*Natural Women*, 1994). During this period, an explosion of new commercial gay magazines catapulted the boys' love (BL) genre into the mainstream (Welker, 2015). In addition, a new generation of gay magazines such as *Badī* (*Buddy*, 1993–2019) and *G-men* (1995–2016), offered new avenues for gay community-building and self-representation.

Mainstream publications also began to feature articles by and about lesbian women (Maree, 2007, pp. 293–294), which challenged the androcentric and heteronormative – that is, often sexualized and pathologizing – representations of same-sex desire and relationships between women up to the 1980s (Sugiura, 2007, pp. 129–133; Welker, 2017, pp. 149–156). In 1987, the special magazine feature *Onna o aisuru onnatachi no monogatari* (*Stories of Women Who Love Women*), the first commercial publication by and about lesbian women, was produced. Many of its articles were written by Sawabe Hitomi, who was one of the organizers of the above-mentioned early lesbian groups, as well as Regumi Sutajio (Regumi Studio) in the late 1980s (Welker, 2018, pp. 59, 66; see also Iino, 2008; Sugiura, 2011). Subsequently, commercial lesbian periodicals such as *Furīne* (*Phryné*, 1995) and *Anīsu* (*Anise*, 1996–1997, 2001–2003) further diversified the representations of same-sex desire between women and provided the lesbian community with additional platforms for discussion and exchange.

This reflected a new phase of visibility in lesbian and gay activism, embodied by the lesbian activist and writer Kakefuda Hiroko and gay writer Fushimi Noriaki, who both came out during the 1990s (Maree, 2007; Welker, 2018). Kakefuda's book *"Rezubian" de aru to iu koto* (*On Being "Lesbian,"* 1992) sparked debates on the issue of heteronormativity both in Japanese feminism and Japanese society at large, as well as on the difficulty of representing oneself as lesbian in these environments, while Fushimi advocated for a radical critique of heterosexism – albeit from an explicitly gay male point of view – in books such as *Puraibēto gei raifu* (*Private Gay Life*, 1991) (McLelland & Suganuma, 2009; Suganuma, 2006).

Discussions of LGBTQ+-related matters also took place in special issues of highbrow magazines such as *Imago* (February 1991, August 1991, November 1995, May 1996) and *Gendai shisō* (May 1997). These included several translations of Anglophone queer theory, such as essays by Gayle Rubin, Eve K. Sedgwick, and Leo Bersani, which provided new theoretical frameworks for feminist and LGBTQ+ writers, scholars, and activists to address and critically engage with the intersections between patriarchy and heteronormativity. Similar to the volume *Kuia studaīzu*

'97 (Kuia Sutadīzu Henshū Iinkai, 1997), these magazines brought together issues of gender and sexuality, and facilitated transnational dialogues between feminist, gay, and queer activism/studies such as in Keith Vincent, Kazama Takashi, and Kawaguchi Kazuya's (1997) *Gei sutadīzu* (*Gay Studies*), or the queer-feminist writing of Takemura Kazuko (1996a, 1996b, 1996c, 1996d, 1996e, 1996 f, 1997), who also translated some of Judith Butler's works into Japanese.

The 2000s: A new era of political visibility for trans people and the "gender-free" backlash

Overlapping with these developments, the early 2000s saw a new era for trans people. In 2003, three years after trans novelist Fujino Chiya won Japan's most prestigious literary award, the Akutagawa Prize, Kamikawa Aya became the first trans politician to be elected to public office, when she won a seat in the election of the Tokyo Municipal Council. The same year, the Law for the Handling of Gender in the Special Cases of People with Gender Identity Disorder (Seidōitsusei Shōgaisha no Seibetsu no Atsukai no Tokurei ni Kansuru Hō) was passed. The legalization of gender-affirming surgery in 1997 had highlighted trans people's need to change their legal gender, which this law made possible for those who underwent surgery. The law's pathologizing language and restrictive requirements, however, have been criticized as violating trans people's human rights (Norton, 2013; Yamada, 2022; see also Stefan Würrer's paper in this volume).

In 2005, Osaka Prefectural Assembly member Otsuji Kanako came out as lesbian in her autobiography *Kamingu auto: Jibun rashisa o mitsukeru tabi* (*Coming Out: A Journey of Self-Discovery*) and ran for a seat in the National Diet in 2007. Though not elected in 2007, she made it into the Diet as the result of a special election in 2013 to fill the vacant seat of a fellow Democratic Party member. This made her the first openly lesbian Diet member in Japanese history, following into the footsteps of such local politicians as Kamikawa, as well as the openly gay Ishikawa Taiga and Ishizaka Wataru, who were elected to the Toshima Ward and Nakano Ward Assemblies, respectively, in 2011.

The late 1990s and early 2000s, however, also saw a social conservative and nationalist backlash, which targeted, among others, feminist initiatives and sexual minorities. It revolved around the term "gender free," which was, as Yamaguchi Tomomi (2014) noted, "originally coined for educators in 1995 and [was] intended to help break down traditional understandings of gender roles" (p. 548). This anti-gender movement was spearheaded by nationalist politicians such as Abe Shinzō with the support of religious groups – primarily Jinja Honchō (Association of Shinto Shrines) and Sekai Heiwa Tōitsu Katei Rengō (Family Federation for World Peace and Unification; widely known as "Tōitsu Kyōkai," or the Unification Church) – and spread through well-organized right-wing grassroots movements that attacked local municipal efforts to introduce new sex-education curriculums and gender equality ordinances (Poritasu TV et al., 2023; Yamaguchi, 2018; Yamaguchi et al., 2012). At the height of the backlash in the early 2000s – which was in part a reaction to the Basic Law for a Gender Equal Society (Danjo Kyōdō Sankaku Shakai Kihon Hō, 1999) and public debates on the sexual enslavement of women by the Imperial Japanese military forces leading up to and during the Pacific War – the social conservatives at the center of the backlash demonized "gender-free" education as erasing biological differences between the sexes and turning underage girls and boys into homosexuals or genderless beings (*chūsei ningen*) (Kazama, 2007, p. 26; Yamada, 2022, p. 502). Responses to this backlash by mainstream feminists largely failed to address the homophobia and transphobia within the conservatives' arguments, revealing not only the difficulty faced by Japanese feminism in addressing issues of gender and sexuality beyond heterosexist and cisgenderist norms, but also a more general indifference in society toward the protection of gender and sexual minorities from discrimination (Kazama, 2007, pp. 28–31; Shimizu, 2007, p. 504; Yamada, 2022, p. 503; Yamaguchi, 2014, p. 570; see also Kawasaka, 2023).

The 2010s and beyond: The emergence of the "LGBT market" and the diversification of political and cultural LGBTQ+ representations

After 2010, the situation for LGBTQ+ people changed in at least three ways. First, LGBTQ+ people increasingly began to be seen as a market by mainstream Japanese businesses. As Kazuyoshi Kawasaka points out in his paper in this volume, in 2012, the weekly business magazines *Shūkan Tōyō keizai* (*Weekly Toyo Keizai*) and *Shūkan daiamondo* (*Diamond Weekly*) featured analyses of the domestic "LGBT market," which the latter estimated to be worth around 5.7 trillion yen (Shūkan Daiamondo Henshūbu, 2013). Further surveys, such as by advertising and public relations company Dentsu's Diversity Lab in 2015, reiterated the market potential of LGBTQ+ people (Dentsū, 2015).

Against the backdrop of this heightened financial interest, Japanese mainstream businesses began to regard LGBTQ+ rights protection as an essential issue of their corporate policies and self-marketing. Since 2011, the organization Work With Pride has evaluated LGBTQ+-related corporate policies and consulted on LGBTQ+ inclusion in the workplace. In 2022, more than 400 companies participated in their evaluation (Pride Shihyō Jimukyoku, 2022). These companies seem to have followed the lead of the highly influential Nihon Keizai Dantai Rengō (Japan Business Federation), which in 2017 recommended to its member companies to develop work environments that support, protect, and encourage understanding of LGBTQ+ people in order to attract diverse human resources and improve their productivity and brand value in a global market.

Mainstream businesses also became a new source of financial support for LGBTQ+ activism, which historically has tended to rely on gay businesses such as bars and clubs (Ogiue, 2012). This allowed LGBTQ+ organizations such as Tokyo Rainbow Pride to organize pride parades and other events on a bigger scale, and to create new LGBTQ+-friendly spaces such as Pride House Tokyo Legacy in central Tokyo. However, while this new support has arguably strengthened the sustainability of LGBTQ+ organizations, the marketization of LGBTQ+ inclusion and activism has been criticized for reducing the issue of human rights protection to that of profitability (Kawasaka, 2015; Shimizu 2013, 2015).

Second, LGBTQ+ activism and the political recognition of LGBTQ+ people have expanded beyond metropolises such as Tokyo and Osaka. Pride events and LGBTQ+ film festivals are now held throughout the five main islands of Japan, rooted in and centered around local communities (Kanno, 2019; Sugiura & Maekawa, 2022). As Kawasaka argues in his paper, this spread of activism was enabled through collaborations of LGBTQ+ organizations with local municipalities and regional business communities which, in their need for rebranding and opening up new sources of capital, followed the lead of the Japan Business Federation and national businesses (see also Kawasaka, 2015).

Another facet of this shift toward inclusivity in local politics is the introduction of ordinances that allow officials to issue partnership certificates to same-sex couples, beginning with the Tokyo wards of Shibuya and Setagaya in 2015, which were followed by over 300 municipalities throughout Japan in the following years. As the papers of Kawasaka, Taniguchi, and Kamano and Khor in this volume argue, these partnership certificates differ greatly from marriage licenses, as they offer only limited, if any, legal benefits or protection. However, while being a mostly symbolic gesture of recognition, they seem to have helped to shed light on the existence of same-sex couples and the need for legal equality. Recent opinion polls suggest that around 60%–70% of Japanese respondents now support same-sex marriage ("Dōseikon ni sansei," 2023; *Kyōdo tsūshin no yoronchōsa*, 2023; Marriage for All Japan, 2020).

Third, the objective of LGBTQ+ activism shifted from a fight with the heterosexist, cisgender norms of Japanese society, toward also advocating for legal change, especially the institutionalization of same-sex marriage and anti-discrimination laws. Same-sex marriage activists are not only lobbying lawmakers in the Diet (LGBT Hōren Gōkai, 2015), but since 2019 have also brought cases around the unconstitutionality of the lack of legal recognition of same-sex marriage to courts in cities such as Sapporo, Tokyo, Nagoya, Osaka, and Fukuoka (*Dōseikon mitomenai*, 2023). As Hiroyuki Taniguchi notes in his paper, while legal scholars have discussed LGBTQ+ rights within the context of the Japanese Constitution since at least the 2000s, these cases brought the discussion to the courts and are important precedents for advancing the human rights protection of LGBTQ+ people in Japan.

LGBTQ+ people and issues also gained more visibility in popular culture again, as exemplified by the television and movie franchise *Ossanzu rabu* (*Ossan's Love*; 2016, 2018), or the television adaptations of the BL manga series *Kinō nani tabeta?* (*What Did You Eat Yesterday*, 2007–present) in 2019 and the lesbian web manga series *Tsukuritai onna to tabetai onna* (*She Loves to Cook, and She Loves to Eat*, 2021) in 2022. However, as Kubo Yutaka writes in his contribution to this volume, while LGBTQ+-related movies and television during the 2010s do offer a wider variety of representations of non-normative sexual orientations and gender expressions, the focus still tends to be on gay men.

Moreover, with the debut of lesbian Taiwanese fiction writer Li Kotomi (the pen name of Lǐ Qínfēng) in 2017, Japanese literature and, more generally, the Japanese public, gained a new outspoken voice for sexual minority rights. Li won the Akutagawa Prize in 2021 and several of her works, including her debut novel *Hitorimai* (*Solo Dance*), were featured in cosmetics company Aēsop Japan's (2022) "Queer Library" project, a selection of around 60 LGBTQ+-themed Japanese novels, which were offered as gifts to visitors of their Shinjuku store, regardless of purchase. Curated by Yasuda Aoi, who organizes Tokyo-based queer reading circle Dokusho Saron (Literature Salon), the selection included other contemporary novels by Matsu'ura Rieko, Nakayama Kaho, Fujino Chiya, and Miyagi Futoshi, alongside older works of queer fiction such as Mori Ōgai's *Vita sekushuarisu* (*Vita Sexualis*, 1909), Tanizaki Jun'ichirō's *Manji* (*Quicksand*, 1928), Kawabata Yasunari's *Shōnen* (*The Boy*, 1948), Mishima Yukio's *Kamen no kokuhaku* (*Confessions of a Mask*, 1949), and Mori Mari's *Koibito tachi no mori* (*The Lovers' Forest*, 1961). While being another example of the increasing entanglement of corporate interests with LGBTQ+ activism, this selection can also be considered a mainstream attempt at delineating, and making visible, a canon of queer Japanese literature.

The corpus of queer studies also grew after 2010 with important contributions to various fields, including, for example,

- queer theory and criticism by Nagashima Saeko (2013, 2019), Fujitaka Kazuki (2018, 2022), Shimizu Akiko (2013, 2015, 2022), and Shimizu Akiko et al. (2022);
- queer history by Akaeda Kanako (2011, 2014), Ishida Hitoshi (2019, 2023), and Mitsuhashi Junko (2018, 2022);

- queer disability studies by Iseri Makiko (2013, 2019, 2020) and Iino Yuriko et al. (2016, 2022);
- the study of LGBTQ+ activism and communities by Moriyama Noritaka (2012), Shingae Akitomo (2013, 2022), Sunagawa Hideki (2015), Thomas Baudinette (2021), Itani Satoko (2021), and Sugiura Ikuko and Maekawa Naoya (2022);
- lesbian studies by Sugiura Ikuko (2011, 2017), Horie Yuri (2015), and James Welker (2017, 2018);
- trans studies by Ishii Yukari (2018), Yamada Hidenobu (2020, 2022), Yoshino Yugi (2020), and Shūji Akira and Takai Yutori (2023);
- legal and human rights studies by Taniguchi Hiroyuki (2019, 2022) and Ayabe Rokurō and Ikeda Hirono (2019).

The three-volume anthology *Kuia sutadīzu o hiraku* (*Exploring Queer Studies*), edited by Kikuchi Natsuno, Horie Yuri, and Iino Yuriko (2019, 2022, 2023), also features a wide range of academic discussions of LGBTQ+-related issues that tend to be overlooked in the recent "LGBT boom" (Kikuchi et al., 2019, pp. 5–6), as did the special issues of the mainstream philosophy magazine *Gendai shisō* (*Modern Thought*) on sexual minorities (2015) and intersectionality (2022). Newly published feminist and queer mainstream magazines such as *Shimōnu* (*Les Simones*, 2019–present), *Etosetora* (*Etcetera*, 2019–present), *Over and Over* (2019–present), and *Iwakan* (*Discomfort*, 2020–present) also provide new avenues for the public discussion of LGBTQ+-related issues and exchange between researchers, activists, and the broader public.

With regard to a specific focus on cultural representation, Mizoguchi Akiko (2015, 2017, 2023), James Welker (2019, 2022), and Hori Akiko and Mori Naoko (2020) have contributed to establishing the study of BL media as a distinct academic field. The mainstream art and culture magazine *Yuriika* (*Eureka*) further popularized the study of BL through two special issues (2012, 2020). Mirroring the increase in LGBTQ+ representation in mainstream movies and drama series, a range of monographs developed queer Japanese film and media studies (e.g., Kanno, 2021, 2023; Kubo, 2022; Maree, 2020) and enriched Japanese literature studies with new queer perspectives (e.g., Angels, 2011; Iida, 2016; Iwakawa, 2022; Kimura, 2010; Kuroiwa, 2016; Takeda, 2018; Vincent, 2012).

However, the increased visibility of LGBTQ+ issues in political discourse and the mass media was also met with a backlash. Unlike the "gender-free" backlash of the late 1990s and early 2000s, it focused primarily on LGBTQ+ people and activism, who were framed as threats to traditional family values by social conservatives and religious right-wing groups. Arguably the most notorious example was Liberal Democratic Party (LDP) lawmaker Sugita Mio's (2018) essay for the magazine *Shinchō 45*, in which she argued, among other things, that LGBTQ+ couples were "unproductive" because they do not procreate, which is why LGBTQ+-related initiatives are not worthy of tax money (pp. 57–58). Her attempt to exploit social anxieties about Japan's low birthrate and aging population to mobilize public support against LGBTQ+ inclusion, however, backfired. Various minority rights groups organized well-attended protests in front of the LDP headquarters in Tokyo's Chiyoda Ward, criticizing Sugita for the anti-LGBTQ+ rhetoric of her essay, and especially for reducing a human's value to its productivity and reproductive capabilities, which was widely supported by major news outlets (Carland-Echavarria, 2022; Okano, 2018; "'Seisansei nai' wa nachi no yūseishisō," 2018).

While the failure of Sugita's anti-LGBTQ+ campaign to gain traction shows, if anything, that Japanese society has become more inclusive toward LGBTQ+ people and their rights, the idea that LGBTQ+ people threaten the social order as they do not form traditional families continues to dominate the political imagination of the ruling LDP. A similar rhetoric was used by prime minister Kishida Fumio in parliament in 2023, when he blocked calls by the opposition to legalize same-sex marriage by saying that this is an issue that requires "extreme caution" because the legalization of same-sex marriage would fundamentally change Japanese society and people's values (Abe & Sugihara, 2023).

Since the public supports the legalization of same-sex marriage, anti-LGBTQ+ discourse in the late 2010s has shifted from homophobia to transphobia. Mirroring, as Stefan Würrer notes in his paper, the global phenomenon of social conservatives and religious right-wing politicians collaborating with mainstream feminists in the name of cis women's rights and safety, social conservatives in Japan – again with the support of the Shinto Association and the Unification Church, as well as, in this case, feminists – have increasingly targeted trans people, especially trans women, whom they frame as usurpers of women's spaces and a potential threat to women's safety (see also Kawasaka, 2023; Poritasu TV et al., 2023). While transphobic discourse intensified on social media after the decision of Ochanomizu Women's University to accept applications by trans students regardless of their legal gender and transition status in 2019, the social inclusion of trans women became a much-discussed topic in the mass media through the opposition of ultra-conservative politicians such as the LDP's Yamatani Eriko – who was also at the center of the "gender-free" backlash of the late 1990s and early 2000s – against the LDP's Draft Bill on the Promotion of Better Understanding of LGBT Issues (LGBT Rikai Zōshin Hōan). Although this law aims only to cultivate acceptance toward LGBTQ+ people and lacks any concrete sanctions for failures to abide by its vague guidelines (Carland-Ecchavaria, 2022, p. 5), Yamatani, together with other politicians, criticized in particular the depathologizing language of the bill as posing a threat to cis women (Ibuki, 2021; "Jimin Yamatani-shi," 2021).

In addition, they criticized the phrase "discrimination on the basis of sexual orientation or gender identity is unacceptable," which they argued would open the door for "legal action to punish or prohibit any speech deemed 'discriminatory'" (Carland-Ecchavaria, 2022, p. 17). Under their pressure, the amended draft that was submitted to the Diet in 2023 stated, "there should be no unjust discrimination," which implies the existence of "just discrimination." It also states that efforts made to promote understanding toward LGBTQ+ people must consider the comfort of all citizens based on guidelines the government will provide. This has been criticized as effectively hindering the bill's objective (Matsuoka, 2023; Satō, 2023).

Overview of the book

During the 2010s, the term "LGBT" became a buzzword in the Japanese mainstream media, mirroring the increased visibility of sexual minority issues in public discourse. However, as Kazuyoshi Kawasaka notes in his paper, while making it easier to generally address LGBTQ+-related issues, the term does not necessarily facilitate a more nuanced understanding, as it avoids differentiating between the people, as well as the struggles and needs, represented by each of the letters it is made up of. As Kikuchi et al. (2019, p. 3) have pointed out, this is also the case with the term *kuia* (queer), which tends to be used as a depoliticized umbrella term for non-normative forms of gender and sexuality, despite its history of representing not only a more inclusive approach toward the self-representation of those labelled "abnormal" by heteronormative societies, but also their manifold cultural and political interventions into the structural discrimination and stigmatization such societies rely upon. Similarly, the expression *tayōsei* (diversity) often is used to pinkwash political and business initiatives that superficially signal inclusion of sexual minorities, but lack concrete measures that would remedy inequity (Kawasaka, 2015, pp. 90–91). In this volume, as its title suggests, we aim to take a look beyond pinkwashed surfaces and offer critical perspectives to stimulate transnational discussions of LGBTQ+ issues in Japan after 2010.

Kawasaka's paper discusses Japanese mainstream pro–LGBTQ+ rights discourses and representations within domestic and international political contexts, and analyzes how these have been influenced by the marketization of LGBTQ+ people and issues, US diplomacy, and the 2020 Summer Olympics and Paralympics in Tokyo. It shows how the institutionalization of LGBTQ+ rights is appearing through Japan's neoliberal, uneven governmentality and how this maintains its male-dominant heteronormative conservatism while impressing upon the international community that Japan is seemingly becoming an LGBTQ+-friendly place that promotes diversity.

Diana Khor and Saori Kamano's paper adds a new perspective to the debates about same-sex marriage, especially the polarizing question of whether its legalization would strengthen or subvert existing heteronormative systems through the inclusion of same-sex couples. Drawing on their previous analyses of same-sex partnerships in Japan, Khor and Kamano analyze interviews with same-sex couples in Japan and explore how they make sense of their partnership, the marital institution, and broader familial ties. They show that these interviews point toward the necessity of more nuanced dialogues about same-sex marriage that take into consideration both the issue of legal equality and problems inherent in Japan's current marriage system.

Hiroyuki Taniguchi examines the history of the intersections between human rights discourses and LGBTQ+-related laws, policies, and court cases in Japan. Demonstrating how the lack of a proper understanding of the concept of human rights hinders the advancement of legal equality, he argues for the promotion and utilization of international human rights laws as a means to improve the legal situation of Japan's LGBTQ+ community.

Azusa Yamashita discusses the experience of LGBTQ+ people during disasters, especially large earthquakes. She emphasizes that such events are not simply natural occurrences, but also have political, socioeconomic, and environmental contexts, and thus reveal existing social inequalities and magnify the vulnerability of certain social groups. Through an analysis of interviews with LGBTQ+ survivors of earthquakes, she shows that although Japanese policymakers have begun to make improvements to reflect the needs of gender and sexual minorities in disaster risk reduction and management policies, LGBTQ+ people continue to experience certain additional difficulties during times of crisis.

Both Genya Fukunaga and Guo Lifu explore contemporary transnational LGBTQ+-related discourses in the context of East Asian politics. Fukunaga analyzes the homonationalism, that is, the intersections of nationalism and pro-LGBTQ+ politics, in the relationship between Taiwan and Japan. As he points out, while homonationalist rhetoric contributes to the mainstreaming of LGBTQ+ rights discourses in Taiwan and Japan and allows these two societies to be classified as "LGBT friendly" and "advanced," it does so in contrast to the "backwardness" of communist China. Meanwhile, Guo takes a closer look at online anti-trans discourses in Japan and China during the Tokyo 2020 Olympics, especially in view of the upcoming Beijing 2022 Winter Olympics. Through a social media analysis of Japanese-language tweets and Chinese-language Weibo posts, he shows how both Japanese and Chinese online trans-exclusionary discourses frame the participation of trans women in sport as a threat to cis women athletes, albeit based on different ideologies.

Stefan Würrer also discusses recent transphobic discourses, focusing on the initially surprising alliance between Shōno Yoriko, one of Japan's leading feminist fiction writers and former Japanese Communist Party supporter, and right-wing social conservative politician Yamatani Eriko, who have both participated in the framing of trans women as a potential threat to women's safety. Würrer shows how this transphobic alliance is both part of a global phenomenon and symptomatic of historical problems within Japanese feminism. He then revisits Shōno's fiction and argues that the numerous characters in her novels who are struggling with their assigned sex and gender do not necessarily contradict Shōno's trans-exclusionary arguments. Rather, Shōno's politics and fiction together have to be understood as part of an always incomplete, performative, and problematic process of reestablishing a coherent and fixed female identity through the abjection of the Other.

Finally, Yutaka Kubo's paper presents a history of LGBTQ+ representation in Japanese cinema from the "gay boom" of the 1990s to the "LGBT boom" of the 2010s and examines how film studies and criticism in Japan have struggled to incorporate a queer perspective. He emphasizes the need for both the Japanese film industry and film studies to become more attentive toward the complexity of minority perspectives and audiences, rather than merely targeting the mainstream, in order to achieve a more diverse representation of Japan's LGBTQ+ people and their lives.

While this anthology covers a wide variety of LGBTQ+-related topics after 2010, we did not collect papers with a specific focus on identity such as lesbian, gay, bisexual, or trans. Rather, our goal was to shed light on the broader entanglement and power dynamics of social, political, historical, economic, and cultural factors that influence LGBTQ+ people, their lives, and their needs in contemporary Japan. The papers presented in this volume offer but a tiny fragment of potential perspectives on LGBTQ+-related developments after 2010 – based on this understanding, we ask our readers to take this anthology for what it is: as an invitation to critically engage with the arguments it presents and as one potential stepping stone in the further advancement of LGBTQ+-related academic research in the context of Japan and, more broadly, East Asia.

References

Abe, R., & Sugihara, S. (2023, Feb. 3). Kishida cautious on gay marriage because it would "change society." *The Asahi Shimbun.* https://www.asahi.com/ajw/articles/14830834.

Aēsop Japan. (2022). *Kuia no koe o hasshin suru: Isoppu kuia raiburarī* [Amplifying queer voices: The Aēsop Queer Library]. https://www.aesop.com/jp/r/pride-jp.

Akaeda, K. (2011). *Kindai Nihon ni okeru onna dōshi no shinmitsu na kankei* [Intimate relationships between women in modern Japan]. Kadokawa Gakugei Shuppan.

Akaeda, K. (2014). Sengo Nihon ni okeru "rezubian" kategorī no teichaku [The establishment of the category of "lesbian" in postwar Japan]. In S. Koyama, K. Akaeda, & E. Imada (Eds.), *Sekushuariti no sengoshi* [A history of sexuality in post-war Japan] (pp. 129–151). Kyōto Daigaku Gakujutsu Shuppankai.

Angels, J. (2011). *Writing the love of boys: Origins of bishōnen culture in modernist Japanese literature.* University of Minnesota Press.

Ayabe, R., & Ikeda, H. (Eds.). (2019). *Kuia to hō: Seikihan no kaihō/kaihō no tame ni* [Queer and law: Liberating/opening up sexual norms]. Nihon Hyōronsha.

Baudinette, T. (2021). *Regimes of desire: Young gay men, media, and masculinity in Tokyo.* The University of Michigan Press.

Carland-Echavarria, P. (2022). We do not live to be productive: LGBT activism and the politics of productivity in contemporary Japan. *The Asia-Pacific Journal 20*(2), Article 5669. https://apjjf.org/2022/2/Carland.html.

Chalmers, S. (2002). *Emerging lesbian voices from Japan.* Routledge Curzon.

Dentsū. (2015, April 23). *Dentsū daibāshiti rabo ga "LGBT chōsa 2015" o jisshi* [Dentsu Diversity Lab conducted the "LGBT survey 2015"] [News release]. https://www.dentsu.co.jp/news/release/2015/0423-004032.html.

Dōseikon mitomenai no wa kenpōihan: Ikenhanketsu wa zenkoku ni-kenme – Nagoyachizai [Not recognizing same-sex marriage is unconstitutional: Nagoya district court becomes the second to rule it unconstitutional]. (2023, May 30). NHK. https://www3.nhk.or.jp/news/html/20230530/k10014082521000.html.

Dōseikon ni sansei 65% jimintō shijisō demo 58% honsha yoronchōsa [65%, even among LDP supporters 58%, in favor of same-sex marriage, says our survey]. (2023, February 27). *Nihon keizai shinbun.* https://www.nikkei.com/article/DGXZQOUA253J70V20C23A2000000.

Frühstück, S. (2022). *Gender and sexuality in modern Japan.* Cambridge University Press.

Fujitaka, K. (2018). *Judisu Batorā: Sei to tetsugaku o kaketa tatakai* [Judith Butler: A fight for life and philosophy]. Ibunsha.

Fujitaka, K. (2022). *"Toraburu" toshite no feminizumu:"Torimidasasenai yokuatsu" ni aragatte* [Feminism as "trouble": Fighting with "the pressure to not lose control"]. Ibunsha.

Fushimi, N. (1991). *Puraibēto gei raifu* [Private gay life]. Gakuyō Shobō

Hori, A., & Mori, N. (Eds.). (2020). *BL no kyōkasho* [A BL textbook]. Yuhikaku.

Horie, Y. (2015). *Rezubian aidentitīzu* [Lesbian identities]. Rakuhoku Shuppan.

Ibuki S. (2021, May 31). *"Inochi o mamoru hōritsu o tsukutte kudasai": Jimintō gi'in no sabetsu hatsugen, ima tōjishatachi ga tsutaetai omoi* ["Please create laws that protect lives": What those affected think of the discriminatory remarks made by members of the Liberal Democratic Party]. Buzzfeed. https://www.buzzfeed.com/jp/saoriibuki/ldp-lgbt-protest.

Iida, Yūko. (2016). *Kanojotachi no bungaku* [The women's literature]. Nagoya Daigaku Shuppankai.

Iino, Y. (2008). *Rezubian de aru "watashitachi" no sutōri* [The story of "us" lesbians]. Seikatsu Shoin.

Iino, Y., Kawashima, S., Nishikura, M., & Hoshika, R. (2016). *Gōriteki hairyo: Taiwa o hiraku, taiwa ga hiraku* [Reasonable accommodation: Opening up dialogues, dialogues that open up]. Yūhikaku.

Iino, Y., Kawashima, S., Nishikura, M. & Hoshika, R. (2022). *"Shakai" o atsukau aratana mōdo: "Shōgai no shakai moderu" no tsukaikata* [A new mode of engaging with "society": How to use the "social model of disability"]. Seikatsu Shoin.

Iseri, M. (2013). Furekishiburu na shintai: Kuia negativitī to kyōseiteki na kenjōteki shintaisei [Flexible bodies: Queer negativity and coercive able-bodiedness]. *Ronsō kuia, 6*, 37–57.

Iseri, M. (2019). "Fuzai" kara no shiza, "fuzai" e no shiza: Disabiritī, feminizumu, kuia [Perspectives from "absence," perspectives toward "absence": Disability, feminism, queer]. *Gendai shisō, 47*(3), 289–298.

Iseri, M. (2020). (Han)-miraishugi o toinaosu: Kuia na tairitsusei to dōin sareru shintai [Rethinking (anti)-futurism: Queer antagonism and mobilized bodies]. *Shisō, 1151*, 70–86.

Ishida, H. (2019). Anzen na jiyū: Hattenba ni yume o takushita jidai ni okeru [Safe freedom: When cruising spots were places of dreams]. In *Kōkai shimpojiumu "'LGBT' wa dō tsunagatte kita no ka"* [Public symposium: "LGBT" connections over the years] (pp. 23–31). Hokkaido University Collection of Scholarly and Academic Papers. http://hdl.handle.net/2115/74609.

Ishida, H. (Ed.). (2023). *Yakudō suru gei mūbumento: Rekishi o kataru torikkusutā tachi* [Vibrant gay movements: Tricksters narrating history]. Akashi Shoten.

Ishii, Y. (2018). *Toransujendā to gendai shakai: Tayōka suru sei to aimaina jikozō wo motsu hitotachi no seikatsusekai* [Trans people and contemporary society: The everyday life of people with ambiguous self-images and the diversification of gender and sexuality]. Akashi Shoten.

Itani, S. (2021). *"Tai'ikukai-kei joshi" no poritikusu: Shintai, jendā, sekushuariti* [The politics of "athletic girls": Body, gender, sexuality]. Kansai Daigaku Shuppanbu.

Itō, S. (2006). Japan. In T. Yamamoto & S. Itō (Eds.), *Fighting a rising tide: The response to AIDS in East Asia* (pp. 119–155). Japan Center for International Exchange.

Iwakawa, A. (2022). *Monogatari to torauma: Kuia feminizumu hihyō no kanōsei* [Narrative and trauma: Possibilities of queer feminist critique]. Seidosha.

Jimin Yamatani-shi "bakageta koto okiteru": Sei jinin meguri [LDP's Yamatani speaking of "ridiculous developments" regarding gender identity]. (2021, May 19). *Asahi shinbun*. https://www.asahi.com/articles/ASP5M52GTP5MUTFK004.html.

Kakefuda, H. (1992). *"Rezubian" de aru to iu koto* [On being a "lesbian"]. Kawade Shobō Shinsha.

Kanno, Y. (2019). Komyunitī o saikō suru: Kuia LGBT eigasai to jōdo no shakai kūkan [Community reconsidered: Queer/LGBT film festivals and affective social space]. In N. Kikuchi, Y. Horie, & Y. Iino (Eds.), *Kuia sutadīzu o hiraku 1: Aidentitī, komyunitī, supēsu* [Exploring queer studies, vol. 1: Identity, community, and space] (pp. 110–133). Kōyō Shobō.

Kanno, Y. (Ed.). (2021). *Kuia shinema sutadīzu* [Queer cinema studies]. Kōyō Shobō.

Kanno, Y. (2023). *Kuia shinema: Sekai to jikan ni betsu no shikata de sonzai suru tame ni* [Queer cinema: To exist in different ways in the world and in time]. Firumu Āto Sha.

Kawaguchi, K., Vincent, K., & Kazama, T. (1997). *Gei sutadīzu* [Gay studies]. Seidosha.

Kawasaka, K. (2015). "Jinken" ka "tokken" ka "onken" ka? ["Human rights" or "privileges" or "benefits"?]. *Gendai shisō, 43*(16), 86–99.

Kawasaka, K. (2023). Queers and national anxiety: Discourses on gender and sexuality from anti-gender backlash movements in Japan since the 2000s. In J. Goetz & S. Mayer (Eds.), *Global perspectives on anti-feminism: Far-right and religious attacks on equality and diversity*. Edinburgh University Press.

Kazama, T. (2007). "Chūsei ningen" to wa dare ka? Seiteki mainoritī e no "fobia" o fumaeta teikō e [Who are those "genderless people"? Toward a resistance that's aware of the phobia against sexual minorities]. *Joseigaku, 15*, 23–33.

Kazama, T. (2009). Sutiguma to (seiteki) kenkō: HIV/eizu ni taisuru shakai(kagaku)teki apurōchi [Stigma and (sexual) health: Social (science) approaches to HIV/AIDS]. *Kaihō shakaigaku kenkyū, 23*, 59–61.

Kazama, T. & Kawaguchi, K. (2003). HIV risk and the (im)permeability of the male body: Representations and realities of gay men in Japan. In J. E. Roberson & S. Nobue (Eds.), *Men and masculinities in contemporary Japan: Dislocating the salaryman doxa* (pp. 180–197). Routledge.

Kazama, T. & Kawaguchi, K. (2010). *Dōseiai to iseai* [Homosexuality and heterosexuality]. Iwanami Shoten.

Khor, D. (2010). The foreign gaze? A critical look at claims about same-sex sexuality in Japan in the English language literature. *Gender and Sexuality, 5,* 45–59.

Kikuchi, N., Horie, Y., & Iino, Y. (Eds.). (2019). *Kuia sutadīzu o hiraku 1: Aidentitī, komyunitī, supēsu* [Exploring queer studies vol.1: Identity, community, and space]. Kōyō Shobō.

Kikuchi, N., Horie, Y., & Iino, Y. (Eds.). (2022). *Kuia sutadīzu o hiraku 2: Kekkon, kazoku, rōdō* [Exploring queer studies vol. 2: Marriage, family and labor]. Kōyō Shobō.

Kikuchi, N., Horie, Y., & Iino, Y. (Eds.). (2023). *Kuia sutadīzu o hiraku 3: Kenkō/yamai, shōgai, karada* [Exploring queer studies vol. 3: Health/illness, disability, body]. Kōyō Shobō.

Kimura, S. (2010). *A brief history of sexuality in premodern Japan.* Tallin University Press.

Kubo, Y. (2022). *Yūyakegumo no kanata ni: Kinoshita Keisuke to kuiana kansei* [Over the sunset: Kinoshita Keisuke and queer sensibility]. Nakanishiya Shuppan.

Kuia Sutadīzu Henshū Iinkai. (1997). *Kuia sutadīzu 97'* [Queer studies 97']. Nanatsumori Shokan.

Kuroiwa, Y. (2016). Gei no kashika o yomu: Gendai bungaku ni egakareru "sei no tayōsei" [Reading the new gay visibility: "Sexual diversity" depicted in contemporary Japanese literature]. Kōyō Shobō.

Kyōdō tsūshin no yoronchōsa de dōseikon ni sansei ga 71% nimo nobori, NHK no yoron chōsa de seiteki mainoriti no jinken ga "mamorarete iru" to kanjiru kata wa tatta no 9% de aru koto ga wakarimashita. (2023, May 4). Pride Japan. https://www.outjapan.co.jp/pride_japan/news/2023/5/3.html.

LGBT Hōren Gōkai. (2015, March 30). *LGBT no kokusei robī rengōkai o hatsu kessei* [Founding of the first national LGBT lobby for governmental affairs] [News release]. https://lgbtetc.jp/news/4.

Lunsing, W. (2001). *Beyond common sense: Sexuality and gender in contemporary Japan.* Kegan Paul.

Mackintosh, J. (2010). *Homosexuality and manliness in postwar Japan.* Routledge.

Maree, C. (2007). The un/state of lesbian studies: An introduction to lesbian communities and contemporary legislation in Japan. *Journal of Lesbian Studies 11*(3–4), 291–301.

Maree, C. (2020). *Queerqueen: Excess and constraints in writing gender and sexuality into popular Japanese media.* Oxford University Press.

Marriage for All Japan. (2020). *Dōseikon ni kansuru yoronchōsa* [Report of our survey about same-sex marriage]. https://www.marriageforall.jp/research.

Martin, F., Jackson, A. P., McLelland, M., & Yue, A. (Eds.). (2008). *AsiaPacifiQueer: Rethinking genders and sexualities.* University of Illinois Press.

Matsuoka, S. (2023, June 6). *Mohaya "LGBT rikai yokusei hō": Yotō to ishin no saishūseian ga shūin naikaku iinkai de kaketsu* [This is actually an "LGBT understanding suppression bill": The House of Representatives Cabinet Committee passes the amended bill of the LDP and the Japan Innovation Party]. Yahoo Japan. https://news.yahoo.co.jp/byline/matsuokasoshi/20230610-00353187.

McLelland, M. (2000). *Male homosexuality in modern Japan: Cultural myths and social realities.* Curzon.

McLelland, M. (2005). *Queer Japan from the Pacific War to the internet age.* Rowman & Littlefield Publishers.

McLelland, M. (2012). Death of the "legendary okama" Tōgō Ken: Challenging commonsense lifestyles in postwar Japan. *The Asia-Pacific Journal, 10*(25), Article 5. https://apjjf.org/2012/10/25/Mark-McLelland/3775/article.html.

McLelland, M., & Dasgupta, R. (Eds.) (2005). *Genders, transgenders and sexualities in Japan.* Routledge.

McLelland, M., & Mackie, V. (Eds.). (2015). *Routledge handbook of sexuality studies in East Asia.* Routledge.

McLelland, M., Nagaike, K., Suganuma, K., & Welker, J. (Eds.) (2015). *Boys love manga and beyond.* University Press of Mississippi.

McLelland, M. & Suganuma, K. (2009). Sexual minorities and human rights in Japan: An historical perspective. *The International Journal of Human Rights, 13*(2–3), 329–344. https://doi.org/10.1080/13642980902758176.

McLelland, M., Suganuma, K., & Welker, J. (Eds.). (2007). *Queer voices from Japan.* Rowman & Littlefield Publishers.

Mitsuhashi, J. (2018). *Shinjuku: "Sei naru" machi no rekishi chiri* [Shinjuku: Historical geography of a sex town]. Asahi Shinbun Shuppansha.

Mitsuhashi, J. (2022). *Rekishi no naka no tayōna "sei": Nihon to Ajia, hengen suru sekushuaritī* [Diverse "sexualities" throughout history: Japan and Asia's transforming sexualities]. Iwanami Shoten.

Mizoguchi, A. (2015). *BL shinkaron: Bōizu rabu ga shakai o ugokasu* [The evolution of boys' love: How BL changes society]. Ōta Shuppan.

Mizoguchi, A. (2017). *BL shinkaron (taiwa hen): Bōizu rabu ga umareru basho* [The evolution of boys' love (conversations): Where BL is brought to life]. Ōta Shuppan.

Mizoguchi, A. (2023). *BL kenkyūsha ni yoru jendā hihyō nyūmon: Kotoba ni naranai "moyamoya" o kotoba de kataru "wakuwaku" ni kaeru, hyōshō bunseki no ressun* [An introduction to gender criticism by a BL researcher: Turning unspoken "confusion" into articulated "enthusiasm" through a lesson on the analysis of visual representations.]. Kasama Shoin.

Moriyama, N. (2012). *Gei komyuniti no shakaigaku* [Sociology of the Japanese gay community]. Keisō Shobō.

Nagashima, S. (Ed.). (2013). *Ai no gihō: Kuia rīdingu to wa nani ka* [The art of love: What is queer reading?]. Chūō Daigaku Shuppanbu.

Nagashima, S. (Ed.). (2019). *Yomu koto no kuia: Zoku ai no gihō* [The queerness of reading: The art of love 2]. Chūō Daigaku Shuppanbu.

Nihon Keizai Dantai Rengō. (2017). *Daibāshiti inkurūjon shakai ni mukete* [Toward a diverse and inclusive society]. https://www.keidanren.or.jp/policy/2017/039_honbun.pdf.

Norton, L. (2013). Neutering the transgendered: Human rights and Japan's law no. 111. In S. Stryker & A. Z. Aizura (Eds.), *The transgender studies reader* (Vol. 2, pp. 591–603). Routledge.

Ogawa, S. (2017). *Producing gayness: The 1990s "gay boom" in Japanese media* [Doctoral dissertation, University of Kansas]. KU Scholar Works. http://hdl.handle.net/1808/27011.

Ogiue C. (2012, April 26). Tayōna ikikata o sonchō shiyō [Let's respect diverse ways of living]. *Synodos.* http://synodos.jp/society/2263.

Oikawa, K. (2007). Tōgō Ken, the legendary okama: Burning with sexual desire and revolt. In M. McLelland, K. Suganuma, & J. Welker (Eds.), *Queer voices from Japan* (pp. 263–269). Rowman & Littlefield Publishers.

Okano, Y. (2018). Sabetsu hatsugen to seijiteki bunmyaku no jūyōsei: "LGBT" shien no do ga sugiru" no konkan [Discriminatory speech and the importance of political contexts: What the argument that "LGBT support goes too far" is really about]. *Sekai, 913,* 140–149.

Otsuji, K. (2005). *Kamingu auto: Jibunrashisa o mitsukeru tabi* [Coming out: A journey of self-discovery]. Kōdansha.

Pendleton, M. (2021). And I dance with somebody: Queer history in a Japanese nightclub. *History Workshop Journal, 90*, 297–310.

Pflugfelder, G. M. (1999). *Cartographies of desire: Male-male sexuality in Japanese discourse 1600–1950.* University of California Press.

Poritasu TV, Yamaguchi T., & Saitō M. (2023). *Shūkyō uha to feminizumu* [The religious right and feminism]. Seikyūsha.

PRIDE Shihyō Jimukyoku. (2022). *Puraido shihyō 2022 repōto* [Pride index 2022 report]. Work With Pride. https://workwithpride.jp/topics/wwpprideindex2022.

Reichert, J. (2006). *In the company of men: Representations of male-male sexuality in Meiji literature.* Stanford University Press.

Roberson, J. E., & Nobue, S. (2003). *Men and masculinities in contemporary Japan: Dislocating the salaryman doxa.* Routledge.

Satō, T. (2023, June 13). LGBT "sabetsu" zōshinhō ni NO: Puraido parēdo sura, dekinakunaru kiki. "Konna hō o tōsu kuni wa, hontō ni saitei desu" [No to the Law for LGBT discrimination: Even pride parades are now at risk. "A country that passes such a law is truly despicable"]. HuffPost News. https://www.huffingtonpost.jp/entry/story_jp_6487b4b5e4b048eb9110f7bb.

"Seisansei nai" wa nachi no yūseishisō: Shikishara hihan, kaigai media mo hōdō [Calling people non-productive is Nazi-style eugenics: Criticism from experts, reports by international media] (2018, July 28). *Mainichi shinbun.* https://mainichi.jp/articles/20180728/mog/00m/040/009000c.

Shimizu, A. (2007). Scandalous equivocation: A note on the politics of queer self-naming. *Inter-Asia Cultural Studies, 8*(4), 503–516.

Shimizu, A. (2013). Chanto tadashii hōkō ni mukatteru: Kuia poritikusu no genzai [Heading properly in the right direction: The current state of queer politics]. In R. Miura & S. Hayasaka (Eds.), *Jendā to jiyū: Riron, riberarizumu, kuia* [Gender and freedom: Theory, liberalism, queer] (pp. 313–331). Sairyūsha.

Shimizu, A. (2015). Yōkoso gei furendori na machi e. [Welcome to the gay friendly town]. *Gendai shisō, 43*(16), 144–155.

Shimizu, A. (2022). *Feminizumutte nandesuka.* [What is feminism?]. Bunshun Shinsho.

Shimizu, A., Han, T., & Iino, Y. (2022). *Poritikaru korekutonesu kara doko e* [From political correctness to where?]. Yuhikaku.

Shingae, A. (2013). *Nihon no "gei" to eizu: Komyūniti, kokka, aidentiti* ["Gays" and AIDS in Japan: Community, nation, identity]. Seikyūsha.

Shingae, A. (2022). *Kuia akutibizumu: Hajimete manabu "kuia sutadīzu" no tame ni* [Queer activism: Queer studies for beginners]. Kadensha.

Shūji, A., & Takai, Y. (2023). *Toransujendā nyūmon* [An introduction to transgender people]. Shūeisha.

Shūkan Daiamondo Henshūbu. (Ed.). (2013). *Kokunai shijō 5.7 chōen:"LGBT (Rezubian/gei/baisekushuaru/toransugenda) shijō" o kōryaku seyo!* [A domestic market of 5.7 trillion yen: Let's conquer the "LGBT market"]. Shūkan Daiamondo (online edition). (Original work published 2012)

Suganuma, K. (2006). Enduring voices: Fushimi Noriaki and Kakefuda Hiroko's continuing relevance to Japanese lesbian and gay studies and activism. *Intersections: Gender, History and Culture in the Asian Context, 14.* http://intersections.anu.edu.au/issue14/suganuma.htm.

Suganuma, K. (2012). *Contact moments: The politics of intercultural desire in Japanese male-queer cultures.* Hong Kong University Press.

Sugita, M. (2018). "LGBT" shien no do ga sugiru [The support for "LGBT" people goes too far]. *Shinchō, 45*(8), 57–60.

Sugiura, I. (2007). Lesbian discourses in mainstream magazines of post-war Japan. *Journal of Lesbian Studies, 11*(3–4), 127–144.

Sugiura, I. (2011). Increasing lesbian visibility. In K. Fujimura-Fanselow (Ed.), *Transforming Japan: How feminism and diversity are making a difference* (pp. 164–176). The Feminist Press.

Sugiura, I. (2017). Nihon ni okeru rezubian minikomi-shi no gensetsu bunseki: 1970 nendai kara 1980 nendai zenhan made [A discourse analysis of lesbian zines in Japan: From the 1970s to the early 1980s]. *Wakō Daigaku gendai ningen gakubu kiyō, 10*, 159–178.

Sugiura, I., & Maekawa, N. (2022). *"Chihō" to seiteki mainoritī: Tōhoku 6-ken no intabyū kara.* Seikyūsha.

Summerhawk, B., McMahill, C., & McDonald, D. (1998). *Queer Japan: Personal stories of Japanese lesbians, gays, transsexuals, and bisexuals.* New Victoria Publishers.

Sunagawa, H. (2015). *Shinjuku 2-chōme no bunka jinruigaku* [A cultural anthropological study of Shinjuku ni-chōme]. Tarō Jirōsha Editasu.

Takeda, S. (2018). *Yoshiya Nobuko kenkyū* [A study of Yoshiya Nobuko]. Kanrin Shobō.

Takemura, K. (1996a). Lesbian kenkyū no kanōsei (1): "Romantikku na yūjō" kara sekusorojī zen'ya made [Exploring the potential for lesbian studies 1: From romantic friendships to the eve of sexology]. *Eigo seinen, 142*(4), 187–189.

Takemura, K. (1996b). Lesbian kenkyū no kanōsei (2): "Noroi no bungaku" kara "gaidobukku bungaku" made [Exploring the potential for lesbian studies 2: From a "cursed literature" to "guidebook literature"]. *Eigo seinen, 142*(5), 262–264.

Takemura, K. (1996c). Lesbian kenkyū no kanōsei (3): Feminizumu to no kakawari [Exploring the potential for lesbian studies 3: The relation with feminism]. *Eigo seinen, 142*(6), 318–320.

Takemura, K. (1996d). Lesbian kenkyū no kanōsei (4): Onna wa "yokubō no shutai" to naru ka – seishin bunseki to shakai kōseiron [Exploring the potential for lesbian studies 4: Can women become "subjects of desire"? Psychoanalysis and social constructionism]. *Eigo seinen, 142*(7), 376–378.

Takemura, K. (1996e). Lesbian kenkyū no kanōsei (5): Kamingu auto monogatari to yūshokujin rezubian no taikō hyōshō [Exploring the potential for lesbian studies 5: Coming out stories and oppositional representation of lesbians of color]. *Eigo seinen, 142*(8), 430–432.

Takemura, K. (1996f). Lesbian kenkyū no kanōsei (6): Sekkusu no "keitaigaku" – rezubian hyōshō/riron no ima [Exploring the potential for lesbian studies(6): The morphology of sex – lesbian representation/theory now]. *Eigo seinen, 142*(9), 475–479.

Takemura, K. (1997). Shihonshugi shakai to sekushuariti: (Hetero)sekushizumu no kaitai e mukete [Capitalist society and sexuality: Toward dismantling (hetero)sexism]. *Shisō, 879*, 71–104.

Taniguchi, H. (2019). *LGBT o meguru hō to shakai* [Law and society in relation to LGBT issues]. Nihon Kajo Shuppan.

Taniguchi, H. (2022). *Seiteki mainoritī to kokusai jinken hō* [Sexual and gender minorities in international human rights law]. Nihon Kajo Shuppan.

Tōgō, K. (1979). *Zatsumin no ronri* [The logic of people]. Epona Shuppan.

Treat, J. W. (1999). *Great mirrors shattered: Homosexuality, orientalism, and Japan.* Oxford University Press.

Vincent, K. (2012). *Two-timing modernity: Homosocial narrative in modern Japanese fiction.* Harvard University Press.

Welker, J. (2015). A brief history of *shōnen'ai, yaoi,* and boys love. In M. McLelland, K. Nagaike, K. Suganuma, & J. Welker (Eds.), *Boys love manga and beyond* (pp. 42–75). University Press of Mississippi.

Welker, J. (2017). Toward a history of "lesbian history" in Japan. *Culture, Theory and Critique, 58*(2), 147–165. https://doi.org/10.1080/14735784.2017.1282830.

Welker, J. (2018). From women's liberation to lesbian feminism in Japan: Rezubian feminizumu within and beyond the ūman ribu movement in the 1970s and 1980s. In J. C. Bullock, A. Kano, & J. Welker (Eds.), *Rethinking Japanese feminisms* (pp. 50–67). University of Hawai'i Press.

Welker, J. (Ed.). (2019). *BL ga hiraku tobira: Henyōsuru Ajia no sekushuaritī to jendā* [Opening doors with BL: Transforming sexuality and gender in Asia]. Seidosha.

Welker, J. (Ed.). (2022). *Queer transfigurations: Boys love media in Asia.* University of Hawai'i Press.

Yamada, H. (2020). Toransujendā no fuhenka ni yoru GID o meguru anbivarensu no masshō [Erasing ambivalence related to gender identity disorder through the universalization of transgender]. *Jendā kenkyū, 23,* 47–65. https://doi.org/10.24567 /00063793.

Yamada, H. (2022). GID as an acceptable minority; or, the alliance between moral conservatives and "gender critical" feminists in Japan. *Transgender Studies Quarterly, 9*(3), 501–506. https://doi.org/10.1215/23289252-9836162.

Yamaguchi, T. (2014). "Gender free" feminism in Japan: A story of mainstreaming and backlash. *Feminist Studies, 40*(4), 541–572.

Yamaguchi, T., Saitō, M., & Ogiue, C. (2012). *Shakai undō no tomadoi: Feminizumu no "ushinawareta jidai" to kusanone hoshu undō* [The confusion of social movements: Conservative grassroots movements and the "lost decade" of feminism]. Keisō Shobō.

Yamaguchi, T. (2018). The mainstreaming of feminism and the politics of backlash in twenty first-century Japan. In J. C. Bullock, A. Kano, & J. Welker (Eds.), *Rethinking Japanese feminisms* (pp. 68–86). University of Hawai'i Press.

Yoshino, Y. (2020). *Dareka no risō o ikirare wa shinai: Torinokosareta mono no tame no toransujendā-shi* [You can't live someone else's ideal: Transgender history for those left behind]. Seidosha.

Kazuyoshi Kawasaka

The progress of LGBT rights in Japan in the 2010s

The 2010s was a monumental decade for the progress of LGBT rights in Japan. LGBT rights and discrimination cases became political topics in the mainstream media, attracting public interest. Contrasting with the political climate of the 2000s, when it was rather exceptional for politicians and local governments to promote LGBT rights, 47 local ordinances had institutionalized same-sex partnership certificates and/or anti-discrimination laws that included sexual orientation and gender identity by March 2020 ("Pātonāshippu seido," 2020). In February 2020, Naruhito became the first Japanese emperor to mention LGBT people, advocating diversity and calling for tolerance toward social minorities in a press conference on his birthday (The Imperial Household Agency, 2020).

These political changes cannot simply be analyzed in terms of the historical discourses of Japanese sexual minorities' activism. In 2016, Shibuya Ward in Tokyo suddenly introduced a same-sex partnership certificate system for the first time in Japan. Before that, Japanese LGBT activists had rarely, if at all, argued for such a system, which is highly symbolic but, as I will discuss in this paper, offers nowhere near the same legal rights as heterosexual marriage (Enoki, 2019). In the 2000s, they had often discussed systems that offered legal rights to same-sex couples, such as the French civil solidarity pact (PACS; *pacte civil de solidarité*), which is very different from contemporary Japanese models such as Shibuya's (Akasugi et al., 2004). Thus, the notable gap in Japan between the activist political agenda of the 2000s and the institutionalization of LGBT rights in the 2010s indicates a discursive and political transformation. This paper will contextualize Japanese mainstream pro–LGBT rights discourses and representations – a new politicization of LGBT issues – within domestic and international political contexts and analyze how general Japanese attitudes toward LGBT issues changed in the 2010s.

Firstly, this paper discusses three factors that have particularly changed LGBT discourses and public attitudes in Japan in the 2010s, contributing to the mainstreaming of LGBT politics in society: the LGBT market; the use of LGBT rights in US diplomacy; and the 2020 Summer Olympics and Paralympics in Tokyo. Secondly, it considers how Japanese local governments have become some of the main actors in the institutionalization of LGBT rights, even though they do not have the legal authority to change the marriage system. Thirdly, it analyzes popular representations of LGBT rights and visibility in Japan, focusing on whiteness, as Japan faces international, not domestic, political pressure to institutionalize LGBT rights and tolerance, which are represented as being originally from the West. The paper concludes with a discussion of how the institutionalization of LGBT rights is appearing through Japan's neoliberal, uneven governmentality, which maintains its male-dominant heteronormative conservatism while impressing upon the international community that Japan is seemingly becoming an LGBT-friendly place that promotes diversity.

1 Transnational contexts of LGBT rights in the 2010s

1.1 The concept of an LGBT market in Japan

In 2012, two business magazines issued a special edition about the "LGBT market" in the same week, estimating it to be worth 5.7 trillion yen (approximately US$50 billion) and describing it as an emerging market that is already influential in the US and Europe ("Kokunai shijō," 2012; "Nihon no LGBT," 2012). Subsequently, Dentsū (2015), a major Japanese advertising and public relations company, estimated the market to be worth 5.9 trillion yen and stated that 7.6 % of the Japanese population identified as LGBT. The latter figure was cited in a report on discrimination against LGBT people in Japan, which was published by a research committee of the upper house of the Diet (Nakanishi, 2017, p. 5). Japanese think tanks such as Keidanren (2017) and Mitsui UFJ Research (Hattori, 2017) have since published similar reports on the Japanese LGBT market and diversity.

In the US and Western Europe, the LGBT market was formed within gay communities, including advertisements in gay community magazines, consumer activism, and LGBT employees' efforts to visualize the market in marketing or advertisement companies (Branchik, 2002; Chasin, 2001; Sender, 2004). Although there are many critiques of the connection between neoliberal consumerism and LGBT activism, such as those using the term "new homonormativity" (Duggan, 2004), LGBT activism and visibility also reflect the history of the LGBT community, lifestyle, and political goals (Maks-Solomon & Drewry, 2021).

In the Japanese case, however, the concept of the LGBT market was largely introduced and emphasized by marketing companies and think tanks as a new emerging market and business model that had already influenced Anglophone societies and global corporations, without much interaction with the local LGBT communities and activism. LGBT economic activities in Japan have been historically closely associated with space – the so-called "gay towns" of Ni-chōme in Tokyo and Dōyama in Osaka, or bars in local towns (Baudinette, 2021; Fushimi, 2019; Sunagawa, 2015). However, marketing discourses disconnected LGBT economic activities from the existing limited space of gay towns with the concept of an "LGBT market," and recharacterized it as a "new" market in which "nobody has yet toughed it" ("Nihon no LGBT," 2012, p. 122): the hitherto-invisible market consists of tens of millions of people. Here, the LGBT market is recognized not by the visibility of LGBT customers but by their invisibility and mystification, which arouses a desire to find and understand them.

The LGBT market has also been associated with the concept of "diversity" (*daibāshitī*) (Keidanren, 2017). Shingae Akihiro (2021), a cultural anthropologist specializing in gender and sexuality, noted that the idea of diversity, including LGBT people, became mainstream around 2015 in Japan in line with the needs of corporate management and diversity marketing that were shaped by shifts in the domestic and international business environment (pp. 38–42). He pointed out that the Abe administration encouraged Japanese corporations to improve their diversity management for innovation and to address the domestic labor shortage caused by the declining population. Thus, Japanese corporations introduced "diversity" management and marketing not to improve equality and human rights issues but to manage and utilize demographic differences for economic benefits (Shingae, 2021, p. 42).

Corporate attention to Japanese LGBT markets has influenced LGBT activism, too. One of the most remarkable forms of activism sponsored by "LGBT-friendly" corporations is arguably Tokyo Rainbow Pride (TRP). Established in 2011, TRP is a new organization managing the pride parade in Tokyo. It split from Tokyo Pride Parade (TPP), which had organized pride parades for a decade, after a dispute over the event's management. In an interview in their first year, TRP organizers pointed out that one of TPP's problems was its financial structure (Ogiue, 2012). According to Ōtsuka Kensuke, one of the TRP organizers, TPP had been too dependent financially (e.g., for ads in gay bars) on the gay community in Nichōme, famous for one of the highest concentrations of gay bars in the world. However, because of Japan's long-running recession, such financial arrangements between TPP and the gay community have become difficult (Ogiue, 2012). TRP's budget was reportedly minimized through the recruitment of multinational members as its core workers, in order to acquire the know-how of overseas pride parades. As a result, from 2013 the visibility of gay bars in Tokyo has been downplayed, and multinational corporations, such as Alfa Romeo, Philips, Google, Audi, Volkswagen, Dentsū, and IBM have become its official sponsors ("Supporters," 2013, 2014).

In terms of a business marketing strategy, however, TRP is regarded as a model case of social activism that can be utilized for corporate branding (Yotsumoto & Senba, 2017, p. 110). Thus, the connection between Japanese LGBT activism and "LGBT-friendly" corporations also did not happen through long-term interactions between the local LGBT community and domestic and international LGBT-friendly corporations. Rather, it was enabled by the efforts of marketing firms to turn LGBT people and their allies into their new potential consumers, while LGBT activists utilized such opportunistic exploitation for their own movements amid the shrinking number of traditional local queer businesses.

The emergence of the LGBT market in the 2010s is a model case of the marketization of marginalized groups for political and economic purposes, such as the "Womenomics" promoted by the second Abe administration.[1] While a similar marketization of the LGBT community and the introduction of the term "LGBT market" had been attempted by marketing strategists in the mid-2000s (Ilye, 2008; Kawaguchi, 2013), it was not as successful as in the 2010s when a different social context emerged around LGBT issues in Japan: the US pro-LGBT cultural diplomacy and the 2020 Summer Olympics and Paralympics in Tokyo.

1.2 US diplomacy for LGBT rights and visibility by the Obama administration

Under the Obama administration, the promotion of LGBT rights became an official goal of US diplomacy (*National Security Strategy*, 2015, p. 20). In her groundbreaking speech "Gay Rights are Human Rights," the then Secretary of State Hillary Clinton (2011) symbolically showed the administration's policy for international LGBT rights promotion. Subsequently, the US embassy in Japan started to promote LGBT-friendly messages through openly gay diplomats, Japanese celebrities, events for LGBT rights, and its presence in local LGBT activism such as TRP.[2] It is notable that the Obama administration is the first US government that internationally used LGBT rights as soft power ("Obama Uses Embassies," 2014).

There are two prominent characteristics of the Obama administration's narrative on LGBT rights. Firstly, it situated LGBT rights as universal values, not Western values specifically. For example, in her abovementioned speech, Clinton (2011) associated protecting LGBT rights with "a phrase that people in the United States invoke when urging others to support human rights: 'Be on the right side of history.'" As Cynthia Weber (2016), a queer theorist in international relations, has noted, by setting up a dichotomy between the "right" and "wrong" sides of history in relation to LGBT human rights, Clinton violently "divided the world into good gay-friendly

---

1 For an analysis of the commodification of feminist discourses under neoliberalism in Japan, see Kikuchi (2019).
2 On the openly gay US diplomat and his promotion of LGBT visibility and rights in Japan, see Linehan and Kanegusuke (2014).

states and bad homophobic states" (p. 135). Secondly, even though LGBT rights are supposedly universal, they are represented through US history and values. The *National Security Strategy* of 2015 includes LGBT rights as "American values" that the US promotes globally (p. 26).

The US embassy promoted LGBT rights as a part of the US historical context, not based on local Japanese activism and agendas. In April 2013, when John Roos, the first US ambassador to Japan under the Obama administration, finished his term and left office, he published an essay about LGBT rights as human rights in the Japanese national and liberal newspaper *Asahi shinbun.* He positioned his and Obama's efforts for LGBT equality in the international community as their legacy. He also presented the historical and cultural projection of international LGBT rights as if LGBT rights had originated from US social struggles and then spread to Japan and the world:

> In recent years, LGBT people have made great strides in the advancement of equality – yet hurdles remain. Let us remember the courage of those men and women at Seneca Falls, Selma, and Stonewall, and let us continue to make clear that the struggle for gay rights is part and parcel of the long-term fight for civil rights that has made better places of America, Japan, and the entire world. (Roos, 2013, p. 17)

His narrative presents civil rights and LGBT equality as universal but also, at the same time, as US values that have emerged through the nation's historical struggles. The US ambassador, who wanted to "enlighten" Japanese people about LGBT issues, paid little attention, if at all, to the historical struggles of sexual and other social minorities in Japan.

Caroline Kennedy, the daughter of the former president John F. Kennedy, was extremely popular as the second US ambassador appointed by Obama to Japan (2013–2017). She was more dedicated to promoting LGBT rights, having expressed support for same-sex marriage since 2008, earlier than President Obama had. She became the first US ambassador to participate in and give a speech at TRP in 2016 ("Activists March," 2016). In addition to Kennedy, who garnered celebrity-like attention from the Japanese media, the US embassy utilized actual celebrities to attract general attention to LGBT issues in Japan. It invited Kuroyanagi Tetsuko, a popular Japanese TV presenter, in 2013, and George Takei and Abe Akie, the Japanese first lady, in 2014, to its party for LGBT pride month. These activities of the US embassy in Tokyo certainly created LGBT visibility and opportunities for LGBT activists, such as giving a platform and support to openly LGBT politicians in Japan. At the same time, however, the Obama administration's pro-LGBT discourses disconnected it from the historical and social contexts of sexual minorities in Japan and contextualized them within US politics and discourses. In addition, celebrities who called for tolerance toward LGBT people contributed to relabeling LGBT issues as something fashionable, rather than human rights issues reflected in the everyday struggles of minorities. Through the Obama administration's efforts for LGBT rights promotion, LGBT rights have gained US connotations and their promotion has been an "Americanization" of LGBT rights in Japan (Kawasaka, 2013).

The subsequent Trump administration was not LGBT-friendly, as evidenced by its rolling back of domestic LGBT rights protections started by Obama, moving toward a trans ban in the US military and supporting "religious liberty" against LGBT equality. In Japan, however, the US embassy still participated in TRP, despite a dramatic decline in the number of its LGBT-related events and messages. The then Secretary of State Mike Pompeo even declared LGBTI Pride Month on 1 June 2018. The Trump administration failed to create a new coherent international narrative on LGBT issues and instead dispassionately, perhaps lazily, merely repeated the narrative of the Obama administration.[3]

1.3 The 2020 Summer Olympics and Paralympics and LGBT visibility

The 2020 Summer Olympics and Paralympics in Tokyo also influenced general attitudes toward LGBT issues in Japan. In September 2013, the International Olympic Committee (IOC) elected Tokyo as the host of the Olympics in 2020. The 2014 Winter Olympics in Sochi had suffered from international criticism and boycotts caused by Russia's anti-gay policy (see, e.g., Sykes et al., 2018; Wiedlack, 2017), and the IOC revised the Olympic Charter to include a ban on discrimination against sexual orientation in 2014. Observing an international affray caused by LGBT rights, Japanese officials recognized the need to promote LGBT rights for a successful Olympics (Maree, 2020b; Nikaidō, 2017). In 2016, the Tokyo Organising Committee (TOC) of the Olympic and Paralympic Games (2016, pp. 4–5) announced the Tokyo 2020 Games Vision and its three core values: "Achieving Personal Best," "Unity in Diversity," and "Connecting to Tomorrow." Connecting the concept of diversity with a positive future, the vision stated:

> Sport has the power to change the world and our future. The Tokyo 1964 Games completely transformed Japan. The Tokyo 2020 Games will bring positive reform to the world. (TOC, 2016, p. 1)

---

[3] For changes in US foreign policy on LGBT rights under the Trump administration, see Carlson-Rainer (2019).

In preparing to host the 2020 Games, the Tokyo metropolitan government passed an anti-discrimination ordinance – the Ordinance for Respect of Human Rights Protected by the Olympics Charter in Tokyo (Tokyō-to Orinpikku Kenshō de Uta-wareru Jinken Sonchō no Jitsugen o Mezasu Jōrei) – focusing on anti-LGBT discrimination and banning hate speech against non-Japanese people in 2018. In this context, LGBT rights were considered an unavoidable international duty for Japan as the host country, even though the conservative Abe administration and the Liberal Democratic Party (LDP) were in favor of protecting "traditional" family values against feminist policies (see, e.g., Yamaguchi, 2014).

LGBT activists also regarded the Tokyo 2020 Games as a great opportunity to make LGBT rights mainstream in Japan. Human Rights Watch in Japan promoted the institutionalization of human rights progress, including LGBT rights for the 2020 Games. It held a campaign for an anti-discrimination law that included banning discrimination based on sexual orientation and gender identity at a national level. However, this human rights approach necessitated "considerable negotiation between pursuit of economic profits and respect for human rights" (Sykes et al., 2018, p. 99). A marketing approach for LGBT awareness was more successful in attracting media attention. Good Aging Yells, a Tokyo-based nonprofit LGBT advocacy organization, announced that it would open a Pride House Tokyo during the Games, which supported the TOC's diversity policies (Pride House, 2017).

However, LGBT activists' efforts to promote diversity and human rights exposed the hypocrisy and resistance of the Japanese elite. The first TOC president, Mori Yoshirō, a former prime minister infamous for gaffes that attract public attention, sparked turmoil by his sexist remark that: "If we increase the number of female board members, we have to make sure their speaking time is restricted somewhat; they have difficulty finishing, which is annoying" ("Tokyo Olympics Chief," 2021). Following Mori's resignation from the TOC and several other sexism scandals involving other TOC members, Hashimoto Seiko, the new TOC president, visited Pride House Tokyo for Tokyo's Pride Week in April 2021 to publicly emphasize the committee's commitment to diversity (Takenaka, 2021). The Japanese Olympic Committee (JOC) also reformed the board to increase female membership, achieving its target of 40 % for gender equality. Despite its supposed commitment to diversity, the JOC elected Sugiyama Fumino, a trans man and one of the TPP directors, as a "female" board member, ignoring his gender identity and commitment to trans activism (Asatsuma, 2021). In this context, the TOC and JOC attempted to cover up the sexism scandals by exploiting LGBT activists as "diversity" branding while ignoring their identities and dignity.

In this way, the globalization of LGBT politics such as the marketization of diversity by multinational corporations, human rights diplomacy, and human rights issues in international sports events, prepared the ground for Japanese society to address LGBT issues. At the same time, however, LGBT political issues are tied to economic benefits by the LGBT market or successful international events such as the Olympics. In the next section, I will discuss how LGBT issues in Japan have been translated into actual policies.

2 The political actualization of LGBT rights in Japan

Japanese local governments have become some of the main actors for the institutionalization of LGBT rights in Japan. After Tokyo was selected as the Olympic host city, Shibuya Ward, one of the city's major commercial and cultural centers, announced that it would be the first local municipality to issue certificates of same-sex partnership in 2014.[4] By March 2020, 47 local municipalities had introduced a similar system ("Pātonāshippu seido," 2020). Following Bunkyō Ward in Tokyo in 2013, approximately 10 local municipalities, Ibaraki Prefecture, and metropolitan Tokyo have passed or are moving toward legalizing an anti-discrimination ordinance, including discrimination based on sexual orientation and gender identity and expression.

The ground for local LGBT rights movements was prepared in the early 2000s by the then Prime Minister Koizumi's neoliberal reforms, which aimed for state decentralization by privatization and reducing the size of the central government's bureaucracy. One of his main goals was to change relations between central and local governments: giving local governments more political autonomy while cutting funds from the central government (Ikawa, 2008). As a result, local governments have needed to govern in the same way as a private company for securing their own funds: making their own mascots to attract people, rebranding their local products, playing the role of a matchmaker (konkatsu) for young people to form families and produce babies to combat the problem of an aging society (Itō, 2015; Walter, 2014).

In this context, some local governments started to regard LGBT rights as an opportunity for their new branding. The introduction of the new term "LGBT" from English has contributed to the representation of LGBT issues as a new, "trending" phenomenon. Shibuya's same-sex partnership certificate system has become a model case that other local municipalities have followed. The system is purely symbolic and provides no legal protections – although some local governments have

---

4 For a background of the institutionalization of this system in Shibuya, see Esumuraruda and Kira (2015).

offered benefits with the certificate, such as the right to apply for public housing – because it is the national government that has the authority to reform the legal marriage system in Japan. Hasebe Ken, the mayor who promoted Shibuya's recognition of same-sex partnerships, openly admitted that the intention was to foster an international image of diversity and culture rather than to improve human rights protections (Esumuraruda & Kira, 2015, p. 23; Kawasaka, 2015, p. 91). Similarly, Iga City, the third municipality and the first outside Tokyo, announced a similar recognition of same-sex partnerships in 2016 as a symbolic international embrace of diversity because its prefecture, Mie, hosted the G7 summit that year. In this context, advancing LGBT rights has been regarded not as a human rights issue but a symbol of internationalism and diversity and a tool for promoting a town's image (Shimizu, 2017).

In such promotions, the term "LGBT" can often be confusing in Japanese. In the early 2010s, the term was introduced to the general public and suddenly became a buzzword (Fotache, 2019). *Kōjien*, one of the most popular Japanese dictionaries, included it for the first time in its seventh edition published in 2017. The media started using "LGBT" without understanding what it really meant. Even the *Kōjien* definition was initially inaccurate, as "people who have a different sexual orientation from the majority," which failed to include "transgender." As the term "LGBT" was confusing even for the dictionary's editors, its introduction as a buzzword promoted confusion and ignorance. As a loanword from English, "LGBT" has sometimes been utilized to refer to sexual minorities to avoid having to explain gender and sexuality issues. For instance, NHK, Japan's public broadcasting corporation, used the description *"seiteki shōsūsha, iwayuru 'LGBT'"* (sexual minorities, so called "LGBT") when referring to a gay man who died by suicide after being outed at Hitotsubashi University (NHK@shutoken, 2016). It avoided using the words *gei* (gay, or gay man) or *dōseiai* (homosexuality). In the Japanese context, the foreign loanword "LGBT" can therefore function to obfuscate gender and sexuality issues even in the news media.[5]

Such linguistic obfuscations of gender and sexuality issues enabled the majority party, the LDP, to discuss LGBT issues. As the social conservative party for "traditional" family values, the LDP has been critical about sexual minorities' issues and has been tied to anti-feminist nationalist movements since the 2000s (Yamaguchi, 2014). Nikaidō Yūki (2017), a journalist who has covered LGBT issues since the 2000s, reported that an MP stated in an internal LDP committee on LGBT issues that "in our view, [LGBT issues] are like observing the sun rising from the west"

---

5 For more details of this incident at Hitotsubashi University and the wider contexts of queer lives in Japanese higher education, see Shimizu (2016).

(p. 167). To draw party consensus on these issues, the LDP focused on people's ignorance and proposed a policy to promote a "proper" understanding of LGBT people among the general public.[6] Nikaidō (2017) pointed out that the LDP policy for
promoting knowledge about LGBT issues was suggested as a political strategy to
stop LGBT political movements from going "too far," such as the legalization of
same-sex partnerships or marriage and the enactment of anti-discrimination
laws at a national level because there are many opponents to LGBT rights within
the party (p. 171).

In English, "LGBT" means lesbian, gay, bisexual, and transgender/sexual, but as
a foreign loanword in Japan it is utilized for a particular political message. "LGBT"
politics is represented as a fashionable, international, new phenomenon, while ob-
fuscating actual Japanese human rights and institutional problems that the government must reform. Thus, the introduction and failure of the translation of "LGBT"
in Japan has functioned to build an information wall between the Japanese and
English contexts: while it is utilized in Japanese contexts to avoid challenging gender and sexual norms, the word "LGBT" can function internationally to give the
impression that Japanese society is making progress in LGBT rights.

The abovementioned compromises have failed to translate into actual policy.
The Abe administration did not revise the school curriculum guidelines of the Ministry of Education to include LGBT issues in 2017. Thus, their discussions about promoting "proper" knowledge about LGBT people are indeed a political performance,
pretending to support LGBT issues as the host country of the 2020 Games. In 2021,
when the pandemic-delayed Games was approaching, the LDP did not even bother
with this pretense. A bill of law on promoting LGBT understanding failed to be
read in the Diet due to opposition from an ultraconservative group within the
LDP, and it was scrapped just before the Games started in 2021. They opposed
the bill for its wording – "discrimination based on sexual orientation and gender
identity shall not be tolerated" – and the media reported that some MPs bluntly

---

6 The imagined Japanese "ignorance" on LGBT issues often functions against LGBT rights in Japan,
justifying the exclusion of gender and sexuality. In June 2020, the Nagoya District Court (2020) rejected a request to recognize those in same-sex relationships that had lasted 20 years as being in de
facto marriages (*jijitsukon*), rendering surviving partners ineligible for victim compensation
claims. *Jijitsukon* is a legal status that is usually recognized if heterosexual couples share a household for more than three years. The court based its decision on the lack of so-called "social conventions" (*shakai tsūnen*) in Japan regarding same-sex relationships, which equate cohabitation
with marital status (Nagoya District Court, 2020). Thus, the court relied on this supposed Japanese
conservatism and ignorance to exclude a survivor whose same-sex partner was murdered from
access to the victims' compensation system.

expressed homophobic views in the LDP internal meeting, such as "LGBT goes against the preservation of the species" (Doi & Kyle, 2021).

3 Cultural representations of LGBT rights

As LGBT rights refer to a new business opportunity, foreignness, internationalism, and diversity, they are often represented through a white male body. Tagame Gengorō is one of the most internationally famous and critically acclaimed Japanese gay erotic artists. His first manga for a general audience beyond gay media, *Otōto no otto* (*My Brother's Husband*, 2014–2017), was exceptionally successful compared to other LGBT-related manga. It received an Excellence Prize at the 19th Japan Media Arts Festival and was turned into a TV drama by NHK. *My Brother's Husband* is a story about a Canadian called Mike, who suddenly visits Yaichi, the twin brother of his deceased husband, in Japan. A single father with a daughter, Yaichi's ignorance and attitude toward gay couples is slowly changed as Mike stays in his house for a few weeks.

In this manga, Canadian (or Western) gay friendliness/knowledge and Japanese homophobia/ignorance are racially marked through the visible difference of Mike's white and Yaichi's Asian bodies. Unsurprisingly, in this story, only Japanese people are destined to learn new knowledge on sexuality issues from the Canadian gay man, while the opposite does not occur, although Mike sometimes enjoys the "unique" Japanese culture and customs such as food and tourism sites. The title of the first episode was "The Black Ships Arrive!" (*Kurofune ga yattekita!*). This refers to the historic arrival of the US Navy warships in Edo Bay (now Tokyo Bay) in 1853, which compelled Japan to change its centuries-old isolationism policy to open its ports to trade with the US and ended up overturning the early modern regime, triggering Japan's modernization. The ships are now used to symbolize the inevitable social changes triggered by Western political, economic, or cultural pressures, although resistance persists in Japanese society. In the history of sexual politics, a similar image of Black Ships was used for the AIDS crisis in the early 1990s, implying that it was a danger coming from the US (Shingae, 2013, p. 134). In the 2010s, however, the representation of LGBT issues in terms of Black Ships implies that LGBT tolerance and friendliness are Western phenomena and Japan is under international pressure to accept these new sexual norms.

Contrasting with Mike's embodiment of Canadian gay-friendly whiteness, the Japanese localness signifies a latent homophobia including the closeting of gay men. While Mike influences Japanese people, especially the children around him, to develop tolerance toward homosexuality, no openly gay or lesbian Asian adults appear in the story. In the scene when Mike is having dinner with Katoyan, a closeted gay friend of his deceased husband Ryōji, Mike shows a lack of empathy toward him. Just after Katoyan explains why he is in the closet to Mike – "Unlike Ryoji I have no intention of coming out. I don't think there's any reason anyone needs to go out of their way to proclaim it" – Mike scorns him in his mind: "Though, you will go out of your way to hide it" (Tagame & Ishii, 2017, p. 132). As Yaichi represents the implicit homophobia among straight people in Japanese society in the early part of the story, Katoyan symbolizes the internalized homophobia among Japanese gay people against their own visibility in society. Being with Katoyan, Mike feels he is also forced back into the closet and thinks: "I understand how Katoyan feels. But to be eating with him and keeping it from Yaichi-san.... I came out of the closet to avoid creating more secrets inside secrets" (Tagame & Ishii, 2017, p. 134). Rather than trying to understand the local or personal situation surrounding the closeted gay Japanese man, Mike, a first-time visitor to Japan, easily believes that he understands Katoyan's feelings but cares more about himself being back in the closet for a few hours. Mike's lack of interest in the Japanese cultural and political contexts shows disregard for the relationship between the Japanese social and cultural structure and the intolerance toward certain sexualities. In this story, Mike is symbolized as the promotion of tolerance for gay people without concern for local contexts, where people either become tolerant by encountering sexual others with cultural authority or remain in the old order. Only Mike is immune to change, even when he encounters cultural others. Such enforcement of cultural changes indeed coincides with the metaphor of the Black Ships.

In this work, while whiteness embodies universal values that can permeate across cultural differences, Japanese people are presented as needing to change and overcome cultural differences. When some Japanese characters fail to do so, they are tied to their localness, representing sexual conservatism such as homophobia and being in the closet. Such representations are actually underlined by both Western-centric universalism and Japanese heterosexist nationalism. Although Tagame's work was clearly intended to tackle homophobia and Japanese ignorance against same-sex couples, it rather reproduces the comfortable Japanese nationalist and heterosexist fantasy by representing LGBT-related issues and knowledge with the white male body: the Japanese and the other are visually different; Japan is a racially homogeneous and stable heteronormative place, while LGBT issues and racial diversity are foreign issues. Racialized and Westernized representations of gay friendliness and sexual diversity ironically strengthen the tie between Japanese localness and heteronormativity, which is what anti-LGBT conservatives are eager to defend.

The representation of LGBT rights and visibility through white men also goes hand in hand with the Japanese marketization of LGBT rights. In 2015, the "Out in Japan" project – a series of exhibitions of 10,000 portraits of LGBT-identifying individuals over a period of five years until 2020 – was launched to "familiarize the Japanese public with the presence of sexual minorities and to share accurate information and knowledge of the LGBT community" ("Concept," 2015). Leslie Kee, arguably the most popular and famous openly gay fashion photographer in Japan, joined the project. In 2016, Kee posted a group photograph on his Facebook page for the Out in Japan exhibition on the theme "To Work," with the following comment in Japanese: "Elite salarymen [businessmen] in leading companies are gay and came out. This one group photograph creates Japan's future." The photograph features dark-suited young men in their late 20s to early 40s, mostly Japanese but with a few white men as well, with a big caption in English "The Gay Elite: Goldman Sachs, IBM, Google, Apple, Dentsu, Mitsui Sumitomo, photographed by LESLIE KEE." This suggests that gay men can be respectful business executives in major corporations, not always the *onē* (queeny) that people see daily on TV.[7] However, at the same time, it also premises the respectability of LGBT people tied to their occupation, class, and embodied straight masculine gender. The dark suits represent the men's assimilation to the existing male-dominated Japanese corporate hierarchy and culture; the photograph is not intended to challenge this culture as the new Japanese IT entrepreneurs did in the mid-2000s with their symbolic gesture of refusing to wear business suits to challenge the "old" Japanese business order and culture.[8] While the gay men in the photograph could easily pass as straight businessmen in Japan, their youthfulness and whiteness represent the new Japanese internationalism, which is different from the existing closed corporate culture. This gay representation therefore does not radically challenge the Japanese social order but adds a new "diversity" and internationalism to it.

Such representations are enabled by the Japanese buzzwords "LGBT" and "diversity" as well. "LGBT" and "diversity" do not necessarily include gender diversity, lesbians, and trans people, in Japanese contexts – as we can see from how the JOC only increased the number of its female board members after the sexism scandals in 2021 – but it can make an impression as an international diversity symbol, represented by mostly Japanese and some exceptional white men working in multinational conglomerates. This means that the term can contribute to the international and domestic image of Japanese society as moving toward Western liberal "diversity," which is becoming symbolically important in Japanese business, as Keidanren (2017), the Japan Business Federation, suggests. At the same time, it actually allows the continuation of Japan's male-dominant, business-centered society. Eve K. Sedgwick (2011) once characterized US gay movements based on identity as sep-

---

7 For popular representations of effeminate gay men on Japanese TV, see Maree (2020a).
8 For an analysis of this symbolic gesture of IT entrepreneurs in Japan, see Warren (2007).

aratist assimilationism claiming "the right of seamless social assimilation for a group of people *on the basis of* a separatist understanding of them as embodying a stable ontological difference" (p. 183). Separatist assimilationism underlines LGBT representations in Japan as well, that is, a separatist understanding of minority for "diversity" and an assimilationist stance toward the Japanese corporate culture and heteronormative family systems.

4 Conclusion

It is true that Japanese society has been moving toward increasing the visibility of LGBT people and institutionalizing LGBT rights in the 2010s, despite the limited effectiveness of these policies. However, the LGBT rights discourses and representations are also well reflected by Japanese neoliberal reforms.

Firstly, as LGBT issues have become a marketing tool, working for LGBT rights is not a legal or social duty but a marketing strategy for private corporations that can bring them profit. This economic framing of human rights issues permits them to avoid working for LGBT issues if they decide not to pursue the market. Thus, the buzzword "LGBT issues" as the international diversity symbol has been invented in Japanese society and presented as no serious challenge to Japanese conservatism and traditional family values.

Secondly, as local governments and private corporations have become the main actors in LGBT rights policy, LGBT issues are now an exception to other human rights issues that governments must universally respect. While the role and principle of the state protecting human rights have regressed, local governments instead appear to protect them partly for their own publicity. At the same time, as the legal effectiveness of local recognitions of same-sex partnerships are limited, private corporations have started to offer actual benefits for same-sex partners, such as redefining "family" for their employees and customers. As a result, LGBT rights are localized and tied with class and education: if you can afford to live in an LGBT-friendly local government area, or if you are lucky to be employed by an LGBT-friendly corporation and have enough knowledge about LGBT-friendly services and legal advice, you can partly protect and enjoy your own rights. This localization and privatization of human rights issues are undermining equality among citizens, and economic principles are being applied to issues of human rights and dignity. Moreover, ineffective and uneven governmentality is appearing in Japan.

These neoliberal LGBT issues contain serious contradictions: between new ideas and values of diversity and Japan's internal conservatism, and between economic and legal principles. Such superficial "LGBT friendliness," characterized by

Western- and economic-centered narratives, is also being pointed out by anti–LGBT rights critics, some of whom are openly LGBT-identifying conservatives. Matsuura Daigo, an openly gay ex-politician, said that LGBT rights are concepts from the West, where society has long been homophobic and has acted to legally, socially, and religiously repress LGBT people (Matsuura & Ozawa, 2018, pp. 232–234). Echoing the LGBT market discourse but using it in an anti–LGBT rights way, right-wing politicians in the LDP have started to insist that LGBT people are "unproductive" as they do not produce children, and therefore the government should not support them (Sugita, 2018, pp. 58–59). Unsurprisingly, such anti–LGBT rights discourses are products of the same discursive dynamism that enabled LGBT-friendly discourses in the 2010s.

Acknowledgments

This paper contains the outcomes of research funded by the Deutsche Forschungsgemeinschaft in the framework of "Sexual Diversity and Human Rights in 21st Century Japan: LGBTIQ Activisms and Resistance from a Transnational Perspective" (Project No. 446477950).

References

Activists march for LGBT rights with Kennedy's support. (2016, May 9). *Asahi shinbun.* http://www.asahi.com/ajw/articles/AJ201605090020.html.

Akasugi, Y., Tsuchiya, Y., & Tsutsui, M. (2004). *Dōsei pātonā: Dōseikon/DP hō o shiru tameni* [Same-sex partners: Understanding same-sex marriage and domestic partner laws]. Shakai Hyōronsha.

Asatsuma, H. (2021, June 29). Japan Olympic Committee didn't check how trans man wanted to be identified on its board. *Mainichi shinbun.* https://mainichi.jp/english/articles/20210629/p2a/00m/0na/020000c.

Baudinette, T. (2021). *Regimes of desire: Young gay men, media, and masculinity in Tokyo.* The University of Michigan Press.

Branchik, B. J. (2002). Out in the market: A history of the gay market segment in the United States. *Journal of Macromarketing, 22*(1), 86–97. https://doi.org/10.1177/027467022001008.

Carlson-Rainer, E. (2019). Will sexual minority rights be Trumped? Assessing the policy sustainability of LGBTI rights diplomacy in American foreign policy. *Diplomacy & Statecraft, 30*(1), 147–163. https://doi.org/10.1080/09592296.2019.1557422.

Chasin, A. (2001). *Selling out: The gay and lesbian movement goes to market.* Palgrave.

Clinton, H. R. (2011, December 6). *Remarks in recognition of International Human Rights Day.* Palais des Nations, Geneva, Switzerland. https://2009-2017.state.gov/secretary/20092013clinton/rm/2011/12/178368.htm.

Concept. (2015). *Out in Japan.* http://outinjapan.com/concept.

Dentsū. (2015, April 23). *Dentsū daibāshiti rabo ga "LGBT chōsa 2015" o jisshi* [Dentsū Diversity Lab conducts the 2015 LGBT survey]. http://www.dentsu.co.jp/news/release/2015/0423-004032.html.

Doi, K., & Kyle, K. (2021, May 21). *A gold medal for homophobia in Japan: Japan's ruling party members slur LGBT community.* Human Rights Watch. https://www.hrw.org/news/2021/05/22/gold-medal-homophobia-japan.

Duggan, L. (2004). *The twilight of equality? Neoliberalism, cultural politics, and the attack on democracy.* Beacon Press.

Enoki, T. (2019). Nihonkoku kenpō ni okeru dōseikon no ichi [The status of same sex marriage in the Constitution of Japan]. *Senshū hōgaku ronshū, 135,* 14–44.

Esumuraruda & Kira. (2015). *Dōsei pātonāshippu shōmei hajimarimashita* [Same-sex partnerships are now recognized]. Potto Shuppan.

Fotache, I. (2019). Japanese "LGBT boom" discourse and its discontents. In C. Cottet & M. L. Picq (Eds.), *Sexuality and translation in world politics.* E-International Relations. https://www.e-ir.info/2019/08/20/japanese-lgbt-boom-discourse-and-its-discontents.

Fushimi, N. (2019). *Shinjuku ni-chōme* [Shinjuku ni-chōme]. Shinchōsha.

Hattori, Y. (2017). LGBT seisaku no dōkō to kigyō no LGBT taiō no jōkyō [Trends in LGBT policy and corporate responses to LGBT issues]. *Seisaku/keiei kenkyū, 4,* 91–101.

Ikawa, H. (2008). *15 years of decentralization reform in Japan.* Council of Local Authorities for International Relations. https://www.jlgc.org.uk/en/pdfs/up-to-date_en4.pdf.

Ilye, A. (2008). *Gei manē ga Eikoku keizai o sasaeru!?* [Is gay money supporting the British economy!?]. Yōsensha.

Imperial Household Agency. (2020, February 21). *Press conference on the occasion of his majesty's birthday.* https://www.kunaicho.go.jp/page/kaiken/showEn/30.

Itō, Y. (2015). Konkatsu shien jigyō ni okeru jichitai no yakuwari: Hyōgo-ken Kasai-shi to Taka-shi o jireini [The role of local governments in the marriage support project: Case studies of Kasai City and Taka City, Hyogo Prefecture]. *Hyōgo chiri, 60,* 29–45.

Kawaguchi, K. (2013). Neoriberaru taisei to kuia-teki shutai [The neoliberal system and the queer subject]. *Hiroshima shudai ronshū, 54*(1), 151–169.

Kawasaka, K. (2013). Amerika-ka sareru LGBT no kenri: "Gei no kenri wa jinken dearu" enzetsu to shinpo to iu naratibu [Americanized LGBT human rights: The narrative of progress and the speech "Gay rights are human rights"]. *Gender and Sexuality. Journal of the Center for Gender Studies, 8,* 5–28.

Kawasaka, K. (2015). Jinken ka, tokken ka, onkei ka?: Nihon ni okeru LGBT no kenri [Human rights, privileges, or benefits? LGBT rights in Japan]. *Gendai shisō, 43*(16), 96–108.

Kee, L. (2016, October 23). *Elite salarymen in leading companies are gay and came out. This one group photograph creates Japan's future* [Status update]. Facebook. https://www.facebook.com/lesliekeesuper/posts/the-gay-elite-x-out-in-japan-photographed-by-leslie-kee-supported-by-goldman-sac/10154629194407363.

Keidanren. (2017). *Daibāsitī/inkurūjon shakai no jitsugen ni mukete* [Toward the realization of a diverse and inclusive society]. https://www.keidanren.or.jp/policy/2017/039.html.

Kikuchi, N. (2019). *Nihon no posuto feminizumu* [Postfeminism in Japan]. Ōtsukisha.

Kokunai shijō 5/7-chō en "LGBT shijō" [The "LGBT market" is worth 5 or 7 trillion yen in the domestic market]. (2012, July 14). *Shūkan daiamondo,* 131–147.

Linehan, P. J., & Kanegusuke, E. (2014). *Fūfu enman* [A happy couple]. Tōyō Keizai.

Maks-Solomon, C., & Drewry, J. M. (2021). Why do corporations engage in LGBT rights activism? LGBT employee groups as internal pressure groups. *Business and Politics, 23*(1), 124–152. https:// doi.org/10.1017/bap.2020.5.

Maree, C. (2020a). "LGBT issues" and the 2020 games. *The Asia-Pacific Journal Japan Focus, 18*(4–7). https://apjjf.org/2020/4/Maree.html.

Maree, C. (2020b). *Queerqueen: Excess and constraints in writing gender and sexuality into popular Japanese media.* Oxford University Press.

Pātonāshippu seido, 47 jichitai ni kakudai [Same-sex partnership system expanded into 47 municipalities]. (2020, March 31). *Marriage for All Japan.* https://www.marriageforall.jp/blog/ 20200331.

Matsuura, D., & Ogawa, E. (2018). Fūsatsu sareta LGBT tōjisha no honne [Repressed voices of LGBT people]. *Gekkan hanada*, December, 232–243.

Nagoya District Court. (2020). Judgment of 4 June 2020, case no. H30-GyoU-76. *Hanrei jihō,* 2465, 13 ff. https://www.courts.go.jp/app/hanrei_jp/detail4?id=89615.

Nakanishi, E. (2017). LGBT no genjō to kadai [LGBT people's current situations and problems]. *Rippō to chōsa, 394*, 3–17. https://www.sangiin.go.jp/japanese/annai/chousa/rippou_chousa/back number/2017pdf/20171109003.pdf.

National security strategy. (2015). White House. https://obamawhitehouse.archives.gov/sites/default/ files/docs/2015_national_security_strategy_2.pdf.

NHK@shutoken [@nhk_shutoken]. (2016, August 5). *LGBT dansei jisatsu de daigaku o teiso* [Sue the university for LGBT man's suicide]. Twitter. https://twitter.com/nhk_shutoken/status/ 761467875760545792?s=61&t=ANkeS2hj9LCwXseTjIwGAA.

Nihon no LGBT [LGBT in Japan]. (2012, July 14). *Shūkan Tōyō keizai*, 122–135.

Nikaidō, Y. (2017). Hyōryū suru LGBT hōan [An uncertain LGBT rights bill]. *Sekai, 5*, 167–172.

Obama uses embassies to push for LGBT rights abroad. (2014, April 28). *The Guardian.* https://www. theguardian.com/world/2014/jun/28/obama-gay-rights-abroad-embassies-activism.

Ogiue, C. (2012, April 26). Tayōna ikikata o sonchō shiyō [Let's respect diverse ways of living]. *Synodos.* http://synodos.jp/society/2263.

Pride House. (2017, April 4). *2020 Olympic + Paralympic Games Tokyo, Japan.* Pride House International. http://www.pridehouseinternational.org/mec-events/tokyo-japa-2020.

Roos, J. (2013, April 27). LGBT no kenri: Kōminken to shite suishin o [Seneca Falls, Selma, and Stonewall: Civil rights and equality for all] (US Embassy, Trans.). *Asahi shinbun*, 17.

Sedgwick, E. K. (2011). *The weather in Proust* (J. Goldberg, Ed.). Duke University Press.

Sender, K. (2004). *Business, not politics: The making of the gay market.* Columbia University Press.

Shimizu, A. (2016). Daigaku wa "daigaku" o mamoreruka: Daigaku ni okeru sekushuaru mainoritī [Can a university defend the mission of universities? Sexual minorities at universities]. *Sekai, 11*, 188–194.

Shimizu, A. (2017). Daibāsitī kara kenri hoshō e [From diversity to human rights protection]. *Sekai, 5*, 134–143.

Shingae, A. (2013). *Nihon no "gei" to eizu* [Gay people and AIDS in Japan]. Seikyūsha.

Shingae, A. (2021). Daibāsitī suishin to LGBT/SOGI no yukue [Diversity promotion and the future of LGBT/SOGI]. In K. Iwabuchi (Ed.), *Tayōsei to no taiwa* [Dialogues with diversity] (pp. 36–58). Seikyūsha.

Sugita, M. (2018). "LGBT" shien no do ga sugiru ["LGBT" support is too excessive]. *Shinchō 45, 8*, 57–60.

Sunagawa, H. (2015). *Shinjuku ni-chōme no bunka jinruigaku* [Cultural anthropological study of Shinjuku ni-chōme]. Tarō Jirōsha Editasu.

Supporters. (2013). *Tokyo Rainbow Pride.* http://www.tokyorainbowweek.jp/supporters.

Supporters. (2014). *Tokyo Rainbow Pride.* http://trw.trparchives.com/?page_id=20.

Sykes, H., Seki, M., & Itani, S. (2018). Homonationalism and sport mega-events: Olympics from Vancouver 2010 to Tokyo 2020. *Journal of Sport and Gender Studies, 16,* 89–111. https://doi.org/10.18967/sptgender.16.0_89.

Tagame, G., & Ishii, A. (2017). *My brother's husband.* Pantheon Books.

Takenaka, K. (2021, April 27). *Tokyo 2020 chief visits LGBTQ centre to emphasise diversity.* Reuters. https://www.reuters.com/world/asia-pacific/tokyo-2020-chief-visits-lgbtq-centre-emphasise-diversity-2021-04-27.

Tokyo Olympics chief Yoshiro Mori "sorry" for sexism row. (2021, February 4). BBC News. https://www.bbc.com/news/world-asia-55929404.

The Tokyo Organising Committee of the Olympic and Paralympic Games. (2016). *Tokyo 2020 action & legacy plan 2016.* https://library.olympics.com/Default/doc/SYRACUSE/166614/tokyo-2020-action-and-legacy-plan-2016-participating-in-the-tokyo-2020-games-connecting-with-tomorro?_lg=en-GB.

Walter, D. (2014, February 4). Japanese mascotization, marketing, and imagined communities. *Japan Sociology.* https://japansociology.com/2014/02/04/japanese-mascotization-marketing-and-imagined-communities.

Warren, L. (2007). The establishment strikes back? The life and times of Takafumi Horie. *International Journal of Entrepreneurship and Innovation, 8*(4), 261–270. https://doi.org/10.5367/000000007782433222.

Weber, C. (2016). *Queer international relations: Sovereignty, sexuality and the will to knowledge.* Oxford University Press.

Wiedlack, M. K. (2017). Gays vs. Russia: Media representations, vulnerable bodies and the construction of a (post)modern West. *European Journal of English Studies, 21*(3), 241–257. https://doi.org/10.1080/13825577.2017.1369271.

Yamaguchi, T. (2014). "Gender free" feminism in Japan: A story of mainstreaming and backlash. *Feminist Studies, 40*(3), 541–572. https://doi.org/10.1353/fem.2014.0033.

Yotsumoto, M., & Senba, H. (2017). *Daibāsitī to māketingu: LGBT no jirei kara rikai suru atarashii kigyō senryaku* [Diversity and marketing: Understanding the new corporate strategy through LGBT case studies]. Senden Kaigi.

Diana Khor and Saori Kamano

Same-sex partnerships in Japan: Would legalization mean deradicalization?

In the first judicial ruling on same-sex marriage in Japan, the Sapporo District Court ruled on 17 March 2021 that it is unconstitutional to deny same-sex couples the right to marry. This ruling was based on Article 14 of the Constitution, which guarantees the right to equality under the law. While same-sex marriage advocates celebrated this, they also lamented that the court appeared to affirm the definition of marriage as a heterosexual union in stating that disallowing same-sex marriage does not constitute a violation of Article 24, which defines marriage as being based on the mutual consent of "both sexes" ("Japan Court Rules," 2021; Kawamura, 2021).[1] Is the ruling to be celebrated or lamented? And for what reasons?

Early efforts to legalize same-sex marriage in the West were accompanied by critical discussions of its potential impact, specifically about whether it would further reinforce the heterosexual, patriarchal institutions of marriage, family, and kinship, or whether it would challenge the foundation of these core social institutions.[2] The surge in the legalization of same-sex partnerships across the world in the past few decades has provided invaluable field data to adjudicate among these claims.[3] It has become apparent that how one argues for it is as, if not more, important, than the actual legalization. Equally important is how same-sex partners negotiate the system and understand their own partnership.

In this paper, we will briefly review recent works on the framing of same-sex partnerships before discussing the situation in Japan. Drawing on our previous analyses of same-sex partnerships in Japan (Khor, 2020; Khor & Kamano, 2021), as well as ethnographic and survey data we have collected in various projects involving same-sex partners (Kamano et al., 2018; Khor & Kamano, 2017, 2019; Tang et al., 2020), we aim to elucidate how same-sex partners make sense of their relationship, particularly in the context of kin relations.[4]

---

1 Unless otherwise indicated, all translations from Japanese in this paper are by the authors.
2 See Sullivan (1997) for an early anthology of the debate and Tang et al. (2020) for a review of the arguments. For arguments criticizing the impact of same-sex marriage in Japan, see Horie (2010) and Shida (2009).
3 As of 2022, over 30 nations and territories have enacted laws legalizing same-sex partnership, over half of which occurred after 2010 (Masci et al., 2019; Neghaiwi & Wiegmann, 2022).
4 This paper was written in the context of a larger project, *Same-Sex Partnership in Hong Kong and Japan: Where Family Studies Meet Queer Studies*, funded by the JSPS Grant-in-aid for Scientific Re-

1 The significance of frames

The arguments used to advocate the legalization of same-sex partnerships in court or in society can not only shape the success or failure of legalization, but also have a broader, long-term impact on the very institution of marriage and the (de)legitimation of sexual diversity. Put very simply, depending on the framing, the legalization of same-sex marriage can make society more inclusive of diverse relationships through reaffirming individual rights, or less inclusive by specifying a standard of monogamous coupledom to which one should conform in order to receive the privileges accorded to such unions. In other words, legalization may radicalize and fundamentally change the institution of marriage and kinship, or it may also simply consolidate it. Thus, it is not whether, but how, one argues for the legalization of same-sex unions that matters. Here, we will tease out the relevant arguments in the extant literature to provide an interpretive framework for Japan.

In an analysis of how the framing of political debates can affect policy preferences, political scientist Deva Woodly (2018) found that "all kinds of families" was the most resonant frame in arguments for same-sex marriage in *New York Times* articles from 1994 to 2014. To counter the anti-same-sex marriage arguments that affirm "family values" rooted in religious teachings and traditions, the "all kinds of families" frame affirms the stability of (same-sex) families and relationships and "the social good of family relations" (Woodly, 2018, p. 31), whereas the "equality frame" argument shifts the focus from religious values or morality to the value of "equal access" as the determinant of social policy (p. 30). Woodly (2018) observed that both frames moved the discussion away from sexual and gender norms, which improved its resonance with the public. Centering her analysis on changes in public opinion in response to how the issue was framed, Woodly (2018) did not discuss the implications for the institution of marriage. Focusing on "the public good of family relations" and the stability of same-sex families can result in a lost opportunity to create a truly inclusive society as the mainstream institution of the family remains uninterrogated. Similarly, an emphasis on "all kinds of families" in the mass media, especially with a focus on love and stability, does not necessarily endorse all types of unions, as they reaffirm mainstream family values and only tolerate same-sex unions if they form the same type of "loving and stable" families.

search (19H1571), Principal investigator: Diana Khor; Co-investigators: Saori Kamano and Yusuke Kamiya; Research collaborator: Denise T. S. Tang.

Legal scholar Macarena Saez (2014) argued that if same-sex marriage were legalized without allowing for other forms of emotional associations, a hierarchy of families would result in which some unions would receive more legal protection than others (p. 128). In contrast, Saez (2014) continued, embracing different forms of family while legalizing same-sex marriage has the potential of dissociating citizenship from marriage and allowing for diverse family forms that all enjoy equal protection from the state so long as they remain committed to respecting the rights of each family member. Following the same line of reasoning, other research, as reviewed below, has examined how the very arguments made in court have a direct impact on whether the heteronormative institution of marriage would be strengthened or weakened by the way same-sex partnership is legalized cross-nationally.

Comparisons have been made between legalizing same-sex marriage and decriminalizing (male) homosexual sex in some states in the US. Political philosopher Marino Croce's (2018) close reading of the legal opinions on *Lawrence v. Texas* (2003) showed that homosexual relations become "speakable" only in coupledom in the private sphere (p. 409). In other words, instead of a liberalizing decision that results in the acceptance of diverse modes of intimacy, the decriminalization of homosexual sex affirms the hegemonic form of monogamous kinship that now admits a mode of same-sex relationship in its image. Croce (2018) cited similar arguments in courts outside the US, including the European Court of Human Rights, which in 2010 affirmed that same-sex couples in a stable relationship should have the right to enjoy a "private and family life"; and the Italian Court of Cassation in 2012, which directly emphasized the "aptness" of some unions to be considered "families" (p. 410). Indeed, citing Pierre Bourdieu (1987), Croce (2018) argued that bringing the issue of same-sex marriage to court appears to have reframed it in a way that conforms to current legal categories – the process of reframing creates a "new homosexual" who meets the standard to claim the rights previously reserved for heterosexuals (p. 418).

Across nations, empirical studies have shown that legal arguments can cut both ways. Arguments affirming the value of marriage can be seen to constitute an assimilationist position that affirms the heteronormative marital institution. Examples include the various cases in the US (e. g., *Geiger v. Kitzhaber*, 2014; *Goodridge v. Department of Public Health*, 2003) that "mandate a particular moral code," prescribing strong, stable marriages that are to be protected above all other emotional associations, to which same-sex couples (must) conform to gain legal recognition (Saez, 2014, p. 137). In contrast, human dignity can be invoked without connecting it to the "goodness" or the importance of marriage. Saez (2014) discussed the case of South Africa, where same-sex unions were legalized with reference to dignity being connected to equality (of worth) and autonomy – the legalization of civil unions that can be entered into by both heterosexual and same-sex couples is indicative of the legal inclusion of diverse family forms, since "it is not marriage *per se* that gives individuals dignity, but instead, dignity is derived from the capacity to *choose* to marry" (p. 150). Similarly, when same-sex marriage was argued in courts in Mexico, Brazil, Colombia, and Spain, the emphasis was on dignity defined as equality and autonomy (Saez, 2014, pp. 194–196).

In 2019, Taiwan became the first, and is to date the only, nation in Asia to have legalized same-sex marriage. Justice Yuan's interpretation of the constitution can be examined for arguments supporting legalization (Constitutional Court R.O.C. [Taiwan], 2017). The freedom of marriage, guaranteed by Article 22 of the Constitution, was seen to include "decisional autonomy" with respect to "whether to marry" and "whom to marry." Such autonomy was argued to be "vital to the sound development of personality and safeguarding of human dignity" and is therefore a "fundamental right" protected by Article 22. As such, while the specific right of freedom of marriage was invoked, the core of the argument was human dignity. Narrowly defining marriage as "permanent unions of [an] intimate and exclusive nature," however, the argument concluded:

> The need, capability, willingness, and longing, in both physical and psychological senses, for creating such permanent unions of intimate and exclusive nature are equally essential to homosexuals and heterosexuals, given the importance of the freedom of marriage to the sound development of personality and safeguarding of human dignity. (Constitutional Court R.O.C. [Taiwan], 2017)

In one breath, "human dignity" was merged with an affirmation of marriage as permanent, intimate, and exclusive, limiting the imagination of alternative unions, even though it was also mentioned that procreation is not part of the definition of marriage and that unions are formed "for the purpose of living a common life" (Constitutional Court R.O.C. [Taiwan], 2017; see also Chen, 2019a, 2019b; Wang & Chen, 2017).

2 Japan

Same-sex marriage has not been legalized in Japan. However, beginning with Shibuya Ward in 2015, over 200 local governments, as of 1 July 2022, have allowed for the registration of same-sex partnerships (Niji Bridge, 2022). These registrations are not legally binding and the right to register is restricted to residents of that ward, city, or prefecture. While these registrations are far from an alternative form of legal same-sex partnerships in terms of legal protection, they might have been instrumental in placing the issue of same-sex marriage on the public agenda. In two recent publications, we examined public arguments for and against same-sex marriage (Khor, 2020; Khor & Kamano, 2021). Suffice it here to point out that activists do invoke the arguments presented by the Japanese state that empha- size the naturalness and importance of the family as an institution (Khor, 2019; Khor & Kamano, 2021), albeit toward a different end. The ruling party's proposed amendment to the Constitution of Japan adds a description of the family as a "nat- ural" and "fundamental" unit of society, in which mutual help is "mandatory" (Su- giura, 2013). Equal Marriage Alliance (EMA) Japan (n.d.), for example, champions same-sex marriage by describing the institution of marriage as a system that "im- proves the stability of the household and society" and arguing that countries that recognize same-sex marriage are further improving the productivity of society as a whole (Khor, 2020, p. 34; Khor & Kamano, 2021). According to EMA Japan (n.d.), to exclude same-sex couples from "the most important legal system for humans and society" is a dire violation of the principle of equality and, in contrast, legalizing same-sex marriage would make it possible for same-sex couples to "take more re- sponsibility toward each other's health and well-being." Not only does this argu- ment reinforce marriage as a natural institution into which same-sex couples are merely incorporated, it also affirms the heteronormative foundation of the state, that is, the married couple as the contributing members of a stable society.

The construction of marriage and the family as a "natural" institution that is the core of a stable society feeds into what Lisa Duggan (2002) termed "the new homonormativity," which is a "politics that does not contest dominant heteronor- mative assumptions and institutions but upholds and sustains them while promis- ing the possibility of a demobilized gay constituency and a privatized, depoliticized gay culture anchored in domesticity and consumption" (p. 179). However, putting the arguments by the state aside, it is understandable that activists and same- sex couples themselves would make arguments for same-sex marriage being "pub- licly acceptable," regardless of their own opinions. It is even conceivable that those who put themselves at the forefront to fight for the legalization of same-sex mar- riage might be ambivalent about marriage itself but committed to securing the legal rights for others for whom it is paramount due to their residence status, eco- nomic needs, or health issues. Therefore, it is important to listen to how same-sex couples themselves talk about same-sex marriage. Here, we draw on three previ- ous studies that we conducted to examine how same-sex couples negotiate legal same-sex partnerships.[5]

5 For relevant works developed from these projects, see Khor and Kamano (2017, 2019, 2021), Khor (2020), Tang et al. (2020), and Kamano et al. (2018).

1. "A Qualitative Analysis of Intimacy in Mother-Daughter Relationships: Negotiating Heterosexual, Gender, and Family Norms" – a comparative study of Japan and Hong Kong – funded by JSPS Grant-in-Aid for Scientific Research (B) (JP26285120) (Principal investigator: Diana Khor). The data drawn upon here were based on interviews conducted in 2015 with five non-heterosexual women about their relationships with their mothers in Japan from two age groups (28–39 and 40–50) recruited through personal acquaintances. They are indicated by "(MD)" in the text.

2. A comparative study of the legalization of same-sex partnerships in Hong Kong, Taiwan, and Japan, funded by the Sumitomo Foundation (158038) (Principal investigator: Denise T. S. Tang). The Japanese sample consisted of nine interview participants, including two lesbian activists who were a couple. The participants were recruited through personal acquaintances via social media posts, and all but one participant in his fifties were in their thirties and forties. The interviews with individuals and couples were conducted in 2017 and focused on their views on the legalization of same-sex partnerships. Data from this study are indicated by "(S)" in the text, after the participants' pseudonyms.

3. A study focusing on the partnership certificate granted by Shibuya Ward in Tokyo, planned by the Shibuya City Office but involving researchers from a JSPS Grant-in-Aid for Scientific Research Project (16H03709) (Principal investigator: Kamano Saori). Sixteen persons were interviewed, 12 of whom (including five couples) were registered as partners in Shibuya and four of whom (including one couple) were interested in doing so. The interviews were conducted in 2017 and focused on their experiences and ideas about their partnership registration. Data from this study are indicated by "(Shibuya)" in the text, after the participants' pseudonyms.

3 Same-sex partners' negotiation of same-sex partnerships

In our most recent analysis invoking philosopher and queer theorist Jasbir K. Puar's (2017) concept of homonationalism to explore how the Japanese state portrays itself as "tolerant" without devoting itself to protecting the rights of sexual minorities, we identified ideas expressed by same-sex couples that inadvertently naturalize and affirm the primacy of marriage (Khor & Kamano, 2021). At the same time, we also noted their ambivalence toward marriage as an institution and their critical assessment of heterosexual unions. Here, we would like to look more closely into this ambivalence and derive implications for the institution of marriage should same-sex unions be legalized. We identified various ideas that affirm the normalcy, legitimacy, and/or significance of the existing institution, but also show a desire for "queer" marriage or an acknowledgment of those queer people who feel left out by the same-sex marriage discourse.

There are various ways of conceiving or talking about same-sex relationships that not only leave the primacy of the marital institution unquestioned, but actually affirm its significance. One common argument is that if heterosexual couples can get married, why not same-sex couples? The equivalence of same-sex partnership to heterosexual marriage is also asserted through invoking symbols of and common practices in the latter.

To some couples, invoking symbols such as the wedding ring, or calling one's partner "wife" or "husband," renders one's same-sex relationship intelligible to others as "marriage." Chie (S), who had lived with her partner for over 10 years when she filed the registration of partnership in Shibuya, elaborated on the significance of the ring:

> We both wear rings now, but we were never really interested in making our relationship public/symbolic like this. At least, I didn't really care when I was married to a man before. I'm now in my 40s and people ask me about my marriage status a lot if I don't wear a ring. I'm happy to answer their questions and tell them about my life history and current same-sex relationship status, but it is just too much to do every time they ask me the same question. If I put on a ring, people would assume that I'm married and I can avoid those stressful situations. The rings are very useful.

Chikako (S), Chie's partner, also in her 40s, concurred:

> I just wanted to be honest with people. Also, I wanted to avoid situations where I need to explain my complicated relationship status. If I'm wearing a ring without the certificate,[6] I feel like I'm lying to people. When they ask me if I'm married because of the ring, I can talk about the partnership certificate....
>
> This makes a difference. I can say to others that I have a serious partner. Nevertheless, there aren't many practical changes. We cannot benefit from the partnership certificate that much.... It is like a weapon to protect ourselves. It gives us some assurance.

---

6 The "certificate" here refers to the Shibuya Partnership Certificate. While not legally binding, it allows the registered partners to apply for joint housing loans, family discount deals for cell phones, and so on. To apply, the partners are required to draw up a notarized partnership contract that proves that they are in a true relationship based on love and trust, and that they are living together, taking responsibility for and supporting each other, and shouldering the obligation to share living expenses (Kamano et al., 2018).

Eri (S), in her late 20s, had started living with her partner just one year before she was interviewed. She explained why she refers to her registered partnership as a "marriage":

> Before we got married, I called her "girlfriend," even though it's perfectly fine to call her "partner" too. Personally, I feel that "partner" is most appropriate but, for me, to say that I am married, I do feel a sense of responsibility, and people around too, well, [think] these two are married. They might feel it a little odd at first, but for these people, we'd like to raise their consciousness, and so I do use terms like "married" and "wife" quite deliberately.

Putting on a ring invokes a shared symbol in a heteronormative society and affirms the legitimacy of the marital institution, even though the partnership registration is not equivalent to a legally sanctioned marriage. The same goes for how one calls one's partner. And, ultimately, it is the legal recognition that authenticates these symbols of marriage and makes them "real." Without this, a same-sex relationship remains unintelligible to others. In other words, the same-sex relationship is rendered intelligible only within the heteronormative paradigm. At times, the reference to marriage as it is practiced now is explicit, and conformity to its norms becomes an indicator of a "real marital relationship," as expressed by Keisuke (Shibuya), a gay man in his late 30s who had registered his partnership a year before the interview took place:

> In a "real" marital relationship, people share their household income. If not, the one with more money might just go and have fun on their own, etc. So, from the beginning, we said, let's put our money together.

That some form of legal recognition seals the relationship, making it more "real," more "important," is an idea iterated by interview participants who might also be critical of heterosexual unions. Using heteronormative marriage as a standard in some way is not to say that same-sex couples consider their relationship inferior to that of heterosexual couples. Indeed, it is quite the contrary. At the same time, however, the claim of authenticity and importance – as if same-sex couples surpass heterosexual couples at their game – inadvertently affirms the heteronormative marital institution.

Fumi (Shibuya), in her early 40s, was self-employed and had lived with her partner for a year at the time of the interview. Their partnership was registered in Shibuya. Fumi compared same-sex partnership registration with heterosexual marriage as follows:

> When heterosexual couples decide to get married, they think about ceremonies, whom to invite, and so on. Not that they don't find importance in each other's feelings and relationships, but for them, [getting married] is just submitting a form. I think it is better for heterosexual

couples to make this type of contract too, [so that they would] think seriously about their lives together.

Chie (S), who was quoted above on the significance of the ring, had been married to a man before and described that experience as "just about filling out a form, and with that the contract was sealed." She felt quite differently about her same-sex partnership, as she and her partner Chikako had gone through the process of making a commitment together.

The authenticity of the same-sex partnership was emphasized by Nao (Shibuya), who identifies as a man and was in his 30s at the time of his interview. He was planning to obtain a notarized partnership contract that would "prove" that he and his partner were committed to supporting and caring for each other. His purpose was to show their children (from his partner's previous relationship) that they "are in a real relationship" and "to give them an example of a positive relationship" (Nao [Shibuya]).

Hanako (Shibuya), in her 40s, likened her partnership registration to marriage, albeit indirectly, and saw the certificate as a tangible "proof" of their relationship:

> Before, proof of our relationship was only our feeling.... People say marriage is "just a piece of paper," but there is a significant weight to it, and that's the same for us.

The natal family was also brought in as a witness to the commitment, affirming the significance of both the commitment and their family ties. Rin (Shibuya), in her 30s, who had lived with her partner for a year before the interview, said:

> We want to do a ceremony upon obtaining the SPC [Shibuya Partnership Certificate]. We have other ties, including our families, and we want to emphasize the importance of our families. We want to show our family members that we are living seriously.

While Rin and her partner, Ryōko, connected marriage to family ties, Kenta and Keisuke, both in their 30s, seemed to consider marriage as inseparable from having children. Kenta connected the approval of same-sex marriage to that of same-sex couples having children, but Keisuke expressed concern that such children would be bullied, saying that the children's well-being should be considered as well when considering marriage. Conversely, Takumi (Shibuya), who had been in a steady relationship for over 10 years, explained that he was "not seeking marriage" because he and his partner did not have children who required legal protection for inheritance purposes.

Others emphasized the importance of genetic ties and having children the "natural" way. For example, Kazu (Shibuya), who had been living with his partner for six years and had registered their partnership in Shibuya, would not have a child unless the child could have both their DNAs. Similarly, Hanako (Shibuya), whose emphasis on the "weight" of the partnership certificate was quoted above, would have children only if she and her partner could become pregnant "naturally," ruling out the use of artificial reproductive technologies.

The interview participants who had registered their partnership, despite the lack of legal status, seemed to find it easier to feel as though they were in a "marriage," compared to those who had not registered their partnership or did not live in a city that provides for partnership registration. Indeed, the interviewees above associated marriage with kinship and having children, including the importance of genetic ties, illustrating how same-sex marriage is envisioned within the paradigm of heterosexual marriage.

The practical benefits of legal recognition were quite frequently mentioned by the participants as a reason why same-sex couples should have access to marriage. However, such a focus precludes thinking about alternatives that can provide security and rights outside of marriage. While the participants problematized the lack of access to marriage and its benefits, they left unquestioned the fact that it is only through marriage that one can obtain rights and benefits. For example, Akiko (S) was worried that if she bought a house and died before her partner, her partner would not have access to the house. The solution to the problem, in Akiko's view, was gaining access to the "current marriage system":

> What is necessary is that the current marriage system should be open to homosexual couples too. At least, we need to have the right to choose whether we want to use it or not. That the marriage system can only be used by heterosexual couples creates a gap between heterosexual and homosexual couples, and this gap needs to be reduced. Furthermore, it would be nice if gender becomes insignificant when practicing marriage. Every adult of any gender should be able to marry if they want to. I think this would be desirable.

At the same time, some interviewees also thought that same-sex marriage, even if legalized, would be less socially accepted. For example, Haru (Shibuya) said:

> Even if same-sex marriage is approved, I don't think we can get the [same] level of social acceptance. Also [we do not have] the [same] type of obligations to the other family. So, in that way, the SPC and same-sex marriage won't make us feel as though we are married [to a man].

Both Akiko and Haru connected the seriousness of their relationship and the need for their parents or family to know about it. In the Asian context, it has been shown that the natal family and the larger kin network are important for many individuals in negotiating their same-sex relationship (see, e.g., Brainer, 2019; Tang et al., 2020). As the natal family in most cases is the bastion of familial heteronormativity, how same-sex couples negotiate their relationship in the kin context becomes important in deriving implications for whether their narrative about their relationship serves to reinforce the marital institution or not. To explore this point, we introduce one case below in which an actual wedding ceremony was held with the blessing of the natal family of one partner while the mother of the other partner refused to attend the ceremony. This unusual case gives insight into how the marital institution can be reinforced through a deliberate display of the same-sex union:

> The mother suggested a traditional Japanese wedding ceremony for the daughter and her partner, arguing that if they were to be together, then they should do it "properly." The partner's mother refused to attend, but two sisters attended. Relatives beyond the immediate families were apparently not invited, but the "wedding" was known to a wider circle of relatives and neighbors. When the daughter went back for a visit, she got comments from neighbors that it was good that she "got married." She didn't clarify [and the neighbors didn't know] that it wasn't a heterosexual marriage. This lack of openness about the same-sex partnership coupled with actual cordial interactions with the daughter's partner and her family, despite the partner's mother's rejection of the partnership, might suggest that the mother was trying to understand and cope with the daughter's partnership within a heteronormative framework. (Khor & Kamano, 2019, p. 23) (MD)

This example shows that supportive parents can also affirm the significance of the institution of marriage. Similarly, Mamoru (Shibuya), who had registered his partnership in Shibuya with his partner from overseas, reported how his mother encouraged them to go ahead with the registration as well as to have children, showing how supportive parents can make same-sex relationships resemble heterosexual marriage:

> My mom calls me every day, and she said to me, "Oh, you guys, one can get something now in Shibuya Ward," and she asked us, "Aren't you going to go for it?" My mom values stability, being in a stable relationship, forming a family, etc. Even about having children, she said, "You know, it seems possible with test tubes these days."

Despite the decreasing marital rate and delay in marriage among heterosexual people (National Institute for Population and Social Security Research, 2017), marriage continues to be a significant social institution and the paradigm through which same-sex marriage tends to be considered. It is important, however, to point out that the interviewees quoted above also recognized that same-sex marriage does not result in full equality for all, and that some would be left out even if same-sex marriage were to be legalized.

Some of the participants who registered their partnership and argued for same-sex marriage said explicitly that they did see problems in the current marriage system. Further, despite the inadequacy of this right to register their partnership and have it recognized, some deliberately acted upon this right in Shibuya so that it would not be taken away for others who might want to have their relationship legally recognized. Some also noted that legalizing same-sex partnership renders sexual minorities visible. Chie (S), cited above, reflected on her personal experience:

> I suffered from my gender identity and sexual orientation for almost 30 years. If I had known that there are people with diverse sexualities and gender identities, not just heterosexual men and women, it would have changed my life. It makes it easier for people to accept themselves for who they are.

Despite her rather strong argument for access to marriage and embrace of the (wedding) ring as an important symbol of commitment, Chie (S) also recognized that marriage was not the only option, citing the French civil solidarity pact (PACS; *pacte civil de solidarité*), heterosexual partnerships without marriage, and so on – indeed, she said, "it's better to expand the options."

Eri (S), who had started living with her partner a year before the interview, referred to a case of non-romantic relationships in which the rights of two sisters living together were also not guaranteed, as one sister could be driven away from the house if it were registered under the name of the other when the latter passed away. The conclusion she drew from this case was that "it's better to have a system that can protect the rights of various people" (Eri [S]). Chikako (S), Chie's partner, mentioned asexual people and people who remain single throughout their life, suggesting that their needs should be recognized as well.

The ideas our participants expressed indicate not only a recognition of alternative relationships, identities, and lifestyles, but also the exclusion of some people from having their rights protected or recognized even if same-sex marriage were legalized. At the same time, it is also true that in the interviews, these ideas were more an afterthought following an appeal for same-sex partnerships or marriage, about which they were clearer. The idea that people who are not in a same-sex relationship should be recognized and taken care of does not connect to a coherent rethinking of the marriage system or the very idea of partnership, legalized or not. The difficulty of imagining an alternative to marriage, or at least the lack of a coherent discourse of how rights can be guaranteed in an inclusive way outside of the marriage system, may be attributed to the strength of the institution of marriage. To further ponder the impact of same-sex marriage on this institution and kinship, we would like to end with an examination of nationwide survey data on heterosexual and same-sex marriages.

4 The desirability of (heterosexual) marriage and support for same-sex marriage

To assess the implications of the ideas about marriage from our ethnographic studies, we need also to examine the desirability of marriage as a way of life and the general public's attitudes toward same-sex relationships and partnerships.

If marriage as an institution or the ideology of marriage as it is practiced today remains strong, it would offer a buffer against changes that might be brought about by the inclusion of same-sex couples. Relevant surveys have shown that despite the decreasing marriage rate and delayed age of first marriages in Japan, the vast majority of respondents expressed an intention to marry. Further, this has remained quite constant through the years (National Institute of Population and Social Security Research, 2017). In another survey, it was shown that remaining single for one's entire life is one of the least preferred ways of living (Kamano, 2018). Japan also had the highest percentage of respondents among four countries (Japan, France, Germany, and Sweden) saying that "it is better to get married," though it also had the highest percentage of respondents saying that "marriage, cohabitation, having a partner" is not necessary (Cabinet Office, Japan, 2020).

These survey findings may reflect the ideological significance of the institution of marriage in Japan, albeit not perfectly so, which suggests two possible scenarios. Conservative politicians and community leaders, as well as those who are currently in a heterosexual marriage or inclined toward it, might want to protect the institution from being "contaminated" by inappropriate members. Alternatively, some of these people who truly believe in the importance of marriage might want to increase membership in such a core institution. The Research Group for the 2019 National Survey on Attitudes Toward Sexual Minorities (2020) found that the majority (64.8%) support same-sex marriage, and an even higher percentage support anti-discrimination laws for sexual minorities. However, the survey also revealed that about a third of those polled find same-sex or bisexual romantic orientation "strange." Slightly less than 50% consider female same-sex sexual behaviors "disgusting," while over 50% consider male same-sex or bisexual sexual behaviors "disgusting." Only a minority (about a quarter) reacted negatively to having a neighbor or colleague who is homosexual, but the majority reacted negatively to having a homosexual sibling (53.1%) or child (61.2%) (Research Group for the 2019 National Survey on Attitudes Toward Sexual Minorities, 2020).

These contradictory findings can be interpreted in different ways. It is possible to see the support for same-sex marriage as support for human rights, no matter how one feels about sexual minorities. The fact that close to 90% of respondents agreed to anti-discrimination legislation might be consistent with this interpretation. Another possible interpretation is that same-sex marriage is imagined abstractly and dissociated from the facts of emotional and sexual intimacy. The support for marriage is arguably not for the intimate union of two individuals, but for them to have a status and position in society. The dominant arguments that show the effects of exclusion from the marital institution might have had an effect on the general public, as it is an argument that is easy to understand and hard to refute. In other words, the support for same-sex marriage is dissociated from how one thinks about sexual minorities. Similarly, the majority of Japanese people might not disagree with the idea of their child marrying a "foreigner" (Institute of Statistical Mathematics, 2017), but this does not necessarily mean that they are accepting of foreigners (see, e.g., Arudou, 2021; Morita, 2015). How these different attitudes are or are not articulated might indeed deserve a deeper analysis.

5 Conclusion

We would like to emphasize that the demand for same-sex marriage does not in itself necessarily reinforce the heteronormative institution of marriage, as the very framing of the demand makes a difference. It is also important to recognize that activists and individuals constructing arguments apparently in support of the naturalness of the marital institution are also aware of how same-sex marriage alone does not address the exclusion of alternative ways of living or, albeit less explicitly, the association of marriage with privileges that disadvantage individuals and partnerships outside of the institution. In other words, the demand for same-sex marriage potentially has a radicalizing effect. At the same time, the public opinion in favor of (heterosexual) marriage, the tendency of the popular media's emphasis on "love" as a rationale for the legalization of same-sex partnership – captured well in the title of a newspaper article, "I Love You, but I Can't Choose Marriage…" (Takagi, 2021) – and, indeed, the theme of love and equality in the 2018 Tokyo Rainbow Pride parade all align same-sex marriage with the ideology of romantic love and marriage as it is known and practiced today.

However, in a context where the state is reluctant to pass any anti-discrimination laws or in other ways guarantee the rights of sexual minorities,[7] an apparent "mainstreaming" strategy of same-sex marriage or any form of partnership might allow sexual minorities a voice in the system, which can potentially challenge the heteronormative marital institution from within, so long as those same-sex couples

---

7 See Khor and Kamano (2021) and Khor (2020) on the ruling party's stance on anti-discrimination legislation in Japan.

who have registered their partnership remain critical of the system despite having become part of it. A more effective strategy to guarantee the rights of sexual minorities, while also dismantling the heteronormative institution of marriage to achieve freedom of choice for all, might consist of meaningful dialogues among all those affected by changes in the institution – dialogues that recognize and find ways to meet the actual needs of all those excluded from the institution, and which are also critically aware of the limitations of seeking rights from a heteronormative state.

References

Arudou, D. (2021). *Embedded racism: Japan's visible minorities and racial discrimination* (2nd ed.). Lexington Books.

Bourdieu, P. (1987). The force of law: Toward a sociology of the juridical field (R. Terdiman, Trans.). *The Hastings Law Journal, 38*(5), 805–853.

Brainer, A. (2019). *Queer kinship and family change in Taiwan.* Rutgers University Press.

Cabinet Office, Japan. (2020). *Reiwa 2-nendo shōshika shakai ni kansuru kokusai ishiki chōsa hōkokusho* [Report on the 2020 international survey on the declining birthrate]. https://www8.cao.go.jp/shoushi/shoushika/research/r02/kokusai/pdf/zentai/hyoushi-mokuji.pdf.

Chen, C. (2019a). Migrating marriage equality without feminism: *Obergefell v. Hodges* and the legalization of same-sex marriage in Taiwan. *Cornell International Law Journal, 52*, 65–107.

Chen, C. (2019b). A same-sex marriage that is not the same: Taiwan's legal recognition of same-sex unions and affirmation of marriage normativity. *Australian Journal of Asian Law, 20*(1), 59–68.

Constitutional Court, R.O.C. (Taiwan). (2017). No. 748 (Same-sex marriage case), 24 May 2017 (S.-C. Kuo, Trans.). https://cons.judicial.gov.tw/en/docdata.aspx?fid=100&id=310929.

Croce, M. (2018). Desiring what the law desires: A semiotic view on the normalization of homosexual sexuality. *Law, Culture and the Humanities, 14*(3), 402–419. https://doi.org/10.1177/1743872114553070.

Duggan, L. (2002). The new heteronormativity: The sexual politics of neoliberalism. In R. Castronovo & D. D. Nelson (Eds.), *Materializing democracy: Toward a revitalized cultural politics* (pp. 175–194). Duke University Press.

Equal Marriage Alliance Japan. (n.d.). *Dōseikon Q&A* [Q&A on same-sex marriage]. Retrieved January 9, 2020, from http://emajapan.org/promssm/ssmqaa.

Geiger v. Kitzhaber, 994 F. Supp. 2d 1128 (D. Or. 2014).

Goodridge v. Dept. of Public Health, 798 N.E.2d 941 (Mass. 2003).

Horie, Y. (2010). Dōseikan no "kekkon" ni kansuru hihanteki kōsatsu: Nihon no shakaiseido no bunmyaku kara [A critical analysis of same-sex "marriage": An investigation of the context of the social in Japan]. *Shakai shisutemu kenkyū, 21*, 37–57.

Institute of Statistical Mathematics. (2017). *The study of the Japanese national character.* https://www.ism.ac.jp/kokuminsei/en/table/data/html/ss9/9_14/9_14_all.htm.

Japan court rules failure to recognize same-sex marriage unconstitutional. (2021, March 17). *The Japan Times.* https://www.japantimes.co.jp/news/2021/03/17/national/crime-legal/same-sex-marriage-landmark-ruling/#.

Kamano, S. (2018). Kekkon pātonāshippu no katachi ni taisuru hitobito no kangaekata: Kodomo ni shitehoshikunai ikikata no bunseki o tsūjite [Attitudes toward marriage and partnership: Analysis of the least preferred way of living for one's children]. *Kekkon/rikon/saikon no dōkō to Nihonshakai no henyō ni kansuru hōkatsuteki kenkyū* [Marriage, divorce, and remarriage in Japan: Trends, causes, and social implications]. Grant-in-Aid for Scientific Research (A), JSPS Kakenhi 25245061, PI: M. Iwasawa. Final research report (pp. 583–596).

Kamano, S., Kamiya, Y., Sugiura, I., & Taniguchi, H. (2018). *Family and partnership: Experiences of and ideas on same-sex partnership certificate in Shibuya.* Paper presented at the XIX ISA World Congress of Sociology, Toronto, Canada.

Kawamura, S. (2021, December 23). "Kon'in no jiyū" dōseiaisha ni mo tekiyō o: Dōseikon soshō hajimaru ["Freedom to marry" to be extended to homosexual people. Same-sex marriage lawsuit hearing begins]. *Asahi shinbun (digital).* https://digital.asahi.com/articles/ASPDR6JY0PDQIIPE02F.html.

Khor, D. (2020). Framing same-sex marriage in Japan. *GIS Journal: The Hosei Journal of Global and Interdisciplinary Studies, 6,* 29–41.

Khor, D., & Kamano, S. (2017). Mother-daughter relationships in Hong Kong and Japan. *GIS Journal: The Hosei Journal of Global and Interdisciplinary Studies, 3,* 1–29.

Khor, D., & Kamano, S. (2019). Same-sex partners and practices of familial intimacy. *GIS Journal: The Hosei Journal of Global and Interdisciplinary Studies, 5,* 19–38.

Khor, D., & Kamano, S. (2021). Negotiating same-sex partnership in a "tolerant" state. *Journal of Gender Studies, 30*(5), 512–524.

Lawrence v. Texas, 539 U.S. 558 (2003). https://supreme.justia.com/cases/federal/us/539/558.

Masci, D., Sciupac, E. P., & Lipka, M. (2019). *Same-sex marriage around the world.* https://pewrsr.ch/3bOqHpO.

Morita, L. (2015). Some manifestations of Japanese exclusionism. *SAGE Open, 5*(3). https://doi.org.10.1177/2158244015600036.

National Institute of Population and Social Security Research. (2017). *Gendai Nihon no kekkon to shussan: Dai 15-kai shusshō dōkō kihon chōsa (dokushinsha chōsa narabi ni fūfu chōsa) hōkokusho* [Marriage and childbirth in Japan today: The 15th Japanese national fertility survey, 2015 (Results of singles and married couples survey)], https://www.ipss.go.jp/ps-doukou/j/doukou15/NFS15_reportALL.pdf.

Neghaiwi, B. H., & Wiegmann, A. (2022). *In Switzerland, first same-sex couples say "I do."* Reuters, https://reut.rs/3bMsFHu.

Niji Bridge. (2022). *Shibuya city office: Nijiiro diversity collaborative study of LGBT partnership coverage in Japan.* https://nijibridge.jp.

Puar, J. K. (2017). *Terrorist assemblages: Homonationalism in queer times.* Duke University Press.

Research Group for the 2019 National Survey on Attitudes Toward Sexual Minorities. (2020). *Oral presentation on the 2019 national survey on attitudes toward sexual minorities.* Grant-in-Aid for Scientific Research (A), JSPS Kakenhi 18H03652, PI: Kawaguchi K. http://alpha.shudo-u.ac.jp/~kawaguch.

Saez, M. (2014). Transforming family law through same-sex marriage: Lessons from (and to) the Western world. *Duke Journal of Comparative and International Law, 25,* 125–196.

Sapporo District Court. (2021). Judgment of 17 March 2021. Case no. (Wa) 267 of 2021, Claim for damages case (Lawyers for LGBT and Allies Network, Trans.). https://bit.ly/3R92LxC.

Shida, T. (2009). Dōseikon hihan [A critique of same-sex marriage]. In O. Seki & T. Shida (Eds.), *Chōhatsu suru sekushuaritī: Hō/shakai/shisō e no apurōchi* [Shaking up law, society, and philosophy: Provocations from sexuality studies]. Shinsensha.

Sugiura, H. (2013). *Jimintō kenpō kaisei sōan/genkenpōtaihi* [LDP's constitutional amendment draft: Comparison with current constitution]. http://www.azusawa.jp/topics/topics-20130413.html.

Sullivan, A. (Ed.) (1997). *Same-sex marriage, pro and con: A reader.* Vintage Books.

Takagi, S. (2021, December 3). *Aishiteiru no ni "kekkon" o erabenai … "dōseikon" ga motomeru mono to pātonāshippu seido no chigai* [I love you, but I can't choose "marriage" … what "same-sex marriage" seeks and the difference between same-sex marriage and the partnership system]. https://www.fnn.jp/articles/-/278487.

Tang, D., Khor, D., & Chen, Y. (2020). Legal recognition of same-sex partnership: A comparative study of Hong Kong, Taiwan and Japan. *Sociological Review, 68*(1), 192–208. https://doi.org/10.1177/0038026119858222.

Wang, H., & Chen, M. (2017). Discourses on non-conforming marriages: Love in Taiwan. *International Journal of Japanese Sociology, 26*, 52–66. https://doi.org/10.1111/ijjs.12063.

Woodly, D. (2018). The importance of public meaning for political persuasion. *Perspectives on Politics, 16*(1), 22–35. https://doi.org/10.1017/S1537592717003127.

Hiroyuki Taniguchi

LGBTQ human rights in Japanese laws and policies

While there has been a global trend to promote LGBTQ human rights, Japan has been slow to do so, especially in terms of laws and policies at the national level. No progress has been made on amending the strict requirements set out in 2003 for legal gender alteration. Same-sex relationships continue to be placed outside of the legal framework. A draft bill that set forth the basic principles of human rights protections regarding sexual orientation and gender identity (SOGI) failed in 2021. Nevertheless, the public sector, including local governments, as well as the private sector and civil society, have made efforts to effect change in education and the workplace.

Despite pledging its commitment to protect human rights since the current Constitution was enacted in 1946, and to promote and protect LGBTQ human rights at the United Nations (UN) since the 2000s, Japan has failed to pass effective legislation. This paper will examine the function and limitations of human rights in Japan by reviewing the laws, policies, and court cases in relation to LGBTQ issues. It will highlight that a proper understanding of human rights, primarily international human rights law, is essential for advancing LGBTQ human rights protections in Japan.

1 Significant LGBTQ-related cases

There have been few LGBTQ-related lawsuits in Japan, partly because of Japanese customs, where it is rare to take problems to court when they arise. This section presents two significant cases concerning sexual orientation, gender identity, and human rights.

1.1 Blue Boy case, 1964–1970

The "Blue Boy case" involved a surgeon who was arrested for performing gender reassignment surgeries for trans women working in show business in 1964. He was convicted for performing surgeries to make a person sterile without cause, which is prohibited under Article 28 of the Eugenics Protection Law of 1948, because he had conducted surgeries without adequate medical examinations and proper processes.

In addition to the legality of gender reassignment surgery, which was the main issue in this case, the relationship between gender reassignment and dignity was carefully discussed. Article 13 of the Constitution provides the right to pursue happiness and self-determination, similar to the right to privacy or respect for private life. According to the Tokyo District Court (1969):

> Sexual freedom is fundamental to human instincts and deeply related to a person's innate right to pursue happiness. It therefore must not be oppressed unless it infringes on the fundamental human rights of others or is harmful to their own life or body.[1]

The court's reference to human rights potentially allows for an interpretation that directly links gender reassignment to a person's right to pursue happiness, since the court's decision was based on the premise that if a surgeon performs gender reassignment surgery through a careful process, it is not a violation of the Eugenics Protection Law. A similar argument for trans people's human rights first occurred in 1979, when the European Commission of Human Rights (1979) found a violation of the right to respect for private life in Belgian law, which prevented a trans man from changing his gender on his birth certificate.

1.2 Fuchu Youth Hostel case, 1991–1997

The "Fuchu Youth Hostel case" concerned a hostel run by the Tokyo Metropolitan Board of Education, which refused a booking from a gay rights activist group called OCCUR. The refusal was based on the principle of providing separate accommodations for men and women, as the facility insisted that it was impossible to allow people who had the potential to be sexually attracted to each other to stay in the same room, and allowing gay people to stay would conflict with its purpose of supporting the "sound upbringing of youths" (The Tokyo Youth Hostel Ordinance, Art. 1). As a part of its litigation strategy, OCCUR consciously cited the progressive efforts of other countries, such as having the then president of the San Francisco Board of Education, Tom Ammiano, who had come out as a gay man in the 1970s, appear as a witness.

The Tokyo High Court's (1997) judgment, which ruled in favor of OCCUR, included the following passage:

---

1 Translated by the author. Unless otherwise indicated, all translations from Japanese in this paper are the author's own.

The administrative authorities, including the [Tokyo] Metropolitan Board of Education, are required to give due consideration to homosexuals, who are a minority, in the performance of their duties and to protect their rights and interests fully. Indifference or lack of knowledge is unacceptable in the exercise of public authority.

The original judgment also said the refusal amounted to sexual orientation discrimination, which is illegal under Article 244 of the Local Autonomy Act of 1947 (Tokyo District Court, 1994). It is important to recall that in the same year the UN Human Rights Committee (1994) found sexual orientation discrimination under Articles 2 and 26 of the International Covenant on Civil and Political Rights (ICCPR) in the case of *Toonen v. Australia* for the first time.

2 Legal gender alteration

While the above two cases offered opportunities to internationalize Japanese legal interpretations in regard to human rights, progress is yet to be made. Despite the potential advances for trans rights that could have been made based on the Tokyo District Court's interpretation of Article 13 in the Blue Boy case in 1969, every request to alter one's legal gender in Japan has since been rejected. The situation remained the same even after the official approval of gender reassignment surgery in the field of medicine in 1997. Article 113 of the Family Register Act of 1947 stipulates that changes can be made to one's family registry (*koseki*) only when there are mistakes or omissions, or if any entry is impermissible under law. In the case of a child with intersex features, the court allows for the alteration of gender because it deems the original registration was a mistake. However, once a person is registered as male or female without intersex features, there is no question of mistakes, omissions, or impermissibility.

2.1 Requirements of the GID Act (2003)

The Act on Special Cases in Handling Gender Status for Persons with Gender Identity Disorder (GID Act) was passed in 2003 and came into force the following year, which enabled the alteration of legal gender markers. As of the end of 2020, approximately 10,000 people have obtained permission to legally change their gender (gid.jp, 2020).

However, the GID Act is infamous for its requirements, which are arguably the strictest in the world (Norton, 2006; Taniguchi, 2013). In addition to diagnoses of

gender identity disorder from two or more physicians, the following five requirements must be fulfilled. The person must:

- have reached the age of majority (which, in Japan, was 20 years of age in 2003,
  and is now 18 years old since 2022)
- be unmarried at the time of the application
- have no minor children (the word "minor" was added in the 2008 amendment)
- be sterile
- have external genitalia resembling those of the opposite sex

The applicant must file the request with the family court, which decides whether
the alteration is acceptable.

2.2 Constitutional challenges

Legal challenges to the constitutionality of the GID Act have been made since its
enactment. In the early cases, there were several judgments that accepted the
drafter's intent in determining the constitutionality of the requirements. This section discusses two recent cases in which the Supreme Court of Japan ruled the GID
Act constitutional.

In the first case, the requirement for sterility was disputed, as the plaintiff
could not obtain permission to alter his legal gender because he had not removed
the ovary from his body. The drafter's intent behind this requirement was that it
was not reasonable for the person to still be able to have children. The Supreme
Court (2019) found the sterility requirement constitutional "at present," but it acknowledged that it raised constitutional issues because it was an invasion of the
body. This indicates the possibility of finding it unconstitutional in a future case.
Further, the two judges concurred clearly that the "invasion of the body" itself
might constitute a violation of the rights under Article 13 of the Constitution,
which is a general provision on dignity and characterized as a residual provision
that does not apply to other rights. They also referred to the judgment of the European Court of Human Rights (2017) and the joint statement by international bodies
(World Health Organization [WHO], 2014).

In another case, an applicant was not able to change their legal gender due to
the presence of a minor child. The drafter's intent for this requirement was to prevent disruptions of the family order and avoid negative effects on the welfare of
any children. The Supreme Court (2021) ruled that this requirement was constitutional, without even moderating it with the phrase "at present." Yet, one judge, Uga
Katsuya, presented a dissenting opinion and carefully acknowledged the unconstitutionality of this requirement. He indicated that the drafter's justification based

on disruptions of the family order was weakened by the 2008 amendment. He also pointed out that the alleged anxiety of a child was based on vague and abstract concerns, because the legal gender alteration itself does not affect the child's acceptance of their parent's changes. He added that the possibility of discrimination at school or other places is not acceptable as a justification, since it is those who discriminate that should be condemned. He concluded that, although the reasons for this requirement can be justifiable, the means were not reasonable because it was solely based on the presence of a minor child.

3 Same-sex relationships

3.1 A legal system premised on the gender binary

As in other countries, the Japanese legal system relating to marriage and the family has traditionally been designed exclusively for opposite-sex partnerships. Article 24 of the Constitution provides that marriage is based solely on the consent of "both sexes." The Civil Code and other laws and regulations on social security use gender-specific terms such as "husband-wife" and "father-mother" as basic units, which assume opposite-sex relationships.

This understanding is also evident in the registration form for marriage. It requires filling in the name of the "person who will be the husband" in the left column and the name of the "person who will be the wife" on the right. Article 3 of the GID Act stipulated the no-marriage requirement for legal gender alteration to prevent any existing married couples from becoming legally married same-sex couples (Taniguchi, 2013).

In June 2019, the four opposition parties submitted a draft bill to the Diet to amend some parts of the Civil Code to allow same-sex marriages. This bill proposed two amendments: adding the words "by parties of the opposite or same sex" to those who can enter a marriage in Article 739; and changing the gender-specific words to gender-neutral terms, such as "father–mother" to "parent" (e. g., Arts. 158, 711, 766) and "between husband and wife" to "between parties to a marriage" (e. g., Arts. 159, 728, 750). However, the ruling Liberal Democratic Party (LDP) has criticized and rejected the bill.

Some local governments now issue certifications for same-sex partnerships, starting with certain wards in Tokyo in 2015. More than 250 local governments have joined them as of late 2022, covering more than 60 % of the population. Though the number is increasing drastically, this certification is not a form of legal protection since the marriage and family legislation falls under national jurisdiction. Its significance is only symbolic, not legal. However, these trends have stimulated litigation regarding the legal protection of same-sex couples.

3.2 De facto marriage as legal protection for same-sex couples

Although there is no comprehensive legislation with regard to de facto marriages (*jijitsukon*), some laws and ordinances have offered protections to de facto partners with regard to public housing (Public Housing Act, Art. 27), domestic violence (Act on the Prevention of Spousal Violence and the Protection of Victims, Art. 1), and workers' compensation (Industrial Accident Compensation Insurance Act, Art. 16), though they do not make explicit provisions, such as for alimony in dissolution, residency permits, and tax deductions. However, these laws presuppose the de facto couple to be a man and a woman.

The courts have been divided in their interpretation of whether or not same-sex relationships should be included in the definition of de facto marriage. For example, the Utsunomiya District Court (2019) approved an alimony claim from a partner for infidelity after deciding that same-sex partners should be afforded the same legal protections as de facto (heterosexual) partners. This decision was based on the fact that the Constitution does not explicitly exclude same-sex relationships in its definition of marriage, and local authorities are increasingly implementing partnership certifications. The Tokyo High Court (2020) upheld the decision, setting a precedent for recognizing same-sex relationships as a form of de facto marriage.

The other example in which the result was the opposite concerns partners of victims of a crime, such as murder, who are eligible to receive benefits from the state to "help the surviving family members to lead a peaceful life again," whether they are married or in de facto relationships. When a man who lost his same-sex partner to murder claimed these benefits, the Public Safety Commission determined that their relationship did not constitute a de facto marriage in legal terms and denied payment. The Nagoya District Court (2020) upheld the commission's decision because "it cannot be said that a socially accepted notion had been formed that the [same sex] relationship could be regarded as a marriage."

Despite differences in the content of the two claims, and the amount of money involved, it is noteworthy that the interpretation of the legal concept of de facto marriage has differed. Without a clear indication of whether same-sex relationships are included in the legal definition of de facto marriage, it is left to the court's interpretation, and same-sex relationships continue to be placed in an ambiguous position.

3.3 "Freedom to Marry for All" litigation

In February 2019, several lawsuits were filed in four district courts, and in another district court in September, across the country to clarify the constitutionality of the current legal system, which does not allow same-sex couples to marry. These are collectively called the "Freedom to Marry for All" litigation, characterized as policymaking lawsuits within the LGBTQ movement.

In its first judgment in March 2021, the Sapporo District Court (2021) ruled that the current legal system, which "does not provide legal means to enjoy even some of the legal effects that arise from marriage" to same-sex couples, amounts to a violation of Article 14(1) of the Constitution. Though sexual orientation is not explicitly mentioned in Article 14(1), the court interpreted it to be one of the prohibited grounds of discrimination. The court also pointed out that the objections against same-sex relationships in society only need "limited consideration," as discrimination based on sexual orientation is subject to strict scrutiny, which requires an inevitable and unavoidable reason to justify the different treatment. Also, it clarified that while Article 24 stipulates "both sexes" as a precondition for marriage, this does not mean that it prohibits same-sex marriage (Sapporo District Court, 2021). However, the court did not specify in its ruling what system would be appropriate for the legal protection of same-sex relationships. It could be the introduction of a specific legal framework, such as civil partnership laws or registered partnerships, or it could eliminate gender restrictions in marriage.

Similarly, in November 2022, the Tokyo District Court (2022) did not specify an ideal system either, when it ruled that the current laws do not allow for same-sex marriage. The court only admitted a violation of Article 24(2), which stipulates that "laws shall be enacted from the standpoint of individual dignity and the essential equality of the sexes" concerning "choice of spouse, ... and other matters pertaining to marriage and the family" (Ministry of Justice, 2023).

4 SOGI discrimination

4.1 Lack of SOGI-related legislations

Japanese laws make no direct reference to SOGI. Article 14 of the Constitution provides for "no discrimination" based on "race, creed, sex, social status or family origin," but does not explicitly refer to SOGI. In addition, there is no legislation on anti-discrimination or human rights protection in general; nor is there any specific act on discrimination based on SOGI. As the Japanese legal system is primarily based on codified rules, in which statutory regulations play the primary role, the absence of reference to SOGI has a more severe impact than in countries with Anglo-American legal systems based on common law.

Some administrative efforts have been made to make up for the legal deficiencies. The Ministry of Justice has been conducting an awareness-raising campaign according to the Act on the Promotion of Human Rights Education and Human Rights Awareness-Raising of 2000. This includes the prohibition of discrimination and prejudice against "sexual orientation" since 2002, and "gender identity disorder" (which was changed to "gender identity" in 2018) in 2004. The campaign is also being conducted at the local government level, and SOGI is explicitly included in some local ordinances and plans related to human rights and/or gender equality. However, the campaign focuses only on raising awareness and does not provide any compensation to victims of discrimination, investigate the alleged cases, or implement specific measures to address or prevent human rights violations. It must be pointed out that current efforts tend to be limited to individual awareness and do not question laws and policies or provide an effective solution for SOGI discrimination.

4.2 Failures in legislation

In 2016, a Draft Bill on the Elimination of Discrimination based on SOGI (LGBT Sabetsu Kaishō Hōan) was submitted to the Diet by four opposition parties. This was a basic law confirming the need for human rights protections for LGBTQ people. Similar legislation already existed in relation to persons with disabilities and those of *buraku* origin. However, this bill failed due to a lack of support from the ruling LDP, which instead announced its intention to submit a Draft Bill on the Promotion of Better Understanding of LGBT Issues (LGBT Rikai Zōshin Hōan) in 2018. While this was intended to cultivate acceptance toward LGBT people and contribute to the realization of a more tolerant society, no concrete proposals were developed and the bill was never submitted to the Diet.

In 2021, a nonpartisan caucus for discussing SOGI-related issues, LGBT Giren, which was composed of members from all the major political parties and had assumed a central role in the debate since 2015, reached a consensus on a new draft bill by incorporating the aims of the 2016 bill. Tokyo's hosting of the 2020 Summer Olympics and Paralympics, which were postponed by one year, encouraged agreement on the bill, as the International Olympic Committee requires the host state to follow the non-discrimination provisions of the Olympic Charter, which explicitly refer to sexual orientation (Maree, 2020). The LDP was the only party that was unwilling to approve the bill, as its general council vehemently opposed one phrase in particular – "discrimination shall not be tolerated" – owing to a concern that it would lead to increased lawsuits and contradict free speech principles. Ultimately, the draft bill was not submitted to the Diet due to a lack of support from the LDP.

5 Recommendations from international monitoring bodies

As described above, there has been no substantive progress on legal gender alterations, legal protections for same-sex relationships, and anti-discrimination legislation based on SOGI. Japan's handling of these issues is subject to constant global scrutiny and criticism.

5.1 Treaty bodies' recommendations

Japan has ratified most major human rights treaties and is subject to the state party reporting system, under which treaty bodies make recommendations to improve compliance with the obligations of each treaty.

For example, the UN's Human Rights Committee, which monitors the implementation of the ICCPR, adopted recommendations relating to SOGI for the first time in 2008. It recommended that the Japanese government consider amending its legislation, such as public housing laws, to include sexual orientation among the prohibited grounds of discrimination. It also requested that equal treatment be ensured between unmarried cohabiting opposite-sex couples and unmarried cohabiting same-sex couples, to comply with Article 26 of the ICCPR (2008, para. 29). After there was no concrete progress, the Human Rights Committee made the following recommendation in 2014:

> The State party should adopt comprehensive anti-discrimination legislation that prohibits discrimination on all grounds, including sexual orientation and gender identity, and provides victims of discrimination with effective and appropriate remedies. The State party should intensify its awareness-raising activities to combat stereotypes and prejudice against lesbian, gay, bisexual, and transgender persons, investigate allegations of harassment against lesbian, gay, bisexual, and transgender persons, and take appropriate measures to prevent such stereotypes, prejudice, and harassment. (para. 11)

This observation indicates that Japan will inevitably need to explicitly include SOGI when it introduces anti-discrimination legislation in the future. In the most recently adopted recommendation, the Human Rights Committee (2022) suggested further specific improvements: strengthening awareness-raising, ensuring the legal protection of same-sex relationships nationwide, amending the GID Act, and improving the treatment of trans inmates.

Other treaty bodies also adopted LGBTQ-related recommendations under their jurisdictions, especially in the context of anti-discrimination measures, legislation, and intersectional forms of discrimination, including the Committee on Economic, Social and Cultural Rights (CESCR, 2013), the Committee on the Elimination of Discrimination against Women (CEDAW, 2016), the Committee on the Rights of the Child (CRC, 2019), and the Committee on the Rights of Persons with Disabilities (CRPD, 2022).

5.2 Monitoring under the Human Rights Council

The UN's Human Rights Council (HRC) was established in 2006 with a new human rights monitoring procedure, the Universal Periodic Review (UPR), which is a state-driven peer-review system monitoring the human rights situation of each UN member state according to internationally recognized human rights standards. Each party can express its acceptance of a recommendation. It takes four and a half years to review all the member states in one cycle; the third cycle ended in late 2022.

In the first cycle, Canada recommended that Japan take measures to tackle SOGI discrimination (HRC, 2008), which the Japanese government accepted. In the second cycle, six countries made recommendations on SOGI issues (HRC, 2012). The government accepted four of them, which were similar to the recommendation in the first cycle, and noted the other two recommendations, which suggested enacting anti-discrimination laws that specifically refer to SOGI. In response to the stagnant legal situation, 13 countries submitted more precise recommendations in the third cycle (HRC, 2017). Interestingly, the Japanese government accepted the recommendation (from New Zealand) to strengthen the measures for eliminating discrimination and to revise the GID Act, while taking note of the other recommendations, including anti-discrimination legislation (from Germany, Honduras, Ireland, the Netherlands, Norway, and the USA), expansion of the hate speech act (from Australia and Mexico), and legal recognition of same-sex marriage (from Canada and Switzerland).

6 International human rights perspectives

Article 98(2) of the Constitution of Japan states that international law should be "faithfully observed," which implies that international law as a whole has the effect of disciplining the conduct of the state. As a specific field of international law, international human rights laws, including human rights treaties and related practices and documents, has binding force in legal practice, such as the formation, conclusion, interpretation, and application of internal laws (Iwasawa, 1999).

6.1 Legal gender alteration

Treaty bodies are relatively silent on the issue of legal gender alteration. Though there has been some constructive dialogue, the concluding observation by CEDAW (2017, paras. 12, 21) does not refer to the GID Act. At the conclusion of the third UPR cycle, the only reference to the GID Act was the recommendation from New Zealand (HRC, 2017, para. 161.70). Japan has agreed to follow up on this recommendation (HRC, 2018, p. 4).

All of the GID Act requirements have been criticized internationally. For instance, five international organizations issued a joint statement on combating forced sterilization and abolishing the sterility requirement for legal gender alterations (WHO, 2014). The Independent Expert on Sexual Orientation and Gender Identity (2018), appointed by the HRC, called for the member states to exclude any third-party and institutional intervention, including medical surgery, from the requirements of legal gender alteration procedures and to respect each person's gender identity as the highest priority. In addition, the European Court of Human Rights (2017) clearly stated that it is a human rights violation to compel surgery or bodily alteration by making it a condition for legal gender alteration.

Some of the private sector have also focused on the GID Act in Japan. Human Rights Watch (2019), a US-based international human rights organization, conducted research and a campaign to recommend a drastic amendment to the GID Act, and the BBC produced and aired programs focusing on the sterility requirement ("Trans in Japan," 2021). Both reflected global trends in relaxing the conditions for altering one's legal gender from human rights perspectives.

Each state report made by the Japanese government refers to the 2008 amendment of the GID Act, from requiring "no child" to "no minor child," as an improvement of human rights with regard to gender identity (Human Rights Committee, 2020, para. 42). However, besides this minor revision, there have been no amendments to improve human rights protections for trans individuals. As mentioned above, the concurring opinion of the Supreme Court in 2019 only referred to some of the global trends. They did not rely on, or even refer to, the fact that the Japanese government had agreed to follow up New Zealand's recommendation at the UPR third cycle to amend the GID Act in 2018.

6.2 Same-sex relationships

The recommendations relating to legal protections for same-sex relationships started in 2008. In its concluding observation on the fifth report, the Human Rights Committee (2008) called for amendments to laws to ensure the equal treatment of opposite-sex de facto marriages and same-sex relationships, mainly focusing on the Public Housing Act and the Act on the Prevention of Spousal Violence and the Protection of Victims. In 2013, the CESCR also expressed concern about laws against same-sex partner relationships (para. 10). Furthermore, in the third UPR cycle, Switzerland and Canada recommended legal protections for same-sex relationships at the national level, and Timor-Leste recommended including same-sex relationships in the Act on the Prevention of Spousal Violence and the Protection of Victims (HRC, 2017). Japan accepted the latter recommendation from Timor-Leste, but it only noted the former, stating that they "require careful consideration" (HRC, 2018).

International human rights standards are not always effective for the legal protection of same-sex relationships. For example, the Human Rights Committee (2002) and European Court of Human Rights (2010) interpret that the right to marry does not oblige state parties to legalize same-sex marriage, and they allow for a broad range of interpretations by each state party. However, they have also indicated that differences in the treatment of opposite-sex and same-sex couples cannot be justified in several cases (European Court of Human Rights, 2003; Human Rights Committee, 2003). Moreover, in recent years, some regional courts have interpreted that international human rights law obliges states to enact some legal frameworks for same-sex relationships (European Court of Human Rights, 2015; Inter-American Court of Human Rights, 2017).

In the ongoing "Freedom to Marry for All" litigation, some judgments resemble these interpretations, though they do not specifically refer to recommendations from international monitoring bodies. The Sapporo District Court's (2021) judgment indicates that the lack of legal protection for same-sex relationships is unconstitutional and that they are very similar to opposite-sex relationships. Furthermore, the Tokyo District Court (2022) stated that formal recognition of their relationships was needed to respect individual dignity.

6.3 SOGI discrimination

Most of the recommendations from international monitoring bodies are focused on SOGI discrimination – some recommend continuing and expanding existing measures, and others recommend enacting general anti-discrimination legislation, which includes SOGI or SOGI-specific anti-discrimination law. The recommendation from the Human Rights Committee in 2014 was the most comprehensive example. Concerning its reply to the UPR recommendations, the Japanese government accepted the expansion of existing measures to SOGI, but only took note to enact anti-discrimination legislation. This directly affected the failure of legislation on the basic laws on SOGI in 2021. The Constitution does not have a definition of discrimination, and restrictions on human rights are only permitted on the grounds of "public welfare," which could be broadly interpreted. Several treaty bodies have also pointed out the need to clarify this vague wording (CEDAW, 2016, para. 11; Committee on the Elimination of Racial Discrimination, 2018, para. 8; Human Rights Committee, 2014, para. 22). Deep-seated opposition to the re-alization of human rights through legal norms can be seen on the part of the Japanese government.

In addition to these normative and systematic limitations, there are also signif-

Another factor in implementing human rights obligations in general is that Japan has no National Human Rights Institutions (NHRIs; Japan Federation of Bar Associations, 2020, p. 7). It is also recommended to introduce such institutions from every treaty body (CEDAW, 2016, para. 15; CESCR, 2013, para. 8; CRC, 2019, para. 12(b); Human Rights Committee, 2014, para. 7). In 1993, the UN General Assembly adopted a resolution, "Principles Relating to the Status of National Institutions," known as the Paris Principles, as core institutional factors for realizing human rights. More than 110 countries complied with this resolution and established NHRIs, which are highly independent of government. A civil rights commissioner system has provided counseling and promoted human rights in Japan since 1949. However, it is under the jurisdiction of the Ministry of Justice, the commissioners do not initially have human rights expertise, and 80 % of them are retired older adults.

In addition to these normative and systematic limitations, there are also significant limitations in recognizing human rights. In Japan, human rights tends to be synonymous with morality and compassion, partly due to the government's awareness-raising campaign. Even human rights education in schools and society is about understanding others and fostering tolerance and attitudes toward diversity. The LDP's Draft Bill on the Promotion of Better Understanding of LGBT Issues in 2018 was based on this concept, which provides no institutional protection for human rights violations. The fact that it was abandoned because of the insertion of the phrase "discrimination shall not be tolerated" is symbolic of the human rights situation in Japan.

7 Conclusion

The groundbreaking arguments of international human rights law are rarely referred to as having legal significance, even though they are spoken of with admiration by the general public. This trend is not limited to LGBTQ issues but reflects the problematic nature of human rights protections in Japan.

Despite some precedents in domestic courts which suggest interpretations in line with international human rights standards, laws and policies on LGBTQ issues in Japan have not kept pace with international trends. There is a vital need to promote greater understanding of LGBTQ human rights, incorporating the points raised by the international human rights monitoring systems to further develop and revise SOGI-related laws and practices in Japan.

References

Committee on Economic, Social and Cultural Rights. (2013). Concluding observation: Japan (3rd report), 10 June 2013, U.N. Doc. E/C.12/JPN/CO/3.

Committee on the Elimination of Discrimination against Women. (2016). Concluding observation: Japan (7th and 8th reports), 10 March 2016, U.N. Doc. CEDAW/C/JPN/CO/7–8.

Committee on the Elimination of Discrimination against Women. (2017). Summary record, 7 August 2017, U.N. Doc. CEDAW/C/SR.1376.

Committee on the Elimination of Racial Discrimination. (2018). Concluding observation: Japan (10th and 11th reports), 26 September 2018, U.N. Doc. CERD/C/JPN/CO/10–11.

Committee on the Rights of Persons with Disabilities. (2022). Concluding observation: Japan (initial report), 7 October 2022, U.N. Doc. CRPD/C/JPN/CO/1.

Committee on the Rights of the Child. (2019). Concluding observation: Japan (4th and 5th reports), 5 March 2019, U.N. Doc. CRC/C/JPN/CO/4–5.

European Commission on Human Rights. (1979). *Van Oosterwijck v. Belgium*, Report of 1 March 1979, Application no. 7654/76.

European Court of Human Rights. (2003). *Karner v. Austria*, Judgment of 24 July 2003, Application no. 40016/98.

European Court of Human Rights. (2010). *Schalk and Kopf v. Austria*, Judgment of 24 June 2010, Application no. 30141/04.

European Court of Human Rights. (2015). *Oliari and Others v. Italy*, Judgment of 21 July 2015, Applications nos. 18766/11 and 36030/11.

European Court of Human Rights. (2017). *A.P., Garçon and Nicot v. France*, Judgment of 6 April 2017, Applications nos. 79885/12, 52471/13 and 52596/13.

gid.jp. (2020). *Seidōitsu seishōgai tokureihō ni yoru seibetsu no toriatsukai no henkōsū chōsa (2020-nenban)* [Research on the number of people who correct their legal gender under the GID Act, 2020]. https://gid.jp/research/research0001/research2021042201.

Human Rights Committee. (1994). *Toonen v. Australia*, Views of 31 March 1994, U.N. Doc. CCPR/C/50/D/488/1992.

Human Rights Committee. (2002). *Joslin et al. v. New Zealand*, Views of 17 July 2002, U.N. Doc. CCPR/C/75/D/902/1999.

Human Rights Committee. (2003). *Young v. Australia*, Views of 6 August 2003, U.N. Doc. CCPR/C/78/D/941/2000.

Human Rights Committee. (2008). Concluding observation: Japan (5th report), 30 October 2008, U.N. Doc. CCPR/C/JPN/CO/5.

Human Rights Committee. (2014). Concluding observation: Japan (6th report), 20 August 2014, U.N. Doc. CCPR/C/JPN/CO/6.

Human Rights Committee. (2020). Japan: 7th report, 28 April 2020, U.N. Doc. CCPR/C/JPN/7.

Human Rights Committee. (2022). Concluding observation: Japan (7th report), 3 November 2022, U.N. Doc. CCPR/C/JPN/CO/7.

Human Rights Council. (2008). UPR (first cycle): Japan, 30 May 2008, U.N. Doc. A/HRC/8/44.

Human Rights Council. (2012). UPR (second cycle): Japan, 14 December 2012, U.N. Doc. A/HRC/22/14.

Human Rights Council. (2017). UPR (third cycle): Japan, 4 January 2018, U.N. Doc. A/HRC/37/15.

Human Rights Council. (2018). Replies by Japan, 1 March 2018, U.N. Doc. A/HRC/37/15/Add.1.

Human Rights Watch. (2019, March 19). *A really high hurdle: Japan's abusive transgender legal recognition process.* https://www.hrw.org/report/2019/03/19/really-high-hurdle/japans-abusive-transgender-legal-recognition-process.

Independent Expert on Sexual Orientation and Gender Identity. (2018). Report to the General Assembly, 12 July 2018, U.N. Doc. A/73/152.

Inter-American Court of Human Rights. (2017). Gender identity, and equality and non-discrimination of same-sex couples, Advisory opinion OC-24/15, 24 November 2017.

Iwasawa, Y. (1999). *International law, human rights, and Japanese law: The impact of international law on Japanese Law.* Clarendon Press.

Japan Federation of Bar Associations. (2020). *Report of JFBA regarding the seventh periodic report by the government of Japan based on article 40(b) of the International covenant on civil and political rights.* https://www.nichibenren.or.jp/library/pdf/activity/international/library/human_rights/iccpr_7en.pdf.

Maree, C. (2020). "LGBT issues" and the 2020 games. *The Asia-Pacific Journal: Japan Focus, 18*(4), https://apjjf.org/2020/4/Maree.html.

Ministry of Justice. (2023). *The constitution of Japan.* Japanese Law Translation Database System. https://www.japaneselawtranslation.go.jp/en/laws/view/174.

Nagoya District Court. (2020). Judgment of 4 June 2020, case no. H30-GyoU-76. *Hanrei jihō*, 2465, 13 ff. https://www.courts.go.jp/app/hanrei_jp/detail4?id=89615.

Norton, L. H. (2006). Neutering the transgendered: Human rights and Japan's law no. 111. *Georgetown Journal of Gender and the Law, 7*(2), 187–216.

Sapporo District Court. (2021). Judgment of 17 March 2021, Case no. H31-Wa-267. *Hanrei jihō*, 2487, 3 ff.

Supreme Court. (2019). Decision of 23 January 2019, Case no. H30-Ku-269. *Saikō saibansho saibanshū minji*, 261, 1 ff.

Supreme Court. (2021). Decision of 30 November 2021, Case no. R2-Ku-638. *Saikō saibansho saibanshū minji*, 266, 185 ff.

Taniguchi, H. (2013). Japan's 2003 gender identity disorder act. *Asian-Pacific Law & Policy Journal*, *14*(2), 108–117.

Tokyo District Court. (1969). Judgment of 15 February 1969, Case nos. S40-GoWa-307, S40-GoWa-339, and S40-TokuWa-927. *Keiji saiban geppō* 1(2), 133 ff.

Tokyo District Court. (1994). Judgment of 30 March 1994, Case no. H3-Wa-1557. *Hanrei jihō*, 1509, 80 ff.

Tokyo District Court. (2022). Judgment of 30 November 2022, H31-Wa-3465. https://www.courts.go.jp/app/files/hanrei_jp/778/091778_hanrei.pdf.

Tokyo High Court. (1997). Judgment of 16 September 1997, Case no. H6-Ne-1580. *Hanrei taimuzu*, 986, 206 ff.

Tokyo High Court. (2020). Judgment of 4 March 2020, Case no. R1-Ne-4433. *Hanrei jihō*, 2473, 47 ff.

Trans in Japan: "I can't change my gender unless I'm sterilised." (2021, April 8). BBC News. https://www.bbc.com/news/av/world-asia-56668349.

United Nations General Assembly. (1993). Principles relating to the status of national institutions, 20 December 1993, U.N. Doc. A/RES/48/134.

Utsunomiya District Court. (2019). Judgment of 18 September 2019, Case no. H30-Wa-30. *Hanrei jihō*, 2473, 51 ff.

World Health Organization. (2014). *Eliminating forced, coercive and otherwise involuntary sterilization: An interagency statement, OHCHR, UN Women, UNAIDS, UNDP, UNFPA, UNICEF and WHO.* https://apps.who.int/iris/handle/10665/112848.

Azusa Yamashita

Being LGBT in disasters: Lived experiences from Japan

Conflict, disaster, or unexpected events such as the COVID-19 pandemic unveil existing social inequalities and magnify the vulnerability of certain social groups, such as uneven access to gender-appropriate supplies and services. Japan is particularly prone to natural hazards, including earthquakes, tsunamis, typhoons, and volcanic eruptions.[1] As such, it may be one of the best places to observe political and legal responses to the resultant disasters, and the manner in which crises and vulnerabilities interact. Japan's national disaster policies started to incorporate an understanding of age-related dimensions of vulnerability in the late 1980s based on the experiences of older adults in disasters (Lee, 2006), and later a gender lens in understanding the ways in which disasters and human experiences converge (Asano, 2012). It was only after the Great East Japan Earthquake in 2011, however, when policymakers, academics, disaster-response NGOs, women's groups, and LGBT communities became aware of the specific vulnerability and needs that some people have in times of disaster because of their sexual orientation, gender identity, and/or gender expression in Japan.

The experiences of LGBT survivors of the Great East Japan Earthquake have been documented widely in research by myself and other researchers (e.g., Sugiura & Maekawa, 2021; Uchida, 2012, 2015; Yamashita, 2012; Yamashita et al., 2017). In this paper, I build on this research by focusing on the lived experiences of LGBT people in three disasters that occurred after the Great East Japan Earthquake: the Kumamoto Earthquakes in 2016, flood and landslides in Hokkaido and the Tohoku region caused by a series of typhoons in 2016, and the Hokkaido Eastern Iburi Earthquake in 2018. I first examine Japan's disaster risk reduction and management (DRRM) policies from an LGBT lens, before introducing the cases of 10 LGBT survivors, whose experiences I documented in a series of semistructured interviews in 2019 and 2020.

---

1 In this paper, I consciously avoid the use of the term "natural disaster," as it perpetuates the perception of disasters as naturally occurring, inevitable events, while overlooking the political, socioeconomic, and environmental context in which they occur (see, e.g., Balthasar, 2023).

1 The Great East Japan Disaster as an opportunity for change

Over the past few decades, Japanese society has gradually come to recognize the hurdles LGBT people face on the basis of their sexual orientation, gender identity, and/or gender expression in different spheres of their everyday life, such as at home, in school, at work, and in healthcare settings. As the only G7 country that does not legalize marriage equality or outlaw discrimination on the basis of sexual orientation, gender identity, and/or gender expression at the national level, Japan remains an outlier with regard to what many Global North nations recognize to be the fundamental human rights of LGBT persons. The realities documented by researchers and the tireless activism of vocal human rights proponents have informed some policies that are more reflective and inclusive of LGBT needs. For example, the law on legal gender marker changes was established in 2003 as a result of advocacy by a group of trans people. The inclusion of gender and sexual minorities in national policies for suicide prevention and anti–school bullying, and the national gender equality plan are such examples. These important efforts have not yet had an impact, however, in crisis situations, such as those that arise in the context of disasters. LGBT experiences of disaster have long been invisible and overlooked in society, policies, and even within queer communities themselves. This is the case in other parts of the world as well (Dominey-Howes et al., 2014), and LGBT perspectives have remained scarce in documentation and policies globally (Gaillard et al., 2017).

The Great East Japan Disaster saw the largest-scale earthquake (magnitude 9.0) in the country's recorded history (International Federation of Red Cross and Red Crescent Societies, 2014, p. 12), and the ensuing tsunamis and nuclear power plant explosions resulted in over 22,000 lost or missing lives (*Higashinihon daishinsai*, 2021), destroyed livelihoods, and displaced over 400,000 people (Kawata, 2011). The economic and social impacts of the disaster will continue for decades to come. Moreover, the disaster has revealed and raised awareness of the existing inequalities that vulnerable populations faced in Japanese society prior to the disasters. In documenting support work for disaster-affected women by other disaster-affected women, Asano (2012) argued that during the response to the Great East Japan Disaster, support for hitherto-neglected groups emerged, including gender and sexual minorities, as well as girls and college-aged women (p. 131).

A literature search supports Asano's point. Few articles about LGBT-specific struggles in the disaster context prior to the Great East Japan Disaster appear when searching newspaper databases and CiNii (a database of Japanese- and English-language academic articles published in Japan) by using various combinations of relevant Japanese words. For example, with the "Great Hanshin-Awaji Earthquake" in 1995, I searched for "homosexuality," "lesbian," "gay," and "trans." I then searched for the same terms with the "Niigata Chūetsu Earthquake" in 2004. The 1990s was a pivotal period in the history of Japan's LGBT communities. A lesbian and gay organization filed the first case against a public authority for discrimination in 1991, and the first pride parade was held in 1994 (Fushimi, 2004, pp. 371–372). However, Japanese society was still not informed enough on LGBT issues to pay attention to LGBT people's disaster experiences. It must be acknowledged that there were LGBT people who survived disasters prior to the Great East Japan Earthquake in spite of the shortage of documentation.

By the time of the Great East Japan Disaster, certain institutional changes to respect LGBT rights were already in place, such as enabling legal changes to one's official gender (2003), the national suicide prevention policy (2012), and the memorandum on the support of gender and sexual minorities in schools by the Ministry of Education (2015). Japan's LGBT communities had benefited from a few decades of activism, and there was greater social awareness of LGBT issues. This made it possible for conversations around the experiences and needs of LGBT people in disasters to take place not only within LGBT communities, but also among DRRM stakeholders such as municipal employees, shelter volunteer groups, and neighborhood associations, who came to realize that LGBT people faced specific challenges and needs not only in times of disaster but also in everyday life. In other words, the 2011 disaster functioned as a turning point to highlight LGBT issues. Scholars in development studies have argued that disaster can function as an opportunity for some form of social transformation (Bănică et al., 2020).

Prior to the Great East Japan Earthquake, Japan's DRRM policies did not consider LGBT needs. In 2013, the Cabinet Office's Gender Equality Bureau made two explicit references to sexual minorities regarding evacuation shelter management in its publication on DRRM guidelines and building better measures from a gender equality perspective:

> To accommodate gender and sexual minorities and others, it is necessary to consider installing at least one universal restroom that both men and women can use. Outdoor universal restrooms are inaccessible for wheelchair users, so installing temporary indoor restrooms would be ideal. (p. 29)[2]

Further, it noted:

---

2 Unless otherwise indicated, all translations from Japanese in this paper are by the author.

> When creating lists [of evacuees], [the evacuees'] agreement to the disclosure of personal information must be confirmed. An abundance of caution is required in managing such information. Gender on evacuees' lists can be recorded in open-ended columns out of consideration for gender and sexual minorities. (Gender Equality Bureau, 2013, pp. 34–35)

It is noteworthy that these references were made only two years after the 2011 disaster. As there were officials from the Gender Equality Bureau and the Gender Equality Team of the Reconstruction Agency who were keen to learn about LGBT experiences and needs during the 2011 disaster, these references were clearly based on such discussions that took place in LGBT communities.

2 LGBT lived experiences after the Great East Japan Earthquake

I conducted semistructured and face-to-face interviews with 10 LGBT survivors of three disasters between February 2019 and January 2020 in order to identify the disaster vulnerability, resilience, and policy needs of LGBT people. As some of the experiences in the Great East Japan Disaster of 2011 had already been documented, my objective was to examine whether subsequent DRRM policies reflected any LGBT struggles and needs that had been highlighted for the first time in 2011. Ten interviewees were chosen because outreach to potential candidates was feasible through LGBT groups with whom I had built trust. Finding LGBT individuals who have been affected by disasters and are willing to talk about who they are and what they went through is not easy. That is why I chose three disaster-affected areas where I have a network with local LGBT groups for this research.

Interviewees were approached through local LGBT groups and given a concise explanation of the research. Before commencing each interview, I explained the objective of the interview, types of questions to be asked, how the interview data would be used, and the interview process (see appendix A) – they could skip questions they preferred not to answer and stop the interview at any time. I also briefly shared with interviewees my own experiences during the Great East Japan Earthquake and my involvement with LGBT communities. Written consent was then obtained from the interviewees, and the interviews were audio-recorded with the interviewees' permission. Sample interview questions (translated from Japanese) are included in appendix B.

The 10 interviewees consisted of two lesbian women, two bisexual women, one pansexual woman, two trans women, one trans man, and two gay men. Details of the interviewees and their interviews are shown in table 1. While potential candidates were approached without any limitations on nationality, all the interviewees happened to be Japanese citizens living in Japan. Therefore, all the interviews were conducted in Japanese, transcribed, and later translated by the author. The interviewees were all adults, whose ages ranged in their twenties to fifties. I use the interviewees' chosen pronouns and identities, as well as their preferred vocabulary.

Table 1: Summary of interviews with LGBT survivors of disasters.

Interviewee	Sexual Orientation or Gender Identity	Experiences	Date of Interview
Kumamoto Earthquakes: Earthquakes from magnitude 5.4 to 7.3 struck Kumamoto on 14–16 April 2016, which resulted in 139 deaths, 2,581 people injured, and 181,373 houses (Fire and Disaster Management Agency, 2016).			
A	Bisexual woman	Water and electricity cut, fled to emergency shelter, and provided support to others.	17 June 2019
B	Trans woman	Housing damaged and fled to emergency shelter.	17 June 2019
C	Pansexual woman	Housing damaged and fled to parents' house with a same-gender partner and children.	18 June 2019
D	Gay man	Water and electricity cut, fled to a friend's house and an emergency shelter, and provided support to others.	17 September 2019
Flood and landslides in Hokkaido and Tohoku: Six typhoons hit Hokkaido and northeast Japan, which caused large-scale floods, 23 deaths, and 6 people missing in August 2016 (Bosai Plus, 2016).			
E	Trans woman	Neighborhood flooded, fled to a friend's house and provided support to others.	1 February 2019
Hokkaido Eastern Iburi Earthquake: A series of earthquakes from magnitude 5.2 to 6.7 (Japan Meteorological Agency, n.d.) struck in September and October 2018, which resulted in 44 deaths, 785 people injured, 49,412 houses damaged, and a large-scale blackout throughout Hokkaido (Hokkaido Government, 2022).			
F	Lesbian	Housing damaged but stayed home with a same-gender partner.	14 September 2019
G	Gay man	Electricity cut and provided support to others.	16 September 2019
H	Lesbian	Water and electricity cut, stayed home, and provided support to others.	25 January 2020

Table 1: Summary of interviews with LGBT survivors of disasters. *(Continued)*

Interviewee	Sexual Orienta-tion or Gender Identity	Experiences	Date of Interview
J	Bisexual woman	Water and electricity cut, stayed home, and provided support to others. (H's partner)	25 January 2020
K	Trans man	Water and electricity cut, stayed home with wife, and provided shelter to his evacuating mother.	26 January 2020

3 LGBT vulnerability during a disaster

The impact of a disaster on an area differs depending on one's vulnerability, as "the characteristics of a person or group and their situation ... influence their capacity to anticipate, cope with, resist and recover from the impact of a natural disaster" (Wisner, 2003, p. 11). Just as social dimensions of difference such as ethnicity, age, or disability can render one vulnerable, one's actual or perceived sexual orientation, gender identity, and/or expression can add to one's vulnerability in disaster settings (Brown et al., 2019). The 10 interviews illustrate the vulnerability and stresses that LGBT people are forced to deal with because of the lack of legal rights and social recognition of LGBT issues in times of disaster. They point to specific challenges faced by LGBT people in times of disasters such as evacuees' lists, restrooms and baths, privacy, housing, medication, inclusion/exclusion, and intersectionality, as described below. These challenges should be seen as a continuation of hurdles faced in daily life. For instance, trans people would feel safer using a restroom in accord with their gender identity and expression at an evacuation shelter if they were already able to do so in schools, at work, and in other public spaces in daily life. Same-gender couples would not hesitate to evacuate to a shelter and would not have to hide their relationship if it were legally recognized and widely accepted in society.[3]

---

3 "Same-sex" tends to reproduce the image of one's sex as being both static and binary. It does not take into account the many nonbinary and trans identities possible in human relationships that may be "read" by others as same-gender relationships but might be, for example, a trans woman and a cis woman. That is why I have chosen to use "same-gender" here, rather than the more commonly used term "same-sex."

3.1 Evacuee lists

When a disaster strikes, emergency shelters are set up by local governments based on Article 49(7) of the Basic Act on Disaster Management. Every shelter has a list of evacuees in advance or creates one when the shelter is set up in order to gather basic information about the evacuees so that the shelter managers can arrange necessary supplies for them, such as food, water, blankets, and clothes, and respond to their specific needs, including the needs of older adults and families with small children. The list usually contains one's name, address, phone number, age, and gender.

Two of the interviewees (B and H) indicated that the evacuees' lists could be a problem for some trans evacuees, at least in their current form. Interviewee B, a trans woman whose legal gender marker says otherwise, fled from her home after earthquakes caused her windows to be broken and electricity to be cut in the middle of the night. She first fled to an open area by car and spent a few days there. She recalled her problems when she and other evacuees were asked to move to a local public center for farmers:

> The list of people [in my village] was already there to check every evacuee. Someone who was probably from a neighborhood association told me that how I dressed looked like a woman but couldn't confirm I was the man [in the list].... They told me they wouldn't be able to guarantee my safety when larger earthquakes occurred during the blackout because of this mismatch [between my birth name on the list and my gender expression]. I understood their intention. I didn't take it as discrimination based on my *sekushuariti* [sexuality] [*sic*].... So, I told them I'd leave the center and I immediately did.

Interviewee B said that the list that included her sex assigned at birth brought her a sense of pain. If she had been able to change her gender marker on the family register, which functions as the base document for other legal documents, the shelter manager at her second refuge would not have questioned her identity. The Act on Special Cases in Handling Gender Status for Persons with Gender Identity Disorder (2003) requires that one should obtain a medical diagnosis of "gender identity disorder" and be an adult, unmarried, without a minor child, and sterilized, and have genitals of the gender that one identifies with (Ministry of Justice, 2023a). Having been unable to obtain such a diagnosis due to her schizophrenia and depression, Interviewee B was also unable to change her legal gender markers even if she wanted. The law has therefore hindered some trans people from changing their gender marker.

From the perspective of international human rights law, pathologizing trans identities is mostly frowned upon since the World Health Organization (WHO) changed its policy and wording, recognizing the damage that this pathologization caused trans people and others with nonconforming gender identities (Human Rights Watch, 2019). The WHO and other UN agencies have criticized the requirement of sterilization for legal gender marker changes, as it violates one's human rights and is against international human rights standards (WHO et al., 2014).

Interviewees H and J, health service providers in a same-gender relationship, did not need to seek shelters when the earthquake hit. They worked at an evacuation shelter for local residents and remembered what its reception was like:

> Evacuees had to check in in front of everyone. There were tables in the hall entrance and [local government] officials would ask evacuees questions and write down [the answers].... Anyone was able to know who's there and hear everything. The evacuees could see other evacuees on the lists.... It would have been difficult for someone who requires special accommodations to speak up about their needs.

Interviewees H and J also said that "what kind of special accommodation may be required [for various groups of vulnerable people] in what ways is not included in the guidance for local government officials or health service providers." This shows that due diligence is not practiced by DRRM stakeholders, such as shelter volunteers and emergency planning officials in local communities, and that there is a lack of awareness of people who would require extra privacy, including trans people. These failures can, as in Interviewee B's case, deny LGBT people's, especially trans people's, access to shelters.

3.2 Restrooms and baths

Access to restrooms and baths is a basic human rights concern and affects one's sanitation and health. The interviewees' narratives suggest that even such basic rights can be inaccessible in times of disaster, especially for trans and other gender-nonconforming people. Interviewee B, a trans woman, was denied access to the women's restrooms. At the initial stage of her refuge, she was told by other women evacuees to use a universal restroom – the church she had evacuated to happened to have one, but not many evacuation shelters are equipped with a universal restroom. As time passed and these women got to know her, she was eventually allowed to use the women's restrooms.

Other interviewees expressed concerns over gender-segregated restrooms and baths. Interviewee E, a trans woman who evacuated to a friend's house amid floods said:

> If I had [had no choice but to evacuate to an evacuation shelter], other evacuees might have wondered who I was when I used a women's restroom. If I was in a women's space and talked

to someone on the phone, people might have wondered who I was because of my male voice. These things would prevent me from going to an evacuation shelter.

Interviewee B spent three weeks without taking a bath because of her gender identity and expression. She explained:

> If you're a trans man or trans woman with a high level of passing, you may be able to find a way to use a public bath. Even when people offer free baths [for evacuees], I can't go. I may be fine in the water but the problem is the changing room. For example, I wear women's underwear. Trans men would be wearing men's underwear. It would look weird if they were to take off their clothes trying to hide their genitalia among other men. So, I couldn't go. I went to a faraway private public bathhouse [i. e., a public bathhouse with a private bath].

Even when one's level of passing, to be perceived or able to blend in according to your gender identity and expression by others, may be high, gender-segregated shared restrooms and baths can remain a concern for trans people. For example, Interviewee K no longer faces "any inconvenience" because his gender identity, gender expression, and gender marker on the family register match, but he still wondered, "what would I do if the Self-Defense Forces set up baths [which are usually shared and gender-segregated]? What would I do with restrooms if [the effects of the earthquake had been] prolonged?"

Restrooms and baths are often regarded as trans people's issues. Interviewee G, a gay man, however, suggests that the issue is not limited to trans people. While he did not have to evacuate to a shelter, he experienced water shortages and electricity cuts in his apartment and workplace. During that time, he worried that other evacuees may be "confused" and "surprised" if he used restrooms and baths at a shelter because of his gender expression:

> I don't want to have my hair cut short. That doesn't mean I want to wear women's clothes. People tell me that I'm feminine and look like a woman. So, I'm used to other people giving me warnings [on which bathroom to use] because it happens often.

This points to the manner in which spaces are constructed as, and productive of, heteronormative and cisgender identities as the presumed state of all human experience, what planning scholar Petra Doan (2010) and others have called "the tyranny of gendered spaces" (p. 635). Only having separate women's and men's restrooms potentially prevents people whose gender identities do not fall into the gender dichotomy from accessing the very basic human need to urinate. Because access to restrooms affects not only one's right to sanitation but also one's right to life with dignity, right to protection and security, and right to receive humanitarian assistance on the basis of need (The Sphere Project, 2018), universal bathrooms that are accessible to people from a wide spectrum of genders and abilities would be an appropriate response to this problem.

3.3 Privacy

In Japan, large arenas, schools, or public buildings usually function as evacuation shelters, where evacuees share spaces often without curtains or tents. This poses serious privacy issues for many, including LGBT evacuees. The interviews revealed that a lack of privacy at evacuation shelters could send LGBT evacuees away. Interviewee F, a lesbian, and her same-gender partner returned to their earthquake-damaged apartment as soon as they observed their nearby evacuation shelter. She said:

> Staying in a car felt very cramped and we couldn't sleep. It felt safe but we couldn't stretch our legs. It was impossible [to stay in a car]. So, we went to an elementary school behind our apartment because we heard it had opened as an evacuation shelter.... We figured that there were families, ordinary families. We thought we wouldn't be comfortable staying with them.... We knew some people but not so closely. I think you feel like talking to someone when you have free time [and that could have happened]. I didn't want to talk to any strangers. I didn't want other people to ask difficult questions [e.g., about our relationship]. I was too tired to evacuate to that crowded shelter.

Interviewee E, a trans woman, also thought of fleeing to an evacuation shelter but chose to go to her friend's house instead because of privacy concerns. She said:

> I wasn't sure if a single woman could have her own space or men would have their separate spaces at the shelter. I imagined I might look like a man when I woke up the next morning because I haven't completed hair removal [and I didn't want that to happen in front of other evacuees] So, I spent three to four nights at my friend's place.

As support providers, Interviewees H and J observed what an evacuation shelter was like. They explained:

> Shelter managers weren't prepared in the beginning. So, all the evacuees slept on the floor together, including older adults and families with children without any privacy. At a later stage, tents and partitions were provided.... They should have been provided earlier.... Spaces were not even gender-segregated at all. We would never want to evacuate to such a shelter.

The right to privacy is recognized under international human rights law, as well as by the Constitution of Japan as a fundamental human right, not only in ordinary times but also in humanitarian settings such as disasters. The Sphere Project

(2018), an initiative led by humanitarian NGOs to set minimum standards and guidance for humanitarian assistance, has articulated that evacuation shelters should be designed to provide privacy. The interviews show that a lack of privacy from LGBT people's perspectives can easily and effectively prevent them from accessing evacuation shelters. As Interviewee F said, "just being physically safe doesn't bring you safety. A sense of safety comes when privacy is respected."

3.4 Housing

After leaving evacuation shelters, evacuees either return to their restored housing or move to temporary housing that is specifically constructed or rented for evacuees who are unable to rebuild their housing based on Article 23 of the Disaster Relief Act (1947), under which municipal governments are responsible for the practical business of providing housing for evacuees. Eligibility for temporary housing often includes being from the same household unless you are a single-person household. Due to this condition, same-gender couples are effectively excluded from public housing because the same household is defined as "the head of the household and one's spouse" or "husband and wife with a child (or children)" (Ministry of Health, Labor and Welfare, 2009). They are substantially excluded because their relationship is not considered spousal under Japanese law.

Although none of the interviewees had to live in the temporary or rented housing for evacuees, concerns regarding housing accessibility were raised specifically by those in same-gender relationships. Interviewee D, a gay man, is considering registering his same-gender partnership in his local municipality, which recognizes such relationships. He said:

> I have never had to apply for public housing in my life before, so it didn't bother me. But I'm aware now that the effects of partnership recognition differ from one local municipality to another and it could affect me when my apartment collapses [by disaster] and I want to apply [for temporary housing for evacuees].

Interviewee F, a lesbian in a same-gender relationship, also questions housing accessibility and the effects of partnership recognition by her local municipality. She said:

> I know that the partnership system in my locality is useless because I was involved in advocating for the system. It's just like a token. We're negotiating with the local government [for the system to be improved effectively] on public housing.... So, the partnership system isn't useful [for housing, including temporary evacuee housing].

She felt that her partner was "treated as nonexistent," not only in housing but also when she applied for allowance for their damaged apartment and consolation allowance for the disaster-affected because the allowances were provided on a household basis.

The same-gender couple Interviewees H and J wondered whether gay couples might face greater problems in applying for temporary housing because they have observed more social acceptance for two women being together than for two men.

Housing is another basic human right. It is recognized as an integral part of right to life by the Japanese Constitution and by international human rights and humanitarian laws. The Office of the United Nations High Commissioner for Human Rights and UN-Habitat (2014) illustrated that the entitlements of the right to housing includes "equal and non-discriminatory access to adequate housing" (p. 3). The interviews indicate that this is not substantially guaranteed to LGBT people, more specifically people in same-gender relationships, both in peacetime and in the aftermath of disasters.

3.5 Medication

Access to medication affects anyone who is on medication regardless of their sexual orientation or gender identity. The interviews revealed that LGBT people, too, could face hurdles in accessing medication in times of disaster. When floods hit her locality, Interviewee E, a trans woman, was unable to pick up her new stock of hormone pills that she had imported from abroad because roads to the nearby post office were disrupted.

Interviewee D, a gay man, remembers that his local health centers became too busy responding to food poisoning that had occurred at evacuation shelters to continue HIV testing. He wondered "there must have been people who were anxious [about their HIV status but couldn't get tested] during that period."

Interviewee A, a bisexual woman who provided support for a trans woman with a disability in the aftermath of the earthquakes said:

> There are things that only the people concerned know, including the issue of hormone medication. Not many would be able to respond even when [hormone] medication is sent to evacuation shelters.... It would help if there were even just one person who knows about the medication that gender and sexual minority people need, including hormones [sent to evacuation shelters], in a team, or if they wore rainbow signs around their arms so that LGBT evacuees can seek to consult them.

3.6 Inclusion/exclusion

As illustrated above regarding the privacy issues, non-inclusive evacuation shelters effectively turn away LGBT people. After having left the second refuge, Interviewee B, a trans woman, moved to a church that had previously asked her to come over to fix electrical facilities as a licensed electrician. She ended up spending one and a half months at the church. Her pastor was informed that she was a trans woman. Other church members, however, were not informed and seemed to wonder about her gender. She said, "I didn't want to stay inside. No one would talk to me other than the pastor, even during meals. So, I told the church to let me park my car [behind the church] and stay there." While this may seem to be her own choice, it points to the likelihood that any LGBT person can be turned away from a non-inclusive environment and suffer substantial exclusion from shelters, even if that were unintended by shelter managers and/or other evacuees.

3.7 Intersectionality

Foundational research on intersectionality, that is, the manner in which various forms of identity intersect with one another in ways that compound, complicate, alleviate, or ameliorate various forms of vulnerability (Crenshaw, 1995), can offer a useful lens with which to view these challenges in the disaster context. Because all human beings are compounds of multiple characteristics, it is these connected axes of identity that produce specific subjects and experiences (Crenshaw, 1995; Hill Collins, 2019). In short, the intersection of LGBT and other identities can increase one's vulnerability. Interviewee A provided care to a trans woman with an intellectual disability, who was forced to use facilities of her sex assigned at birth, not of her gender identity, during her refuge. Interviewee A recalled:

> Around the seventh day since we evacuated, a nearby gym offered all evacuees at our evacuation shelter free baths.... At the gym, baths were gender-segregated. [I wondered] what can I do for her and what does she want? She could surprise other women [as a trans woman in transition].... She screams when she is happy because of her intellectual disability, which itself is not a problem. If she screams in a changing room when other people, especially when many older adults are around, however, it is difficult to explain [her condition to others] and we [care providers] weren't ready.... In the end, her male care provider convinced her to use the men's bath, saying that care providers weren't ready and she was still in a male body anyway.

Interviewee A said that able-bodied trans people might be able to flee to an accepting friend's house but that was often not an option for sexual and gender minorities with disabilities.

Interviewee F, a lesbian, lives with a physical disability. When asked whether she thought of fleeing to one of the welfare evacuation shelters, she said "until just now, I didn't know there are such things as welfare evacuation shelters." These shelters were designed for evacuees who require special accommodations based on the Basic Act on Disaster Management (1961), in which Article 8–2(2)15 defines people requiring special accommodation as "the elderly, disabled persons, infants, and others requiring special care" (Ministry of Justice, 2023b). She could have evacuated to one of the welfare evacuation shelters as a person with disability but she was not aware of their existence. Future research is required to determine whether such shelters are welcoming of LGBT evacuees with disabilities or whether "others requiring special care" includes able-bodied LGBT evacuees.

4 Resilience

It has become evident that LGBT interviewees and their community members showed their resilience through not only having coped with difficult situations presented by disasters but having helped others in the aftermath of disasters. For example, as illustrated above, Interviewee A, a bisexual woman, kept providing care for a trans woman with a disability. Interviewees H and J served local evacuees at an evacuation shelter as medical service providers. In addition to helping her church as an electrician, Interviewee B, a trans woman, volunteered in a soup kitchen, showed the way to disaster medical assistance teams, and put back fallen furniture for older adults. Interviewee C, a pansexual woman, cared for her children who were frightened by the earthquakes and the aftershocks that followed. Interviewee G, a gay man, kept providing care for people with disability in his workplace even during the power outages.

Interviewee F, a lesbian, and Interviewee K, a trans man, witnessed gay and lesbian bars helping LGBT people and local community members. Interviewee F recalled:

> A gay friend of mine who owns a gay bar texted me asking me if we were OK. I texted back saying my cellphone's battery may run out soon. Then he told me to come over to charge [the phone] with his car. He also told me to come to his bar if we were hungry because he was planning to open a soup kitchen [for the disaster affected]. So, my partner and I went there at around 9:00 p.m. the next day after the earthquake.... When we arrived, there were many women and children inside the bar. These women were saying that they felt safe being around a man even if he may be gay.

Interviewee K also said that he knew a gay bar that opened its space for anyone in need, including for those who wanted to use a bathroom safely.

Interviewee D, a gay man, played a key role at an evacuation shelter where he stayed. While he continued going to his office during the day, he negotiated with the shelter managers to allow him to open a soup kitchen at the shelter with vegetables, rice, and other food he asked his friends to bring. In addition, he disseminated information via social media to tell any LGBT survivors that he was at the shelter if they needed support. Early during his refuge, he saw a poster of an LGBT event on the shelter wall, and he talked to one of the shelter managers to connect him with any LGBT evacuees who might need help. He said to the manager:

> I'm gay. I'm part of the event whose poster is up on the wall and involved [in LGBT communities]. I don't know what kind of difficulties LGBT people face, but please talk to me if you know any evacuee who may need someone to talk to. They may not come to me because I'm a stranger, but they might come to you as you're a shelter manager. There may be something I can help with.

After experiencing floods, Interviewee E, a trans woman, took a training course to become a *bōsaishi* (certified DRRM officer) "hoping to create evacuation shelters where I would feel safe evacuating to" in future disasters. She even joined an association of women *bōsaishi*, hoping to change aspects about evacuation shelters and their management that affected trans people.

In disaster studies, resilience is a key concept coupled with vulnerability. Resilience is understood as "the ability of individuals, communities and countries in highly disruptive events, like disasters, to maintain relatively stable psychological and social functioning, allowing for the capacity to access and organise resources, and 'spring back' in a timely and efficient manner" (Dominey-Howes et al., 2014, p. 908). The concept has been criticized, as it has been used by neoliberal ideologies that attempt to limit state involvement and increase self-reliance (Cretney, 2014). NGOs, local community groups, and activists, however, have been using resilience in order to address social issues. Resilience in a disaster context still has value for its belief in the human capacity to be, to cope with, and to make things better in difficult circumstances.

Women are recognized not only as being susceptible to disasters but also as resilient change agents (Global Facility for Disaster Reduction and Recovery, 2018; Moreno, 2020; Moreno & Shaw, 2018). The interviewees' narratives of resilience suggest the same for LGBT people. While LGBT disaster survivors experience specific struggles in cis-heteronormative disaster responses, they help themselves and others. The rights of all evacuees, including LGBT people, must be protected, but at the same time it is essential that LGBT people are not perceived simply as sufferers or victims in a disaster context because it diminishes their agency and disempowers them. Furthermore, diminishing potential contributors of disaster responses and reconstruction impedes the resilience of communities and of society (Yamashita et al., 2017, p. 66). In addition to specific measures to systematically re-spond to barriers that LGBT people experience at different stages of disasters, the importance of "meaningful consultation with LGBTQI individuals and organiza-tions at each stage of humanitarian response" (The Sphere Project, 2018) is high-lighted as a standard in global humanitarian responses from both community and individual resilience perspectives.

5 Problems with the current DRRM policies from an LGBT lens

Some research has revealed how much local governments respond to LGBT needs in their post-2011 DRRM policies. According to Ōsawa (2019), only 12.8% of all 47 prefectures and 1.7% of 1,171 municipalities (64.8% of all municipalities in Japan) included "consideration of LGBT [people]" in their guidelines on evacuation shelter management as of early 2018 (p. 35). There has since been a rapid increase from 12.8% to 63.8% of all 47 prefectures in 2021 ("Saigai hinan," 2021). In 2020, it was revealed that only 9.6% of six prefectures and 77 of 227 local municipalities in the Tohoku region have such references ("Saigaiji seiteki shōsūsha," 2020). Among the 31 local municipalities that have introduced the same-gender partnership sys-tem in the Tokyo area, 41.9% have these references ("LGBT hairyo," 2021).

 Slow changes at a local municipality level, in contrast to prefectural-level changes, can be attributed to: (a) the lack of a gender lens in various policies and their implementation, (b) a narrow gender framework that is based on the gender binary and heterosexism, and (c) a lack of DRRM initiatives by the national government. Firstly, 5.9% of local municipalities with LGBT references in their DRRM policies have a division in charge of promoting gender equality that collab-orates with the disaster management division. In those without the references, the number decreases to 0.8% (Ōsawa, 2019, p. 16). This suggests that collaboration be-tween these divisions can help to make DRRM policies more equitable in terms of gender and thereby increase the chance of LGBT perspectives being considered.

 Jendā (gender), however, seems to remain narrowly defined as (cis, heterosex-ual) women's issues in DRRM policy areas in Japan. This is reflected in the guide-lines for disaster response published by the Gender Equality Bureau in 2020, whose title refers only to "women's perspectives" (*josei no shiten*). While the guide-lines do state that taking DRRM measures from women's perspectives "should contribute to the accommodation of various people such as children, young people, older adults, people with disabilities, and LGBT people" (Gender Equality Bureau, 2020, para. 2), they fail to outline the specific barriers that LGBT people face or the necessary measures to be taken.

These 2020 guidelines show how little initiative the national government is taking to include LGBT people's needs in national DRRM policies and consequently local policies. The primary responsibility to protect the lives, livelihood, and rights of people in the country lies with the state. Based on the current national DRRM policies, however, the Japanese government is not fulfilling this responsibility. It could provide leadership to local governments, especially local municipalities, through DRRM laws and policies that consider the specific barriers faced by LGBT people, which have been elaborated and expanded with suggested measures in the Sphere Project's (2018) *Sphere Handbook: Humanitarian Charter and Minimum Standards in Humanitarian Response.* The experiences described by the interviews with individuals in the present study underscore how national and local DRRM policies must respond to LGBT people's needs based on their lived experiences, which have become evident since the Great East Japan Earthquake.

6 Conclusion

While the Great East Japan Earthquake caused serious damage to Japanese society, it has functioned as an opportunity for LGBT communities to make their barriers and needs more visible. The barriers and needs are often continuations of existing hurdles that legal, policy, and social situations present to LGBT people in their daily lives.

In this paper, 10 interviews held with LGBT survivors of three disasters after the Great East Japan Earthquake – the Kumamoto earthquakes, typhoons in Hokkaido and the Tohoku region, and the Hokkaido Eastern Iburi Earthquake – have reaffirmed that LGBT people experience various challenges in disasters – evacuee lists, restrooms and baths, privacy, housing, medication, inclusion/exclusion, and intersectionality – which can be attributed to a lack of responsiveness to their needs in national and local DRRM policies.

One key common theme that emerged is that all of the interviewees had at least one person in their life to whom they were out about their sexual orientation and/or gender identity. Those who sought refuge at a parents' house, friend's house, or evacuation shelter indicated that having already come out made it easier for them to ask for help. This does not by any means indicate that LGBT people should come out in preparation for disasters. Rather, what it suggests is that when LGBT people have a supportive person in their life to whom they have come out, this decreases the stress of having to manage the secrecy around their sexual orientation and/or gender identity and having to deal with struggles by themselves. Thus, it can increase their resilience in disasters.

One important element that did not emerge from the interviews is sexual and gender-based violence. While gradually accumulated evidence from different parts of the world, including Japan, show that the reports of such violence increase after disasters (International Federation of Red Cross and Red Crescent Societies, 2018), further research is needed to investigate the realities that LGBT people face in the aftermath of disasters.

Lastly, Japan's DRRM policies have begun to reflect the needs of LGBT people since the 2011 disaster, as seen in a growing number of prefectural policies. However, municipal (at a city, town, and village level) and national policies in particular still do not recognize LGBT people as a vulnerable community or as individuals with resilience and agency. There is a continuing need for DRRM policies at all levels of government in Japan to be based on an understanding of the diversity of sexual orientation, gender identity and/or expression to protect the lives, livelihood, and rights of all.

Acknowledgments

I would like to thank the editors Kazuyoshi Kawasaka and Stefan Würrer for their patience and insightful feedback. I also thank the late Dr. Paul Chamness Iida for his contribution to this book and warm guidance. I am grateful to all the interviewees and the organizers of the local LGBT groups, who made the interviews possible, as well as Dr. Natasha Fox, who provided me with research advice and constant guidance. This paper contains the outcomes of the "Research on Vulnerability and Resilience of Sexual Minority Disaster Survivors and Potential of DRRM Policies," funded by the Grant-in-Aid for Early-Career Scientists of the Japan Society for the Promotion of Sciences (18K13965), Principal investigator: Yamashita Azusa.

References

Asano, F. (2012). Atarashii shien no futatsu no ugoki: Sekushuaru mainoritī to gāruzu sedai o taishō ni [Two new developments in support: Targeting sexual minorities and the "girls' generation"]. In Miyagi no Joseishien o Kirokusurukai (Eds.), *Josei tachi ga ugoku: Higashinihon daishinsai to danjo kyōdō sankaku shiten no shien* [Women on the move: The Great East Japan Earthquake and support from gender equality perspectives] (pp. 131–140). Seikatsu Shisōsha.

Balthasar, B. M. (2023, February 12). Words matter: Stop using the phrase "natural disasters." *Asian Development Blog*. https://blogs.adb.org/blog/words-matter-stop-using-phrase-natural-disasters.

Bănică, A., Kourtit, K., & Nijkamp, P. (2020). Natural disasters as a development opportunity: A spatial economic resilience interpretation. *Review of Regional Research*, 40, 223–249. https://doi.org/10.1007/s10037-020-00141-8.

Bosai Plus. (2016, September 19). *"Tokui na tsūjōsaigai" taifū: "Kansoku o hajimete irai hatsu" wa kanarazu nurikaerareru* [A "unique ordinary" typhoon: The "first in recorded history" will definitely be rewritten]. http://www.bosaijoho.jp/institution/item_7466.html.

Brown, S., Budimir, M., Upadhyay Crawford, S., Clements, R., & Sneddon, A. (2019). *Gender and age inequality of disaster risk: Research paper*. UNICEF and UN Women. https://www.unwomen.org/en/digital-library/publications/2021/11/research-paper-gender-and-age-inequality-of-disaster-risk.

Crenshaw, K. (1995). *Critical race theory: The key writings that formed the movement*. New Press.

Cretney, R. (2014). Resilience for whom? Emerging critical geographies of socio-ecological resilience. *Geography Compass*, 8(9), 627–640. https://doi.org/10.1111/gec3.12154.

Doan, P. L. (2010). The tyranny of gendered spaces: Reflections from beyond the gender dichotomy. *Gender, Place and Culture: A Journal of Feminist Geography, 17*(5), 635–654.

Dominey-Howes, D., Gorman-Murray, A., & McKinnon, S. (2014). Queering disasters: On the need to account for LGBTI experiences in natural disaster contexts. *Gender, Place and Culture, 21*(7), 905–918. https://doi.org/10.1080/0966369X.2013.802673.

Fire and Disaster Management Agency. (2016). *Kumamoto jishin no higai to taiō* [The Kumamoto earthquakes: Damage and responses]. In *Shōbō hakusho* [White paper on firefighting services], pp. 1–9.

Fushimi, N. (2004). *Gei to iu "keiken" zōhoban* [The "experience" of what we call gay (enlarged ed.). Pot Shuppan.

Gaillard, J. C., Gorman-Murray, A., & Fordham, M. (2017). Sexual and gender minorities and disasters. *Gender, Place & Culture, 24*(1), 18–26. https://doi.org/10.1080/0966369X.2016.1263438.

Gender Equality Bureau. (2013). *Danjo kyōdo sankaku no shiten kara no bōsai/fukkō no torikumi shishin kaisetsu jireishū* [Commentary and case book on DRRM guidelines and rebuilding measures from the perspective of gender equality]. https://www.gender.go.jp/kaigi/senmon/kansi_senmon/wg01/pdf/giji_03_3.pdf.

Gender Equality Bureau. (2020). *Saigai taiōryoku o kyōkasuru josei no shiten* [Women's perspectives that strengthen disaster responses]. https://www.gender.go.jp/policy/saigai/fukkou/guideline.html.

Global Facility for Disaster Reduction and Recovery. (2018). *Gender equality and women's empowerment in disaster recovery*. https://www.gfdrr.org/sites/default/files/publication/gender-equality-disaster-recovery.PDF.

Higashinihon daishinsai kara 10-nen: Shisha yukuefumeisha "kanrenshi" fukume 22,000-nin ni [Ten years since the Great East Japan Earthquake: The deceased, missing, and "related deaths" amount to 22,000 people]. (2021, March 10). NHK. https://www3.nhk.or.jp/news/html/20210310/k10012907171000.html.

Hill Collins, P. (2019). *Intersectionality as critical social theory*. Duke University Press.

Hokkaido Government. (2022, March 2). *Heisei 30 Hokkaido Iburi Tōbu jishin ni yoru higai jōkyō nado ni kansuru oshirase* [Damage and other issues in the 2018 Hokkaido Iburi Tōbu earthquake]. http://www.pref.hokkaido.lg.jp/sm/ktk/300906jisin/top.htm.

Human Rights Watch. (2019, May 27). *New health guidelines propel transgender rights: World Health Organization removes "gender identity disorder" diagnosis*. https://www.hrw.org/news/2019/05/27/new-health-guidelines-propel-transgender-rights.

International Federation of Red Cross and Red Crescent Societies. (2018). *The responsibility to prevent and respond to sexual and gender-based violence in disasters and crises*. https://www.preventionweb.net/publication/responsibility-prevent-and-respond-sexual-and-gender-based-violence-disasters-and.

Japan Meteorological Agency. (n.d.). *Heisei 30-nen Hokkaidō Iburi Tōbu jishin no kanren jōhō* [Information regarding the 2018 Hokkaido Iburi Tōbu earthquake]. Retrieved June 1, 2023, from https://www.jma.go.jp/jma/menu/20180906_iburi_jishin_menu.html.

Kawata, A. (2011, April 23). *Higashinihon daishinsai to Kantō daishinsai, Hanshin Awaji daishinsai to no chigai* [Differences among the Great East Japan Earthquake, Great Kanto Disaster, and the Great Hanshin-Awaji Earthquake]. https://www.cas.go.jp/jp/fukkou/pdf/kousou2/siryou5.pdf.

Lee, Y. (2006). *Saigai ni okeru yōengosha gainen no saikō: "Saigai jakusha" kara "saigaiji yōshiensha" e no apurōchi* [Reconsidering the concept of people who need assistance in disasters: Changing our approach from "vulnerable people in disasters" to "people with special needs in disasters"]. *Journal of Japanese Association for an Inclusive Society, 8*(1), 38–48.

LGBT hairyo no saigai taiō mada mada [LGBT-responsive disaster responses not enough yet]. (2021, February 22). *Tōkyō shinbun*. https://www.tokyo-np.co.jp/article/87372.

Ministry of Heath, Labor and Welfare. (2009). *Setai* [Household]. https://www.mhlw.go.jp/toukei/list/dl/20-21-yougo_h25.pdf.

Ministry of Justice. (2023a). *Act on special cases in handling gender status for persons with gender identity disorder (Act no. 111 of 2003)*. Japanese Law Translation Database System. https://www.japaneselawtranslation.go.jp/en/laws/view/2542/en.

Ministry of Justice. (2023b). *Basic act on disaster management (Act no. 223 of 1961)*. Japanese Law Translation Database System. https://www.japaneselawtranslation.go.jp/en/laws/view/3982.

Moreno, J. (2020, November 4). From victims to agents of change: How women recovered from the 2010 Chile tsunami. *DRR Voices Blog*. https://www.preventionweb.net/experts/oped/view/74535.

Moreno, J., & Shaw, D. (2018). Women's empowerment following disaster: A longitudinal study of social change. *Natural Hazards, 92*, 205–224. https://doi.org/10.1007/s11069-018-3204-4.

Office of the United Nations High Commissioner for Human Rights and UN-Habitat. (2014). *Fact sheet no.21: The right to adequate housing*. https://www.ohchr.org/en/publications/fact-sheets/fact-sheet-no-21-rev-1-human-right-adequate-housing.

Ōsawa, M. (2019). *Bōsai, gensai to danjo kyōdō sankaku* [DRRM and gender equality]. The University of Tokyo ISS Research Series, vol. 66. University of Tokyo Press.

Saigai hinan de LGBT hairyo 70%: Todōfuken seireishi chōsa [70% accommodating LGBT needs: Research on prefectural and designated cities]. (2021, April 24). *Saga shinbun*. https://www.saga-s.co.jp/articles/-/666638.

Saigaiji seiteki shōsūsha no "hairyo" ichiwari mitazu Tōhoku no jichitai [Less than 10% of Tohoku municipalities "consider" sexual minorities during disasters]. (2020, December 8). *Kahoku shinpō*. https://kahoku.news/articles/20201208kho000000091000c.html.

Sphere Project. (2018). *Sphere handbook: Humanitarian charter and minimum standards in humanitarian response*. https://handbook.spherestandards.org/en/sphere.

Sugiura, I., & Maekawa, N. (2021). *Tohoku chihō no sekushuaru mainoritī dantai katsudō chōsa hōkokusho* [Research report on the activities of sexual minority groups in the Tohoku region]. Seikyūsha.

Uchida, Y. (2012). *Sekushuaru mainoritī no hinan seikatsu: "Kojin" toshite sonchō sareru shakai e* [The refuge life of sexual minorities: Toward a society where one is respected as an "individual"]. In Miyagi no Joseishien o Kirokusurukai (Eds.), *Joseitachi ga ugoku: Higashinihon daishinsai to danjokyōdō sankaku shiten no shien* [Women on the move: The Great East Japan Earthquake and support from gender equality perspectives] (pp. 100–113). Seikatsu Shisōsha.

Uchida, Y. (2015). *Higashinihon daishinsai ni okeru sekushuaru mainoritī tōjisha no hisai jōkyō oyobi nīzu/Kadai ni kansuru chōsa hōkokusho* [Research report on the situation, needs, and challenges of sexual minority people in the Great East Japan Earthquake]. Seikatsu Shisōsha.

WHO, OHCHR, UN Women, UNAIDS, UNDP, UNFPA, & UNICEF. (2014). *An interagency statement: Eliminating forced, coercive and otherwise involuntary sterilization.* https://apps.who.int/iris/handle/10665/112848.

Wisner, B. (2003). *At risk: Natural hazards, people's vulnerability and disasters.* Routledge.

Yamashita, A. (2012). *Saigai to sekushuaru mainoritī* [Disaster and sexual minorities]. In M. Takenobu & C. Akaishi (Eds.), *Saigai shien ni josei no shiten o!* [Women's perspectives for disaster support!] (pp. 41–42). Iwanami Shoten.

Yamashita, A., Gomez, C., & Dombroski, K. (2017). Segregation, exclusion and LGBT people in disaster impacted areas: Experiences from the Higashinihon dai-shinsai (Great East-Japan Disaster). *Gender, Place and Culture, 24*(1), 64–71. https://doi.org/10.1080/0966369X.2016.1276887.

Appendix A: Participant consent form (English translation)

"Research on vulnerability and resilience of sexual minority disaster survivors and potential of DRRM policies" funded by Grant-in-Aid for Early-Career Scientists of the Japan Society for the Promotion of Sciences

Things I would like your understanding on before you take part in this research:
This form contains information regarding this research such as research objectives and potential risks and benefits by taking part in this research.
- Generally, the main objective of conducting research is to contribute to the overall body of knowledge by gaining knowledge about a certain phenomenon
- Generally, research outcomes will be published in conference presentations and academic journals. In this research, the research outcomes will be published in a way that interviewees will not be identified.
- Participation in this study is not compulsory. You may change your decision even after you have agreed to participate in this study.
- Please read this form and feel free to contact the researcher if you have any questions or concerns.
- There will be no disadvantages for you if you decide not to take part in this research.

1 Research objective

In Japan, since the Great East Japan Earthquake, large-scale disasters have continued to occur throughout the country, including the Kumamoto Earthquakes and the torrential rains in Hokkaido and Tohoku. Research on the experiences of sexual minority disaster survivors is limited. In addition, it has not yet been verified whether the perspectives of sexual minorities are reflected in the support provision for disaster survivors and disaster reduction and management policies – the importance of which has been pointed out since the Great East Japan Earthquake – in other disasters.

Therefore, this research aims to contribute to the field of disaster reduction and management policy and humanitarian policy in Japan and abroad by identifying struggles faced by sexual minority survivors of disasters in Japan after the Great East Japan Earthquake, and by identifying how much the international standards (the Sphere Principle) on the right to a life with dignity and non-discrimination are reflected in disaster reduction and management policy, as well as factors that make it difficult to reflect the principle.

2 Researcher

Yamashita Azusa, Assistant Professor, Hirosaki University

3 Details of participation in this research

You will be interviewed about your experiences as a gender and sexual minority during disasters. During the interview, please answer only the questions that you feel you can answer. One or two people each who have experienced the torrential rains in Hokkaido and Tohoku, the Kumamoto earthquakes, and the Hokkaido Iburi Tobu Earthquake are asked to participate. The interviews will last about an hour.

4 Potential risks of participating in this research

There are potential risks associated with this study, such as the possibility of personal information leakage and the possibility that some of the questions in this study may cause you psychological discomfort or upset. In such a case, please inform the researcher immediately. You will be referred to the appropriate contact person for assistance.

In addition, the possibility of personal information leakage will be minimized through the following procedures. The recording of the interview survey will be converted to text and destroyed within one month. To ensure anonymity, pseudonyms will be used for all research data. The consent form and the honorarium payment form may serve as identifiable documents of the research participants, but these forms will not be linked to the textual research data in any way. All data related to the research will be stored in a lockable room after the research is completed. Ten years after the completion of the research, all data related to the research will be disposed of.

5 Benefits of participating in this research

It is unlikely that participation in this study will bring you direct benefits. This study, however, will contribute to increasing knowledge about the disaster experiences of sexual minorities in Japan and abroad, as well as to general knowledge about diversity-informed disaster management policies.

6 Contact

If you have any questions or concerns about this research, please contact me below.
Yamashita Azusa
Phone: [redacted text]   Email: [redacted text]

7 Handling of research data

If you agree to participate in this study, you will be interviewed privately. The interview will be audio-recorded. After the recording, the data will be converted to text by the researcher within one month. Pseudonyms will be used for the textual data. After that, the recording will be erased and any notes taken at the interview will be destroyed. Therefore, the participants' identities will not be confirmed by any reference to them in the interviews. This form and the receipt of the honorarium may serve as verifiable documentation of the participant's identity; therefore, any information revealed by the participant in the interviews will not reveal your identity. After the completion of this study, all data will be stored in a lockable room and will be disposed of appropriately after 10 years.

8 Changing your mind about participating in this research

Participation in this study is completely voluntary. You will not be disadvantaged in any way by refusing to participate in the study. You may refuse to answer certain questions. If you do so, you may be asked the reason for your refusal. You may also choose to discontinue your participation in the research. In this case, the recorded information will be destroyed. If you experience mental discomfort or similar problems during the interview, the researcher may decide to terminate your participation in the study. In this case, you may be referred to an appropriate contact person to help you deal with the mental discomfort or upset.

9 Cost of participating in this research

There is no cost to participate in the interview survey. You will receive an honorarium (a book coupon) for your participation in the research.

10 Consent to participate in this research

By signing the form below, you give your consent to participate in this study. Your signature below indicates that you have decided to participate in the study, that you understand the implications of your participation in the study, and that you have carefully read and understood the information above.

Name (signature) of the interviewee:
Name (signature) of the interviewer:
Date:

Appendix B: Interview questions (English translation)

- What disaster(s) were you affected by?
- When the disaster(s) occurred, where were you and what were you doing? Please share the damages caused to you.
- Did you experience any struggles and/or anxiety when you were affected by the disaster(s)? If yes, can you describe the struggles and/or anxiety?
- Please tell me about your sexuality and coming out status.
- Were you connected to any support group when the disaster(s) occurred? If yes, please share since when and in what way were you connected to the support group?
- How important is the connection with the group to you?
- Did you receive any support from a sexual minority support group when the disaster(S) occurred? If yes, please tell me what kind of support it was and whether it was helpful.
- Did you receive any support from a group other than a sexual minority group? If yes, please tell me what kind of support it was and whether it was helpful.
- Were there any other kinds of support and/or environments you wished to receive/have but couldn't?
- What kind of support and/or environment did you want or would you want (for future disasters)?
- Have you shared your experiences of surviving a disaster with someone or have you taken any actions as a result of being affected by the disaster?
- Can you tell me your age, education, occupation, who you're living with, and nationality?

Genya Fukunaga

Queer politics and solidarity: Post–Cold War homonationalism in East Asia

In the twenty-first century, sexual orientation and gender identity (SOGI) was internationally recognized as a component of human rights.[1] Human rights protections for sexual minorities became a key political issue across East Asia, and
new LGBT-friendly political elites have accelerated the process of securing these
rights from the perspective of lawmaking and legislative reform. In other words,
in East Asia the era of discrimination against sexual minorities has passed, and
in its place "LGBT-friendly societies" are beginning to emerge.

LGBT movements in East Asia are using massive, high-visibility events such as
pride parades as platforms for establishing solidarity. At these events, however, it
is not unusual to discern a nationalistic tone in the language celebrating advances
in LGBT rights and activism, as in the case of slogans such as "Taiwan: Marriage
Equality First in Asia."[2] Rather than resisting the authority of states and their respective administrations, LGBT activists have arguably begun to do the opposite,
helping to perpetuate government authority in an ongoing attempt to transform
it into a tool to advance LGBT rights and further activist agency.

The present paper will investigate the forging of intimate solidarity between
LGBT movements in Japan and Taiwan and the extent to which this was facilitated
by the historical and political context in East Asia. It begins by exploring the mainstreaming of the LGBT-friendly discourse in Taiwanese society since the 2000s, as
well as the homonationalism underlying the movement. It then examines the links
between Japanese LGBT activists' interest in Taiwan and Japan's imperialist desires
under the post–Cold War world order. It highlights how the collusion between homonationalism and imperialism allows these two societies to be classified as
"LGBT friendly" and "advanced" in contrast to the "backwardness" of China. In
conclusion, the paper summarizes the dynamics of queer politics and competing
nationalisms in the East Asian geopolitical context, emphasizing the need to de-
colonize and de-imperialize the LGBT movements and discourses.

A sociological methodology is used to analyze primary sources (e.g., pamphlets
and other print media, official websites and related staff blogs, and photographs)

---

1 Earlier versions of this paper have been presented at conferences and universities in Japan, Taiwan, Hong Kong, China, and South Korea from 2020 to 2022.
2 This slogan was emblazoned on the banners of the Taiwan Alliance to Promote Civil Partnership
Rights (TAPCPR) at the Tokyo Rainbow Pride parade in 2018.

gathered from pride parades, film festivals, and other manifestations of queer activism in Japan and Taiwan between 2011 and 2021. The two case studies of this research – Tokyo Rainbow Pride and Taiwan LGBT Pride – have been observed since 2013.

Images and representations of sexual minorities in newspapers, online news, magazines, films, advertisements, and social media are also examined, including media representations of Taiwan in Japan and vice versa. Articles published between 1990 and 2017 from four major Japanese newspapers – *Asahi shinbun, Mainichi shinbun, Yomiuri shinbun,* and *Sankei shinbun* – and two Taiwanese newspapers – *United Daily News* and *China Times* – are the primary objects of this analysis, as well as all articles with titles that contain the terms "Taiwan" or "Republic of China" in four Japanese conservative-leaning magazines: *Bungeishunjū, Seiron, Mansurī WiLL,* and *Boisu (Voice).* Japanese articles from the late 1990s onward are particularly significant because they reflect the increasing interest in Taiwan on the part of Japanese conservatives.

1 The emergence of Taiwanese homonationalism

1.1 The birth of an LGBT-friendly Taiwan

After the 1990s, the social conditions of sexual minorities in nations across East Asia changed dramatically, but nowhere more so than in Taiwan, which has become known as "the most LGBT-friendly in Asia" (Hao, 2010).[3] In recent years, the English-language media has also highlighted the notion of Taiwan as a "beacon" for Asia (Jacobs, 2014). From the 2010s, Taiwanese activists have adopted this domestically and internationally crafted image of an LGBT-friendly Taiwan to advance their cause. For example, the Taipei City Government proudly congratulated the city's pride parade, which has grown into one of the largest in Asia, and Taiwanese marriage equality activists carried a large banner declaring "First in Asia," in English, through the streets during the 2018 Tokyo Rainbow Pride.

This discourse of an LGBT-friendly Taiwan originates, in fact, from the nation's political elite. Notably, Ma Ying-jeou of the Kuomintang projected a gay-friendly image as early as the 1998 Taipei mayoral elections (*United Daily News*, 1998) and repeatedly used the term *tóngzhì yǒushàn* (LGBT friendly) in his presidential campaigns during the 2000s. Following Ma's presidency (2008–2016), his successor, Tsai Ing-wen, also expressed support for same-sex marriage in her election cam-

---

3 Unless otherwise stated, all translations from Chinese and Japanese in this paper are my own.

paigns (Fukunaga, 2016). An example on a local level is the continued official funding of the Taipei LGBT Festival from 2000, which led the city's mayor, Hau Lung-pin (2010), to declare that "Taipei has become known throughout Asia as an LGBT-friendly Rainbow City" (pp. 4–5). Thus, in the 2000s, politicians from the mayor to the president diligently projected an image of LGBT friendliness while failing to address the rapidly expanding backlash against gay rights by Christian conservatives.

The LGBT-friendly discourse is therefore inextricably connected to the strategic performances of the political elite to muster electoral support, which cannot solely be aimed at securing the LGBT vote, given the low estimated number of sexual minorities in Taiwan. Rather, expressing an LGBT-friendly position is an attempt to impress a certain image upon the *majority*. According to Chu Wei-cheng (2005), after martial law was abolished in Taiwan,

> support for minority activism, including that of the LGBT movement, came to be regarded as liberal and progressive. As the tides shifted toward a more progressive society, politicians introduced "image politics" and began to respond positively to the demands of the LGBT movement. (pp. 7–8)

Support for minority human rights came to be considered an indicator of the nation's democratization as it worked to transition out of authoritarianism and integrate democratic principles into society. In short, the protection of LGBT human rights garnered political attention when the Democratic Progressive Party (DPP) was attempting to overthrow the Kuomintang's single-party rule and advance a policy of democratization.

1.2 Taiwanese homonationalism

In the early 2000s, President Chen Shui-bian spearheaded a series of policies under the moniker of a "Nation of Human Rights," which included protections for SOGI – a prominent part of the political discourse at the time. Having espoused ideas of "democracy," "freedom," and "human rights" after defeating martial law, his party, the DPP, saw LGBT rights as having a high affinity with its progressive policy direction. Taiwan's marginalized position in international society was also significant. According to Satō Kazumi (2007), an expert on the DPP's human rights diplomacy, these Nation of Human Rights policies

> were in pursuit of a new balance of power, attained through two major shifts: namely, a shift in power relations with China and the use of the US as an axis by which to change the relationship between Taiwan and the mainland. (p. 133)

After China's emergence as an economic superpower in the post–Cold War era, Taiwanese dependence on China rose dramatically – a dependence that only deepened with China's increasingly central position in US foreign policy. China had blocked Taiwan from receiving international recognition since the 1970s, and the DPP's Nation of Human Rights was a soft power strategy – based on the mutual interplay of Taiwan–US and Taiwan–China relations – to expand the nation's international presence (Satō, 2007). SOGI, which had accrued significant international attention, served as a tool for Taiwan to catch up to the US as a country with advanced human rights while differentiating itself from the notoriously oppressive Chinese government.

Alongside Israel and South Africa, Taiwan has been considered one of the protectorates of the US empire under the Cold War world order (Kǎ, 2018), coming to play a significant role in US policy. After the island's incorporation into the Cold War system during the Korean War, the US "did not just decide Taiwan's identity – it also became its most important cultural symbol" (Chen, 2006, p. 71). Taiwanese queer politics was similarly drawn clearly into the sphere of US influence (Fukunaga, 2022).

Amid the dramatic influx of media interest in LGBT issues in the 2000s, Taiwan's portrayal of itself as LGBT friendly was accompanied by a rise in the number of articles decrying China as "homophobic" and "backward" (e. g., *United Daily News*, 2005).[4] An analysis of the *United Daily News* and *China Times* revealed that only a few articles (6 and 12, respectively) on sexual minority rights in China appeared in the 1990s. But from the 2000s, the number leaps to over 137 articles, the majority of which are dedicated to the contrast between the LGBT-friendly Taiwan and the regressive China (Fukunaga, 2017).

Particularly useful for this analysis is the conceptual framework of homonationalism, which Jasbir Puar (2007) used to critique the mainstream gay rights movement's assimilation into nationalism after 9/11. She argued that the War on Terror was justified through two mutually reinforcing concepts – (1) the connection of Islam to "terrorist bodies" and (2) the reinforcement of US moral superiority through the mobilization of homosexual subjects in the service of nationalism – which created a condition she termed "homonationalism" (Puar, 2007, p. 13). According to Puar (2017), homonationalism uses "acceptance" and "tolerance" for gay and lesbian subjects as the barometer by which the legitimacy of, and capacity for, national sovereignty are evaluated (p. 51). In the US, the rise of homonationalism subsumed queer bodies into an assertion of the nation's modernity and "sex-

---

4 Note that by the "government of China" here, I refer to the administration of the Chinese Communist Party (CCP) rather than the special administrative regions (SARs) of Hong Kong and Macau.

ual exceptionalism," while relegating Muslims into terrorist bodies (Puar, 2007, p. 2). In Taiwan, the debut of homonationalism was connected to the Nation of Human Rights strategy, which used the US as a model to posit Taiwan as unique in "Asia" – "The most LGBT-friendly in Asia" (*China Times*, 2014, October 31) – a narrative inseparable from the portrayal of China as the irreconcilable "other."

As has been argued, the now internationally popular discourse of Taiwan as the most LGBT friendly in Asia was originally passed down from the nation's political elite throughout the 1990s and 2000s. The following section examines how this homonationalist discourse has been received by the Japanese media and activists.

2 Imperial desires

2.1 The competition for Asian hegemony

Taiwan's homonationalist discourse was popularized in Japan in the 2010s. A recent *Mainichi shinbun* article, for example, linked the creation of an LGBT-friendly Taiwan to the concept of democratization ("'Dōshi' ni yasashii Taiwan," 2017). In fact, Japanese LGBT activists have had a longstanding interest in Taiwan that predates this trend. Internalizing the narrative of an exceptionally LGBT-friendly Taiwan, these activists have sought to surpass or catch up to Taiwan, pursuing ideological supremacy in Asia through their activism.

Perhaps the most striking example of this is Tokyo Rainbow Pride (TRP), which revealed its roadmap in 2014 in the lead-up to the 2020 Summer Olympics and Paralympics. Although the roadmap has since been deleted from the TRP website, its goals could be divided into roughly two levels:
1. to become the largest LGBT event in Asia by 2017; and
2. to "expand the movement" from "Japan to the world" by 2020. (TRP, 2014)

Taiwan's LGBT Pride was not mentioned in the roadmap, but it is clear from writer and radio host Ogiue Chiki's (2012) interview with TRP staff that these goals – particularly the first –was based on Taiwan's LGBT Pride.

This roadmap reveals three major points about TRP's strategy. First, by using the rhetoric of the largest LGBT event in Asia – placing Taiwan (and its LGBT Pride) on a pedestal as both exemplar and competitor –TRP engaged in a struggle for ideological hegemony in Asia, which would fuel the growth of Taiwanese homonationalism.

Second, the US plays a significant role as its point of reference. The Stonewall Riots and the first pride parade in New York were used as historical benchmarks in the TRP roadmap (Tokyo Rainbow Pride, 2014). Using cyberethnography, Itakura (2015) pointed out that TRP considers the US to be "the origin of sexual liberation" (p. 17) and pride parades in Japan or other parts of the world to be contributions to US moral supremacy (p. 16). Indeed, its rhetoric distinguished the US from the rest of "the world," confirming the myth of US sexual exceptionalism.

The third significant point is TRP's efforts to assimilate into the national status quo. This is visible in its emulation of Taiwan's LGBT Pride under the auspices of influencing Asia by 2017, and even more so in its second goal of expanding to the world by 2020. TRP's activism is not based on resistance to the government, but rather draws agency from the advancement of Japan as a "queer-friendly nation" (Itakura, 2015, p. 18) that commands praise and recognition from Asia and the world.

In 2014, the same year of TRP's roadmap, signs of solidarity between TRP and Taiwan's LGBT Pride became increasingly visible in the donation of parade floats, organizer exchanges, and so on. Now, organizers from both countries have begun to vie openly for ideological supremacy in Asia. In 2017, when the constitutional court in Taiwan ruled that the laws forbidding same-sex marriage were unconstitutional, TRP members at Taiwan's LGBT Pride carried a flag that declared "Celebrating Taiwanese Marriage Equality. Press Forward Japan!" At TRP the following year, as mentioned earlier, Taiwanese activists flourished banners proclaiming, "First in Asia." In this way, Japanese homonationalist desires and Taiwanese homonationalist discourses are interdependent and mutually reinforcing.

2.2 A pro-Japanese Taiwan in the post–Cold War era

As demonstrated, lurking behind Japanese activists' obsession with the LGBT-friendly Taiwan is an ideological competition for supremacy in Asia. This is predicated by the dominant Japanese view of Taiwan as pro-Japanese, which is a perspective broadly shared in activist circles as well. For example, Gotō Jun'ichi (2012), director of Out Japan, an LGBT marketing firm, described Japanese gay men's fascination with Taiwan as follows:

> Every year, about 1,000 gay Japanese individuals travel to Taiwan en masse to participate in Taiwan's LGBT Pride.... You might wonder why in the world so many Japanese people would head to Taiwan.... The biggest reason is a feeling of gratitude toward our allies and friends in the Taiwanese gay community for their outpouring of support after last year's earthquake. *In other words, the greatest reason is that Taiwanese people are Japan-friendly* [emphasis added]

.... To us [Japanese gay individuals], Taiwan is like a paradise. It's a place where you can open-ly express yourself and set your heart and body free.

The significant financial support provided by the Taiwanese in the immediate af-termath of the Great East Japan Earthquake of March 2011 has been seen as proof of their "pro-Japan" standing – a topic of continued discussion in both countries.[5]

However, the discourse of a pro-Japanese Taiwan only became popular in Japan in the late 1990s. In the Japanese newspapers and periodicals analyzed for this paper, support for Taiwan's sovereignty claims appears to have been non-existent from the 1950s until the 1980s, as were depictions of it as either pro- or anti-Japanese. In fact, I was unable to find rhetoric classifying any government or region as either pro- or anti-Japan until the 1990s – the few exceptions I was able to confirm pertained to sporadic trade or diplomatic tensions with the US or southeast Asia (see, e.g., "Bankoku kara," 1979; "Tokekomanu Nihonjin," 1973). In the late 1990s, when the right-wing media's portrayal of China and South Korea as anti-Japanese became mainstream, a complementary discourse posi-tioned Taiwan as a pro-Japanese state.

Amid the scholarly literature on the dramatic growth of conservative dis-course in Japan in recent years (e.g., Hayakawa & Nogawa, 2015; Jomaru, 2011; Kur-ahashi, 2018) is the simultaneous emergence and growth of rhetoric portraying China (or South Korea) as anti-Japanese and Taiwan as pro-Japanese. The latter rhetoric was quickly adopted and popularized (in both Japan and Taiwan) as part of a growing movement to reevaluate the Japanese colonial rule of Taiwan.

Despite the collapse of the Soviet Union in 1991, the Cold War system in East Asia – as seen in the divided Korean Peninsula and the Third Taiwan Straits Crisis (1995–1996), for example – became even more entrenched, with the US presence in the region strengthening to such an extent that political conditions have been called part of a "pseudo–Cold War system" (Oguma, 2014). When South Korea and Taiwan emerged as democracies with feminism and other social movements, strife over historical consciousness – best exemplified by the "comfort women" issue – took center stage.

For Japan, which had benefited from its special relationship with the US in the postwar decades, the democratization and rapid economic growth of its former colonies made it impossible to continue evading responsibility for the colonization of its neighbors and wartime atrocities. Japan pursued a large-scale historical re-visionist project, redefining the Greater East Asian War as a "defensive war," de-

---

5 For a critique of the politics surrounding Japan–Taiwan mutual support following large-scale disasters, see Zhào (2018).

nying both its aggression in the lead-up to the war and crimes committed therein. Moreover, a deep-seated anticommunist ideology facilitated the conservative stigmatization of China as anti-Japanese (see, e.g., Kō, 2012a, 2012b; "Nittai dankō 20-nen," 1992). This also arguably stemmed from fear after the bubble burst, which devastated national pride as an economic superpower, just as China was emerging as "the world's factory" in the late 1990s. Consequently, as Japan faced pressure from China and South Korea to assume responsibility for its war crimes and colonization, its right-wing media responded by asserting that Taiwan is a pro-Japanese nation (e.g., "Atarashii Nittai kankei," 2000; "Rī moto Taiwan sōtō," 2008; "Taiwan oishisa," 2000).

In Taiwan, the democratization of the 1990s and 2000s was accompanied by a new definition of nationalism and a dramatic increase in public support for the Taiwanese independence movement. The historical context deserves a brief explanation. After Japan's defeat in WWII, the Kuomintang seized power in Taiwan, positing themselves as the legitimate rulers of "China" and watching carefully for opportunities to launch a continental counteroffensive. The Kuomintang single-mindedly pursued Sinicization through educational and cultural initiatives, but the nation's democratization and China's rise to global prominence spelled the end for its One China policies by the 1990s. The transition from the Kuomintang to the DPP in 2000 was, importantly, accompanied by a shift in national identity from the "Republic of China" to "Taiwan" (Wakabayashi, 2008). A reactionary movement then emerged, aiming to reevaluate the heretofore-critiqued history of Japanese colonization.

The main leader of this movement was Lee Teng-hui, president of the Republic of China. Born and raised under Japanese colonialism, Lee began to actively campaign in both Taiwan and Japan from the late 1990s under the position that Japanese colonization had contributed significantly to Taiwan's modernization (Ching, 2019). Both Lee and his reevaluation of the so-called "Japanese Era" were ecstatically welcomed by Japan's right-wing media (e.g., Kobayashi, 2000, p. 31). There was a rapid increase in Japan's conservative discourse justifying Japanese imperialism and colonialism, an integral part of which was an emphasis on Taiwan's status as a pro-Japanese state. This, in turn, became one of the wellsprings of the modern Japanese perception of Taiwan as pro-Japanese.

3 East Asian modernity

This paper has so far investigated how the discourse of a pro-Japanese Taiwan was created by the right-wing media in the context of a renewed imperial consciousness in Japan. But how is this discourse connected to queer politics?

First, it is necessary to investigate the origins of the discourse which claims that Taiwan and Japan are an *unmei kyōdōtai* (sharing a common destiny) characterized by "modernity." For example, an article in a major Japanese newspaper, *Sankei shinbun*, in the early 1990s based its argument on an "anti-Japanese united front" born from the "anti-Japanese nationalism" of China and South Korea, concluding that, "strategically, it would be far better to strengthen ties with Taiwan – with whom we share a closer sense of values – than China" ("Nittai danko 20-nen," 1992). Here, it should be noted that in the 2000s the ambiguously defined "sense of values" came to stand for *minshu* (democracy), *jiyū* (freedom), and *jinken* (human rights) – all terms that indicate modernity. For example, according to Kō Bun'yū (2007), also known as Peter Wenshiung Huang, a Taiwanese independence advocate who has long been active in Japanese society, Japan and Taiwan have "shared fates, shared communities" based on "their mutual pursuit of the universal human values of democracy, freedom, and human rights" (p. 85). As a counterpoint, Kō (2012a, 2012b) defined China, the propagator of anti-Japanese sentiment, as an irreconcilable, unforgivable other.[6] Following in his footsteps, the Japanese right-wing media discussed Taiwan as a supportive comrade with a shared community and shared fate, while simultaneously decrying Chinese crimes against freedom and human rights (see, e.g., "Nittai danko 20-nen," 1992).

Thus, the conservative discourse has come to follow a clear pattern in presenting China as oppressive to minorities and encroaching upon freedom and human rights, in direct contrast to a democratic and free Taiwan, which protects human rights and is thereby equipped with a modern sense of values. Significantly, Japan's LGBT movement has also adopted this perspective, and China has come to be portrayed as "uncivilized" or "delayed." A man who works as a go-go boy at the East Asia Gay Club Party was the target of an article in TRP's (2017) official magazine, which stated, "Chinese people have a somewhat serious, animalistic, and scary image," while "in comparison, I thought Taiwanese people were nice" (Kenta, 2017, p.7). In this way, the Japanese homonationalist gaze not only racializes Taiwanese and Chinese people, but also establishes a racial hierarchy between them.

In another example, Gotō Jun'ichi (2010) cited a Japanese review, published on a popular gay men's website of which he is the editor-in-chief, of the Chinese gay romance film *Chūnfēng chénzuì de yèwǎn* (*Spring Fever*, 2009) which had just been screened in Japan:

---

6 Alongside Taiwanese independence activists based in Japan, such as Kō Bun'yū and Kin Birei, other figures have also garnered support for a positive view of Japanese colonialism in the Japanese right-wing media from the 1990s. For a scholarly exploration, see Mori (2001).

> Modern Japanese gay men may find that *Spring Fever* paints a somewhat surprising picture of the difficulties of same-sex male romance. Many might wonder if this is truly the current reality in China....
>
> It's totally different from what you might see in a gay [*gei*] film from the West, where there exists a strong gay community within which same-sex marriage and even children are included in an optimistic outlook on gay life.
>
> Amid the severity of living in a society that does not accept homosexuals [*dōseiaisha*], the protagonists nevertheless throw themselves body and soul into an excruciating romance, isolated and alone. This renders the open love between the two men practically a revolutionary act. In this sense, it is a work that seems to keenly convey the heavy weight of freedom.

The original film uses the Mandarin Chinese term *tóngzhì* (comrade) to render male–male romantic relationships, which is similar to the Japanese term *gei* (gay) in that it has come to be associated with a positive identity. In referring to the protagonists as *dōseiaisha* (homosexuals), the above review missed these nuances in the film and presented male–male love in China as the polar opposite of the West with its "strong gay community" and "gay life" (even though the Japanese subtitles for the film used the term *gei* to translate *tóngzhì*). This review implied that, in China, gay people are to be pitied as "homosexuals," a rhetoric that aligns perfectly with the discourse of Taiwanese homonationalism.[7]

As demonstrated, the connection between Taiwan and Japan is strengthened through a twofold system, with the ideals of democracy, human rights, freedom, and other so-called modern values on one level, and the denouncement of the purportedly anti-Japanese China as backward – or even hostile to these values – on the other. Discourse painting Taiwan as pro-Japanese originated from the Japanese right-wing media's revisionist interpretations of imperialism and colonialism, ultimately shaping the mainstream image of Taiwan in Japan. The Japanese LGBT movement is no exception, contrasting the image of a modern pro-Japanese Taiwan with the putative China – a discourse that has a strong affinity with Taiwanese homonationalism.

4 Gender/sexuality politics in post–Cold War Asia

This section will investigate gender/sexuality politics in East Asia from the post–Cold War perspective. After World War II, East Asia was incorporated into the Cold War regime, and the East Asian order was reorganized by the US, which seized hegemony in the region (Chen, 2006). The demise of the Empire of Japan

---

7 See, for example, "Zhǐyǒu gémìng tóngzhì" (1996), a Taiwanese newspaper article that argued that only revolutionary *tóngzhì* (comrades) exist in China, not gay *tóngzhì*.

did not bring decolonization to East Asia. In the Cold War era, the US "displaced, replaced, and subsumed the Japanese empire," and transitional justice was not realized in the process (Ching, 2019, p. 7). In building an anticommunist bloc, the US restored Japan as the economic linchpin of the Pacific Rim alliance, which brought about a division of labor – Okinawa, Taiwan, South Korea, and the Philippines were to bear the brunt of US military functions and installations, which enabled economic growth in mainland Japan (Ching, 2019).

US intervention in the Asia Pacific went beyond simply containing communism to seizing hegemony in the region at the level of knowledge production (Yoneyama, 2016). This enabled the US to assume the highest level of responsibility for directing and supervising the countries of the region with regard to "progress, democracy, and modernity," which was supported by the perception of it as an exceptional nation that offered democracy and freedom. The military regimes in Taiwan and South Korea thoroughly suppressed the demands of the people for democracy in the name of anticommunism. And rather than protecting the local people, the US supported these regimes while positioning itself as the protector of democracy through the Cultural Cold War (Kishi & Tsuchiya, 2009).

According to Lisa Yoneyama (2016), who is well known in transpacific Cold War and post–Cold War studies, gender politics played an important role in this Cold War process of knowledge production. In fact, women's rights and gender equality are key components of US exceptionalism, which holds that the US is an exceptional nation that transcends even international human rights standards in terms of achieving democracy and freedom. An important historical basis for this is the success of the Allied Occupation policies that brought women's suffrage and liberation to Japan (Yoneyama, 2016, pp. 83–84). In the post–Cold War period, this exceptionalism has come to encompass discourses on sexuality. This relates to Puar's (2007) argument, noted earlier, that US hegemony and imperialism are supported by "homonationalism" – a conceptual frame for understanding how mainstream gay politics in the US have become associated with nationalism after 9/11, which has also manifested as racism against Muslims.

As I have pointed out recently, assimilationist discourses became mainstream in the Taiwanese gay movement for marriage equality, which had started as a radical social movement in the 1990s that emphasized the differences between homosexual and heterosexual people. When faced with a conservative backlash in the 2010s, however, the activists began to argue that homosexual people were quite ordinary, not so different to others. The discourse of inclusion in the institution of marriage became mainstream. When homonormative lesbians and gays who do not deviate from heteronormativity claim to be "good citizens," they do not assimilate into the "Republic of China" with its historical background in mainland China, but "Taiwan," a nation that is now inclusive of homosexuality and boasts of its modernity and tolerance toward the international society. Thus, the homonationalism that praises "LGBT-friendly Taiwan" is also gaining support in East Asia as a discourse that shares values with the US and other former Western Bloc countries but, at the same time, differentiates itself from homophobic China.

5 Final thoughts: Homonationalism as a historical shift

Recently, Japan and Taiwan's LGBT movements have been using metropolitan pride parades as important stages on which to develop "solidarity." The present paper has argued that a close reading of the TRP's strategy reveals that its focus on Taiwan is the result of an underlying desire for and competition over Asian ideological hegemony. Moreover, it pointed out that the TRP's internalization of US sexual exceptionalism further complements Taiwanese homonationalism. The Japanese LGBT movement's perception of Taiwan as pro-Japanese has its roots in the conservative discourse that justifies Japanese colonialism and imperialism. In recent years, Taiwanese nationalism has also subsumed gay rights issues, which are now proudly displayed as part of Taiwanese homonationalism (Kă, 2018).

According to Puar (2017), homonationalism is not simply a synonym for racism, but also indicates a "historical shift" – that is to say, homonationalism's origins and expansion are tied to a nation-state's transition from a strict adherence to heteronormativity to the inclusion of homonormativity (p. 51). In the present paper, the theoretical framework of homonationalism was used to analyze the mainstream acceptance of Taiwan's LGBT movement. The homonationalistic discourse in Taiwan, sparked by US homonationalism, has gained considerable importance, such as the slogan declaring Taiwan to be "the most LGBT-friendly in Asia." But most crucial, perhaps, is the fact that it – purposefully – does not fully reject US sexual exceptionalism, and instead seeks to assert a Taiwanese version of the concept – hence the stress on "Asia." In short, as demonstrated throughout this paper, Taiwanese homonationalism and LGBT movement adopted US sexual exceptionalism with very few modifications, and they are defined by the nation's self-portrayal as modern and progressive in direct contrast to the "othered" China. The homonationalistic desire of Japanese gay activists to make Japan a queer-friendly nation to be admired in the "world" resonates with the Taiwanese homonationalist discourse through the racialization of Taiwanese and Chinese people and the establishment of racial hierarchies between them.

Puar (2017) critiqued a particular aspect of homonationalism – "pinkwashing" –defining it as the strategic use of LGBT rights to improve the image of a given administration. Indeed, Israel's use of pinkwashing was a global PR success, rooted not only in the actions of the individual nation-state, but also in the historical and geopolitical context of the US-led world order in which it was enacted. Likewise, Taiwanese homonationalism did not appear from a vacuum: rather, it emerged from the East Asian order defined by an ideology that Yoneyama (2016) has called the "American Cold War geopolitical imaginary" (p. 85).

6 Conclusion

In an attempt to expand and develop Puar's (2007) conceptual framework of homonationalism in the East Asian geopolitical context, this paper has analyzed the influence of US sexual exceptionalism and homonationalism on Taiwan and Japan. The LGBT movements in Taiwan and Japan have worked to establish collaborative ties in recent years, but underlying this solidarity is the former's hegemonic desires toward Asia and the latter's imperial desires under the post–Cold War world order. This collusion between imperialism and homonationalism allows Japan and Taiwan to be classified as "LGBT-friendly, advanced societies," while simultaneously decrying nations like China as "undeveloped" and "half-savage" in regard to sexuality. This provides an important perspective for understanding the current escalating hostilities between China and the US and its supporters, Japan and Taiwan. Such a discussion also shares a view with a study by Liu and Zhang (2022), who, in a paper titled "Queer Subjectivities and Homotransnationalism Across Sinophone Societies," examine the transnational struggles of LGBTQ groups in their respective societies, highlighting the dynamics of queer politics and competing nationalisms in China, Taiwan, and Hong Kong. Their discussion also points out that Puar's homonationalism bears geopolitical limitations in describing the dynamics of sexuality in a single national context.

US sexual exceptionalism has been supported in post–Cold War East Asia. As discussed in Fukunaga (2022), perceptions of homosexuality in Taiwan, South Korea, and Japan have always referred to external standards – these East Asian societies have transformed their domestic discourses on homosexuality by referring to trends in the US and international human rights norms that have been institutionalized mainly by the United Nations (UN). The US has always occupied a special position in all their LGBT movements. In fact, at the 2019 Seoul Queer Parade, a speech celebrating the 50th anniversary of Stonewall included a reference to the US as "an important starting point for the global queer movement," reflecting the perception of the US as a progressive and exemplary nation in terms of gay rights.[8]

According to Chen Kuan-Hsing (2006), a Taiwanese scholar of inter-Asian cultural studies, the decolonization of East Asia is yet to be realized, as prevailing structures of the Global Cold War and the postwar international order have affected, or continue to affect, East Asia in the post–Cold War era. He also advocated the parallel pursuit of three projects: decolonization, de-imperialization, and de-Cold War in Asia. This paper's approach to examining the politics of sexuality in East Asia in the context of the post–Cold War regime was one attempt to respond to this call.

Since the late 2000s in Taiwan, South Korea, and Hong Kong, the Protestant right, inspired by trends in the US, has led a backlash that has primarily targeted gay rights. Religious studies scholar Nami Kim (2016) cautions, however, that critical interventions against the backlash must be practiced in ways that do not inscribe a colonial–imperialist logic that presents gay rights only as an indicator of modernity or democracy (pp. 82–83). Otherwise, a state that does not support gay rights will be seen as backward, "uncivilized," and undemocratic, thus reinforcing US imperialism, which is secured by sexual exceptionalism. Therefore, we must distance ourselves from discourses that enable disconnection from local politics by identifying gay rights as a marker of civilization. Moreover, it is essential to critically examine how discourses of gay rights or LGBT human rights have developed in the local, national, and global politics of post–Cold War East Asia, and how discourses of sexuality have been linked to nationalism and imperialism.

Acknowledgments

The present paper is a result of research conducted under the Japan Society for the Promotion of Science (JSPS) Kakenhi Grant JP16 J08328. I am grateful to the JSPS Overseas Challenge Program for Young Researchers for allowing me time to write during my time at Taiwan's National Central University, where I was a visiting scholar thanks to an invitation from Prof. Ning Yin-Bin and Prof. Josephine Ho. I would like to thank those who provided invaluable comments on various drafts of this paper. I have also learned a great deal from queer activism in the diverse so-

---

8 This quotation is from a speech made in Korean by the MC on a stage set up in Seoul Plaza at the Seoul Queer Parade in South Korea on 9 June 2019.

cieties of East Asia, without which I would not have been able to complete this work.

References

Atarashii Nittai kankei: Kyōtsū no rieki o kiban ni [New Japan–Taiwan relations: Mutual interests as a foundation]. (2000, April 19). *Asahi shinbun*, 14.
Bankoku kara: Fuehajimeta rōshi funsō han-Nichi sainen ni kikenna me [From Bangkok: Labor-management disputes have begun to increase, the danger of a resurgence of anti-Japanese sentiment]. (1979, July 27). *Yomiuri shinbun*, 8.
Chen, K. (2006). *Qù dìguó: Yàzhōu zuòwéi fāngfǎ* [Asia as method: Toward de-imperialization]. Éditions du Flaneur.
Ching, L. T. S. (2019). *Anti-Japan: The politics of sentiment in postcolonial East Asia.* Duke University Press.
Chu, W. (2005, June 4). *Gōngmínquán lùnshù yǔ gōngmín shèhuì zài Táiwān* [Discourse of citizenship and civil society in Taiwan] [Paper presentation]. Meeting for Citizenship/Governmentality, Tunghai University, Taiwan. https://pussleng.files.wordpress.com/2010/05/a019.pdf.
"Dōshi" ni yasashii Taiwan [LGBT-friendly Taiwan]. (2017, June 15). *Mainichi shinbun.*
Fukunaga, G. (2016, January 20). Saieibun wa kon'in byōdō o shiji shimasu: LGBT seiji kara miru Taiwan sōtō senkyo [Tsai Ing-wen supports marriage equality: Taiwan's presidential election and queer politics]. *Synodos.* https://synodos.jp/international/15953.
Fukunaga, G. (2017). "LGBT furendorī na Taiwan" no tanjō [The emergence of an "LGBT-friendly Taiwan"]. In K. Sechiyama (Ed.), *Jendā to sekushuariti de miru Higashi Ajia* [Gender and sexuality in East Asia] (pp. 187–225). Keisō Shobō.
Fukunaga, G. (2022). *Posuto reisenki Higashi Ajia ni okeru sekushuariti no seiji: Taiwan to Kankoku no jirei kara* [Post–Cold War sexual politics in East Asia: From the perspective of Taiwan and South Korea] [Unpublished doctoral dissertation]. University of Tokyo.
Gotō, J. (2010). *Eiga "Supuringu fībā"* [Film review: "Spring Fever"]. g-lad xx. http://gladxx.jp/features/2010/entertainment/848.html.
Gotō, J. (2012, November 12). Gei no "rakuen" o motomete [Looking for a gay "paradise"]. All About Japan. http://allabout.co.jp/gm/gc/402677.
Hau, L. (2010). Yōngbào qīngchūn mèng, gòngshǎng cǎihóng huā [Embrace the dream of youth and enjoy the rainbow flowers]. In *Táiběi 2010 tóngzhì gōngmín yùndòng: Rènshi tóngzhì shǒucè* [LGBT civil rights movement, Taipei 2010], 4–5.
Hayakawa, T., & Nogawa, M. (2015). *Zō no kōkoku* [Hate speech advertising]. Gōdō Shuppan.
Itakura, K. (2015). Making Japan "out-and-proud" through not-yet-consensual translation: A case study of Tokyo Rainbow Pride's website. *Queer Cats Journal of LGBTQ Studies, 1*(1), 3–30.
Jacobs, A. (2014, October 29). For Asia's gays, Taiwan stands out as beacon. *The New York Times.*
Jomaru, Y. (2011). *"Shokun!" "Seiron" no kenkyū: Hoshu genron wa dō henyō shitekitaka* [Research on "shokun!" and "seiron": The transformation of conservative discourse]. Iwanami Shoten.
Kǎ, W. [Ning, Y.]. (2018). Fěnshì yǔ tóngxìngliàn mínzú zhǔyì zhīhòu: Yǐyìzhìyí xià de zhīshì shēngchǎn [Pinkwashing, homonationalism and the politics of colored people knowledge-production]. *Táiwān shèhuì yánjiū jíkān, 111*, 231–248.
Kenta. (2017). Bokura no sekai o motto akaruku shitai [I want to make our world a brighter place]. Tokyo Rainbow Pride. *BEYOND: Tokyo Rainbow Pride official magazine, 3*, 6–7.

Kim, N. (2016). *The gendered politics of the Korean Protestant right.* Palgrave Macmillan.

Kishi, T., & Tsuchiya, Y. (Eds.). (2009). *Bunka reisen no jidai: Amerika to Ajia* [Decentering the Cultural Cold War: The US and Asia]. Kokusai Shoin.

Kō, B. (2007). Nihonjin ni tsugu: Taiwan to iu "Shinnichi kokka" ga kietemo iinoka [Tell the Japanese: Is it OK for Taiwan, the "pro-Japanese nation," to disappear?]. *Seiron, 424,* 78–87.

Kō, B. (2012a). *Han-Nichi kanjō o ayatsuru Chūgoku no shōtai* [The propagator of anti-Japanese sentiment, China]. Nihon Bungeisha.

Kō, B. (2012b). *Kokoro o yurusenai rinjin: Chūgoku to Chūgokujin wa kono gomoji de wakaru* [An irreconcilable, unforgivable other: Understand China and Chinese people with these five characters]. Wac.

Kobayashi, Y. (2000). *Shin gōmanizumu sengen supesharu: Taiwan-ron* [Neo gōmanizumu manifesto special: On Taiwan]. Shōgakkan.

Kurahashi, K. (2018). *Rekishi shūsei shugi to sabukaruchā: 90-nendai hoshu gensetsu no media bunka* [Historical revisionism and subculture in Japan: Conservative discourse and media culture in the 1990s]. Seikyūsha.

Liu, W., & Zhang, C. Y. (2022). Homonationalism as a site of contestation and transformation: On queer subjectivities and homotransnationalism across Sinophone societies. In A. Sifaki, C. L. Quinan, & K. Lončarević (Eds.), *Homonationalism, femonationalism and ablenationalism* (pp. 48–65). Routledge.

Mori, Y. (2001). *Taiwan/Nihon: Rensa suru koroniarizumu* [Taiwan/Japan: The chain of colonialism]. Inpakuto Shuppankai.

Nittai danko 20-nen: Taiwan, tairiku, soshite Nihon [The 20-year Japan–Taiwan divide: Taiwan, mainland China, and Japan]. (1992, October 8). *Sankei shinbun.*

Ogiue, C. (2012, April 26). Tayōna ikikata o sonchōshiyō: "Tokyo reinbō puraido 2012" kaisai chokuzen intabyū [Respect diversity: Interview with Tokyo Rainbow Pride 2012]. *Synodos.* https://synodos.jp/society/2263.

Oguma, E. (2014). Kokusai kankyō to nashonarizumu: "Fōmatto-ka" to giji reisen taisei [The international environment and nationalism: "Formatting" and the pseudo–Cold War regime]. In E. Ōguma (Ed.), *Heiseishi* [A history of the Heisei period] (pp. 499–583). Kawade Shobō Shinsha.

Puar, J. (2007). *Terrorist assemblages: Homonationalism in queer times.* Duke University Press.

Puar, J. (2017). Homonationalism as assemblage: Viral travels, affective sexualities. In S. Oishik & J. Dipika (Eds.), *New intimacies, old desires: Law, culture and queer politics in neoliberal times* (pp. 50 70). Cuban Publishers.

Satō, K. (2007). Minshinto seiken no "jinken gaikō": Gyakkyō no naka de no sofutopawā gaikō no kokoromi ["Human rights diplomacy" under the DPP administration. An attempt at soft power diplomacy to overcome unfavorable Taiwan-strait relations]. *Nihon Taiwan Gakkaihō, 9,* 131–153.

Táiběi tóngzhì yóuxíng, Dà lù dà xiànmù [China's LGBT people stare with envy at Taipei's LGBT Pride]. (2005, December 17). *United Daily News.*

Taiwan oishisa nigiwai wa kenzai: Fukkō chakuchaku kankō PR ni yakki [Taiwan's deliciousness and liveliness: Reconstruction steadily progressing, eager to promote tourism]. (2000, January 13). *Mainichi shinbun,* 6.

Tokekomanu Nihonjin: Tai han-Nichi undō de Bankoku chōsa gaisha kaichō kōen [Intolerant Japanese: Speech by the chair of a Bangkok research agency on the anti-Japanese movement in Thailand]. (1973, January 17). *Mainichi shinbun,* 7.

Tokyo Rainbow Pride. (2014). *Nihon no puraido pareido* [Japan's pride parade]. http://trp2014.trparch ives.com.

Tokyo Rainbow Pride. (2017). *BEYOND: Tokyo Rainbow Pride official magazine*, *3*.

Wakabayashi, M. (2008). *Taiwan no seiji: Chūkaminkoku Taiwan-ka no sengoshi* [The "Republic of China" and the politics of Taiwanization: The changing identity of Taiwan in postwar East Asia]. University of Tokyo Press.

Rī moto Taiwan sōtō no shizuka na rainichi: Chūgoku wa tsuyoi hinan sezu [Former Taiwanese president Lee's quiet visit to Japan: No strong criticisms from China]. (2008, September 24). *Yomiuri shinbun*, 9.

Yoneyama, L. (2016). *Cold war ruins: Transpacific critique of American justice and Japanese war crimes*. Duke University Press.

Zhào, Q. (2018). "Tái-rì yǒuhǎo" de qínggǎn zhèngzhì xué [The affective politics of the "Taiwan–Japan friendship"]. *Coolloud*. https://www.coolloud.org.tw/node/90219.

Zhǐyǒu gémìng tóngzhì, méiyǒu bōlī tóngzhì [Only revolutionary comrades exist, gay "tongzhi" do not]. (1996, April 3). *United Daily News*.

Guo Lifu
Medals and conspiracies: Chinese and Japanese online trans-exclusionary discourses during the 2020 Tokyo Olympic Games

The 2020 Summer Olympics (Tokyo 2020 Games) were held amid concerns, protests, and controversies. The Games were postponed for a year owing to the global COVID-19 pandemic (Oi, 2021). It was not only the form of the event, but also political and human rights issues that garnered public attention. For example, despite the International Olympic Committee (IOC) ban of political, religious, and racial protests, US shot-putter Raven Saunders raised her arms in the shape of an X on the podium to show her support for all oppressed people (Wells, 2021). Furthermore, in February 2021, the then president of the Tokyo Organising Committee (TOC), Mori Yoshirō, made a sexist remark about meetings with women "dragging on" because they talk too much, which resulted in his resignation and public concerns about gender issues at the Games (McCurry, 2021; Sieg, 2021).

The Tokyo 2020 Games also saw the first openly trans athlete – weightlifter Laurel Hubbard from Aotearoa New Zealand – competing in Olympic women's events, which made global headlines. The announcement of her participation immediately triggered heated debates over the fairness of the Olympic Games and trans rights, spreading like wildfire online. These debates, coupled with other incidents such as the Odakyū train stabbing (*Man Out to Kill*, 2021; *Tokyo Train Stabbing*, 2021), contributed to a marked growth in trans-exclusionary discourses online, not only in Japanese, but also in Chinese. As I will argue in this paper, despite the fact that the Chinese government uses its wins in the Olympic Games to showcase its international power and resistance against the ideological West (which includes Japan), the trans-exclusionary discourses in China and Japan actually have similar political implications.

This paper investigates how trans-exclusionary discourses have been framed and mobilized against the geopolitical background of East Asia in the post–Cold War era, focusing on a social media analysis of Japanese-language tweets and Chinese-language Weibo posts during the Tokyo 2020 Games.

The Tokyo 2020 Games were chosen for three primary reasons. First and most obviously, it was the first time a trans woman athlete competed in Olympic women's events.[1] Second, so-called "sex frauds" have always been under heightened surveillance to sustain the "fairness" of the Games, which rests on protectionist gender politics and the assumption that women's bodies are naturally weaker than their male counterparts (*Laurel Hubbard*, 2021), often citing biology and natural science as evidence (Heggie, 2017; Itani, 2021). Third, as one of the largest and most popular sporting events in the world, the Olympic Games function not only as an avenue for sports competition but also as a space for international politics, thereby providing an ideal case to examine the intersection between gender/sexuality and international politics. In particular, among the many East Asian countries, states, and polities that participate in the Olympics, China is inarguably the most significant competitor in both the sporting and geopolitical arenas. Especially with the impending 2022 Winter Olympics in Beijing, there was intense competition between China and Japan on which nation would be the better organizer of international events.

Twitter and Weibo were chosen for two reasons:

1. Easy data access: they provide open application programming interfaces (APIs) for collecting data,[2] unlike other social media platforms such as Facebook and WeChat, and their content is public (except for Twitter profiles that are set to private).
2. Twitter and Weibo are among the most widely used social media platforms in Japan and China, respectively.[3]

In the following sections, I first review the literature on trans-exclusionary discourses and politics, especially the way they are framed in distinct contexts. Second, I present my research methodologies and a sample of my findings. Third, I analyze how the Twitter and Weibo discourses frame the participation of trans

---

1 Although the IOC has allowed trans athletes to compete since the 2000s and the criteria of participation have changed several times, the Tokyo 2020 Games were the first Olympics in which an openly trans athlete competed.
2 APIs allow users to access the Twitter and Weibo databases and pull large amounts of data. However, compared to Twitter, which provides researchers with academic accounts that can pull large amounts of data free of charge, Weibo's free service only allows a limited number of requests. Instead, I pulled the source code in ".json" format, which contains all the information on the webpage to filter out useful data such as username, publication date and time, Weibo content, and location.
3 According to Statista (2022), Weibo had approximately 57,300,000 monthly active users by 2022, while Twitter had approximately 43,600,000 monthly active users worldwide. According to StatCounter's (2023) statistics for July 2022, Twitter in Japan occupied 50.34% of the social media market share.

women in sport as a threat to cis women athletes. Finally, I discuss the transnational connections of the trans-exclusionary discourses in East Asia.

1 Trans-exclusionary discourses and politics

Any discussion of trans-exclusionary discourses must inevitably consider the phenomenon of trans-exclusionary radical feminists (TERFs). First coined in 2008, the term was used by trans allies to criticize trans-exclusionary discourses and politics, especially those delivered by cis women who claim to be feminists (Pearce et al., 2020, pp. 4–8).

The depiction of cis women as victims of violence by trans women, albeit with little supporting evidence, is a prominent way to rationalize these TERF narratives, which often center around the idea that women-only facilities are intended to protect biologically female bodies. For example, in the debate over trans women's use of public bathrooms, TERF campaigners often claim that trans women, especially those who have not undergone sex reassignment, are males who are potential criminals disguised as women (Pearce et al., 2020, pp. 6–7).

However, the idea that these women-only facilities are "safe spaces" has been carefully examined and critically analyzed. Koyama (2006) examined the trans-exclusionary politics in the 1970s Michigan Womyn's Music Festival, arguing that the safety of these safe spaces is in fact part of a wider protectionist politics, which recognizes only idealized female bodies (i. e., white female bodies), as worthy of protection. She further argued that these politics are widely supported by cis white women activists because they assume that women's oppression is the most extreme and fundamental of all social inequalities, and all women's experiences, especially when facing violence, are the same. In other words, these cis white women activists understand violence against women as only coming from biological males, who they essentialize according to the "presence of a penis." Ignoring decades of efforts by feminist and queer scholars to deconstruct gender and sex, these arguments resurrect the dated binary notion of biological sex and socialized gender.

After the debate over trans issues in feminist theory and activism, these narratives found support among political and religious conservatives (Pearce et al., 2020, p. 7). This trend is most significantly manifested in the use of terms such as "gender critical" and "gender ideology" by TERF campaigners. These terms in English have specific historical and political backgrounds. For example, what prompted the debate in the UK was a plan submitted in 2017 to reform the Gender Recognition Act (GRA) of 2004, while in the US, it was the "Bathroom Bill" in North Carolina proposed in 2016. "Gender ideology" was originally used by far-right activists to condemn the coalition of liberals, feminists, and queer activists as a conspiracy of global elites (Korolczuk & Graff, 2018, pp. 807–809). Research has also located the first use of these terms on trans-exclusionary websites, where conservative groups were referred to and then widely shared within the trans-exclusionary online communities (Moore, 2019).

In Japan, feminist theorist Senda Yūki (2020) argued for a redrawing of the women's boundary, igniting heated academic debates over the transphobia manifested in her essay. Philosopher and trans theorist Fujitaka Kazuki (2021) criticized Senda for positioning trans issues as postfeminist, which is a framework that many TERF campaigners adopt. More recently, queer studies scholar Fukunaga Gen'ya (2022) has investigated the adoption of TERF narratives by the young generation of South Korean feminists, who distinguish themselves from the trans-friendly earlier generation of feminists. In China, these debates have not been theorized at the time of writing. But according to my own observations of China's communities of sexual minorities since 2015, there appears to be a clear change after 2020, reflected by an emphasis on biological bodies among feminist online influencers and the creation of various women-only online spaces (*chún nǚ kōng jiān*).

Building on the abovementioned academic studies (Fujitaka, 2021; Fukunaga, 2022), this paper endeavors to provide a contextualized discussion of transnational TERF narratives in East Asia.

2 Methodology and findings

This study examines Japanese tweets and Chinese Weibo posts related to trans athletes' participation in sports within the period of the Tokyo 2020 Games (23 July–7 August 2021). To obtain as much relevant data as possible, I used the method of fuzzy search with the following keywords in Chinese: for Weibo, I searched *kuà xìng bié* (transgender) and *biàn xìng* (meaning "changing sex," which could appear in other compound words such as *biàn xìng shǒu shù* [sex reassignment surgery] or *biàn xìng rén* [trans people]), as well as the English "trans." For Twitter, I initially limited the search to Japanese and used *toransu* (trans) in katakana as the keyword, since it covers all words translated from English that contain the affix "trans." I then searched for the English keyword "trans" as well.[4] This search elicited 4,123 Weibo posts and 67,344 tweets.

---

4 I added the English term "trans" to the search because the communities in China and Japan use it in their daily speech.

The Chinese keywords elicited more accurate results compared to their Japanese counterparts, since Japanese users are more likely to use the short form *toransu* instead of *toransujendā* (transgender). As Japanese words that contain this katakana prefix are very common, the search elicited not only words such as "trans community" but also irrelevant words such as "transformers" and "transmitters," which required a dedicated process of data cleaning.

Forwarding is the Weibo equivalent of retweets on Twitter, which allows users to copy and repost other users' contents on their own timeline. I take this function as an indicator of how widely the content is being disseminated (Fang & Rapnikova, 2018, pp. 6–8). I extracted the most forwarded Weibo posts and retweeted tweets after filtering out the noise data that were irrelevant for my analysis – for example, posts containing keywords such as "transformers," as well as advertisements and posts sent by bots, which randomly pick up trending hashtags that might contain references to "transgender."

For Weibo, I filtered out 154 posts from the 200 most forwarded posts (with the maximum number of forwards being 16,113, and the lowest being 4), while for Twitter, I filtered out 156 tweets from the 1,000 most retweeted tweets (with the maximum number of retweets being 2,085, and the lowest being 10). Tables 1 and 2 show the top five most forwarded Weibo posts (25 February 2022) and retweeted tweets (22 February 2022), respectively.

Table 1: Top 5 most forwarded posts on Weibo (as of 18 March 2022).

	Weibo posts	No. of times forwarded
1	On the 24th [of July], former US President Trump bombarded #跨性别举重运动员# [#TransWeightlifter# / #*kuà xìng bié jǔ zhòng yùn dòng yuán*#] participating in women's sports in a speech. He took aim at the Olympic women's weightlifting contestant, New Zealand trans weightlifter Hubbard. Trump has claimed that trans athletes can easily "crush" records set by female athletes, and that allowing trans people to compete in women's games is a violation of women's rights: "They're taking your rights, it's a feminist movement, and we can't let that happen." Hubbard turned from male to female in 2012. Many weightlifters have opposed her participation, and some former sports stars have spoken out against male-born athletes competing in elite women's sports. Despite the criticism, the International Olympic Committee (IOC) has backed Hubbard to compete with women, saying she can compete under the current rules. (@观察者网 [*guān chá zhě wǎng*], 26 July 2021, 13:30)	16,113
2	Today, the Olympic weightlifting competition will be held in the over 87 kg category. Chinese female weightlifter Lǐ Wénwén will compete with New Zealand trans athletes. This Hubbard didn't even have sex reassignment surgery, he just took medicine to	2,090

Table 1: Top 5 most forwarded posts on Weibo (as of 18 March 2022). *(Continued)*

	Weibo posts	No. of times forwarded
	keep his hormone levels low. Calling himself a "female athlete" is nothing short of the greatest insult to fairness in sports. I have no issues with trans people but have a big issue with a biological male participating in women's sports. He is taking advantage of his physiology to violate the rights and interests of all female athletes. I hope Lǐ Wénwén can defeat this New Zealand "trans person" and take revenge for all the women around the world. (@张忆安-龙战于野 [*zhāng yì ān-lóng zhàn yú yě*], 2 August 2021,10:12)	
3	New Zealand weightlifter Laurel Hubbard will compete in the women's weightlifting competition at the Olympics, competing with the young Chinese athlete Lǐ Wénwén. But it is worth mentioning that Hubbard is the first trans athlete in history to compete in the Olympic Games. Before the age of 35, he did not perform well internationally as a male weightlifter, but when he became a trans woman and competed in the women's games, he became competitive.... (@英国报姐 [*yīng guó bào jiě*], 27 July 2021, 14:00)	1,832
4	A New Zealand trans athlete was selected for New Zealand's Tokyo Olympic team on the 21st [of July 2021]. She will compete in the women's 87 kg class, becoming the world's first trans person to participate in the Olympics. Our young athlete Lǐ Wénwén, who holds a high possibility of winning a gold medal, is in this event. (@今日看点 [*jīn rì kàn diǎn*], 26 July 2021, 13:37)	1,514
5	The Tokyo Olympics women's 87 kg weightlifting competition has a #跨性别举重运动员# [#TransWeightlifter# / #kuà xìng bié jǔ zhòng yùn dòng yuán#] from New Zealand. In this class, our athlete Lǐ Wénwén would dominate the competition. Lǐ is going to face a trans! Come on! (@娱乐资讯头条 [*yú lè zī xùn tóu tiáo*], 26 July 2021, 10:56)	1,499

Note: All the posts in this table have been translated from Chinese by the author.

Table 2: Top 5 most retweeted tweets on Twitter (as of 18 March 2022).

Tweets	No. of retweets
1 For the first time in history, transgender women have been allowed to participate in the Tokyo Olympics. Laurel Hubbard (43), a New Zealand weightlifter. However, since she originally had the strength of a man, she might have an advantage over other players. I'm not convinced. Don't use diversity to cheat. (@toshio_tamogami, 2 August 2021, 17:43)	2,085
2 The IOC has decided that even with "male genitalia," if the testosterone level in the blood is within the range that can extend to 28 times that of a normal girl, it is possible to participate as a "female athlete." We need to know more about LGBT issues. (@HachimotoKotoe, 30 July 2021, 20:00)	1,121
3 China's best women athletics team are being tested as real women by a professional doctor. There are rumors that they have been modified with hormones to win against the world by the Chinese Communist Party. (@P6AX3Er3HqoQynY, 29 July 2021, 18:40)	865
4 In 2015, the IOC removed sex reassignment surgery from the entry requirements. It seems that there are few people who are brave enough to oppose the trans woman problem for fear of being named a hater, but female athletes are raising their voices. In sports, it is not fair for a person with a female body to compete with a person with a male body. At the end of the day, the true misogynist is the IOC. (@kotamama318, 1 August 2021, 11:18)	640
5 The fact that all nonbinary, female, male, and other self-identified athletes try to compete in the women's games is living proof that competing as women is more advantageous for them. There are physical differences between genders. Please don't cheat. (@traductricemtl, 29 July 2021, 23:13)	491

Note: All the tweets in this table have been translated from Japanese by the author.

I categorized each of these posts/tweets according to whether they were trans-exclusionary, hard to define, or trans-inclusionary. Altogether, 79.19 % of the results were trans-exclusionary on Twitter, while Weibo showed a slightly higher rate of 85.52 %. Hard-to-define tweets and Weibo posts showed similar proportions: 7.6 % and 5.38 %, respectively. Conversely, 9.1 % on Weibo and 13.21 % on Twitter were positive. The result shows an overall similar attitude on both platforms, with Weibo being slightly more trans-exclusionary.

Furthermore, I analyzed the topic models of the text of the posts through natural language processing (NLP). A topic model is a text-mining tool for analyzing the topics of a collection of texts. The algorithm in NLP is based on the frequency of the words that appear in the document. NLP technologies are well developed and more accurate when dealing with the English language but still under development for the Chinese and Japanese languages. Fortunately, I narrowed down the sample to a scale that I can double-check manually. Therefore, after the NLP calculations, I checked and corrected errors in the results. The program also gives back a proportion of each topic in the collection of the text.

The results from Weibo contained four major topics: "Donald Trump's opinion" (69.18%), "China's national security and pride" (14.44%), "Debate over the proper female subject" (13.02%), and "Fairness of the Games" (3.37%).

The results from Twitter also contained four major topics: "Debate over the proper female subject" (39.26%), "The leftists and global elites" (24.85%), "Fairness of the Games" (20.37%), and "Chinese sex fraud" (15.52%).

Even though both Weibo and Twitter showed negative attitudes, they were framed in significantly different ways. On Weibo, the most dominant topic was "Donald Trump's opinion," as represented by the most forwarded content in table 1, and Chinese netizens were more interested in how trans athletes would affect the number of China's gold medals rather than the intrusion of trans women into women-only spaces. Conversely, on Twitter, the most dominant topic was the "debate over the proper female subjects," and Japanese Twitter users framed their criticism of trans women in the typical TERF narratives (e.g., they do not share the female social experience; they are intruders in women-only spaces; or they are potential criminals), clearly mobilizing concerns against the liberalist ideology of gender/sexuality diversity.

Although there are many topics to be discussed, I would like to highlight the way these contents depict cis women athletes as victims and trans women as opportunists demolishing the fairness of the Games. Although the discourses of reverse victimhood are present in both Chinese and Japanese online spaces, the exact power relations are reversed and their geopolitical implications are significantly different, as will be identified in the following sections.

3 Weibo: Gold medals and white leftists

One way in which trans women are framed as a threat on Weibo is the depiction of the Chinese nation-state as the victim of an unfair competitive system. A large number of posts depict the Chinese weightlifting medal contender Lǐ Wénwén as being cheated by Laurel Hubbard, who was taking advantage of the rules, that is, the hypercorrect LGBT-friendly environment in Western countries. For example:

> #跨性别举重运动员# [#kuà xìng bié jǔ zhòng yùn dòng yuán# / #TransWeightlifter#] is so unfair. This is obscenity! Letting a male trans [man who is supposedly trans] participate in the women's 87 kg competition just for a win? This New Zealand weightlifter Hubbard originally participated in the men's weightlifting competition, and after his 30s he began to participate

in the women's games through a sex change. Due to his physical advantages, he achieved good results of "six golds and one silver" after participating in the women's games. This time in the women's 87 kg weightlifting competition at the Tokyo Olympics, we have Lǐ Wénwén, our favorite to win the championship. That is a typical double standard, where is there any fairness at all? Come on! Lǐ Wénwén! Lǐ Wénwén has competed with this so-called trans athlete in the past and won against him. This time, we must win against him again with our strength to prove our power. Even if you try to set up obstacles and conspiracies, we can still win. #87 公斤举重队员李雯雯# [#87 *gōng jīn jǔ zhòng duì yuán lǐ wén wén* # / #87kgWeightlifterLiWenwen#] (@娱圈十三妹 [*yú quān shí sān mèi*], 26 July 2021, 14:19)[5]

From this excerpt, it is not hard to identify a narrative that posits trans athletes in opposition to Chinese national achievement in an international competition. First, there is the typical misgendering, where Hubbard was referred to as a male and by the pronouns "he/him." There is also misinformation. The post claimed that Hubbard had "good results" when "he" was a male to emphasize that Hubbard has a strong male body, but it omits the fact that Hubbard had actually been competing as a woman in international competitions since 2017 (Smith, 2021). Behind this misgendering and misinformation is a misogynistic logic that posits women as the perfect victims because female bodies are naturally weaker than male bodies.

This victimhood of the female body is then framed for the incitement of national pride. In the above excerpt, the vulnerability of Lǐ Wénwén's female body is reframed to justify the trans-exclusionary discourse, while Hubbard is positioned as a threat to not only cis women athletes in general, but also those who represent China.

This rhetoric does not stop at naming the threats but emphasizes the destiny of "trans threats" when they are against the Chinese state. The above post refers to Lǐ Wénwén as someone who can win against Hubbard, which then contributes to the imagined bravery of the state in facing injustice.[6] Even if Lǐ does not win, Hubbard being described as a "cheater," a fake woman with a man's body, gives Lǐ and the Chinese state the power to claim victimhood. Lǐ's gender identity is not questioned, even with her record of having won against Hubbard ("the strong male body") in the past.

This rhetoric manifests a complicated depiction of the female body. First, the power relations between cis and trans women are being reversed. Given that trans

---

5 Unless otherwise indicated, all Weibo posts have been translated from Chinese to English by the author. This post had been forwarded 60 times as of 4 March 2022, which is comparatively low, but the rhetoric in this excerpt contains the typical patterns of speech related to national pride.

6 It is also worth mentioning that in the second most forwarded post in table 1, Lǐ's ability and mightiness in winning against Hubbard is not only linked to the state's bravery, but also to the revenge of all women around the world.

women athletes were excluded from the institution based on the scientifically rejected biological evidence on the sex binary (Fuentes, 2022), cis women's unquestioned eligibility in participating in women's games is itself a privilege. This reversal of victimhood is based on the idea that only biological women without a penis should be considered a legitimate female subject to claim victimhood. However, as Jones and Slater (2020) have stated, this very power of claiming victimhood is the power cis women have over trans women. Second, this victimhood of cis women is reclaimed by the nation-state. Although it might seem like the rhetoric of depicting cis women as victims is lobbying for women's rights in TERF politics, the linkage of Lǐ's victimhood to China's national pride reflects that this rhetoric is not even for women's rights in a TERF sense, but an example of China's unremitting tenacity.

This tendency to link women and sexual minorities to national security needs to be understood against the background of China–US relations. The following excerpt provides a valuable example.

> This time I support the king who knows all [*dǒng wáng*][7]: Trump bombarded trans athletes for participating in women's sports, which infringes on the rights of female athletes! Trump harshly criticized the New Zealand trans athlete in a speech. He claimed that trans athletes can easily "crush" records set by female athletes, and that allowing trans people to compete in women's games is a violation of women's rights. "They're taking your rights, it's a feminist movement, and we can't let that happen." But that's what the IOC agreed to. The IOC is just a brainless white leftist in this matter. A male trans [man who is supposedly trans] can't change his natural muscular advantage. It makes no sense to let him compete with female athletes. This is just messed up. (@HW前HR[HW qián HR], 26 July 2021, 19:44)[8]

Political scholars Yang Tian and Fang Kecheng (2021) have stated that the term "white leftist" (*bái zuǒ*) is crucial in the narratives of Chinese online nationalist communities (pp. 6–8). "White leftist" literally refers to white liberals. These people are perceived as those who superficially lobby for the rights of minorities for an empty image of progressiveness, which is often waged as a weapon against China. Although the US is considered an ideological enemy, Trump's speech is frequently cited by Chinese online nationalists. In other words, while the US government is depicted as the ultimate enemy dominated by white leftists, Trump is depicted as a savior who really cares about feminism.

Although women's rights is emphasized in the above excerpt, Chinese online nationalists have long criticized feminism for being a hypocritical performance

---

7 This term was originally used ironically by Chinese speakers for Trump's know-it-all attitude, but in this post it is used in a positive way, implying that this time, Trump really understands the truth.

8 This post had been forwarded 77 times as of 4 March 2022.

of white leftists. I searched for and calculated the number of Weibo posts containing the keyword "feminism" from 2011 to 2021, and found that the number of posts had grown from 886 in 2011 to 18,788 in 2021. After 2017, there were several drastic ups and downs, with 13,570 in 2019 and 5,124 in 2020. Given the Chinese government's tendency to censor heated debates online (King et al., 2012, pp. 15–16), it is safe to conclude that the discussion about feminism on Weibo might have drawn the government's attention and resulted in a huge deletion of Weibo posts in 2020. This matches the emergence of Chinese online nationalist activism in 2016 (Fang & Rapnikova, 2018, pp. 8–11). The term that is often used by the nationalist community to condemn feminism is *nǚ quán* (woman's fist). It is often used together with the term "white leftist," indicating that feminists are supposedly calling for gender equality but are attacking men's rights, that is, punching (men) with their fist. For example, commenting on actor Emma Watson's refusal to cooperate with author J. K. Rowling again for the latter's trans-exclusionary attitude, a Chinese Weibo user posted: "White leftist and white left-wing extremist, a good example of magic defeating magic. What can defeat the feminist's fist? Answer: LGBT" (@Sponge11i, 27 June 2022, 15:51).[9]

In fact, the association of feminism, as well as sexual minority activism, with external threats has a broader historical, political, and institutional context. The economic reform initiated at the end of the 1970s not only stimulated the Chinese market economy, but also vitalized the emergence of diverse gender and sexual identities (Rofel, 2007). The influx of foreign people and capital also inspired the formation of sexual minority communities (Guo, 2021). Despite a growing third sector, the Chinese government placed a double threshold to control and censor its social organizations to eliminate the so-called "external powers" that were thought to overthrow the Chinese Communist Party (Hildebrandt, 2013). Since sexual minorities' organizations were denied direct access to official support and resources for being morally improper, they survived through support from foreign embassies and foundations, which then made them susceptible as instruments of "external powers" (Guo, 2018).

After Xí Jìnpíng's ascension to leadership, the Chinese government switched to a more intransigent attitude. The newly issued Charity Law of 2016 restricted the types of NGOs that are allowed in China to those that pass the ideological test.[10] The ideological and economic conflicts between China and the US intensified as

---

9 This post had not been forwarded as of 18 March 2022, but was a response to a post about J. K. Rowling and Emma Watson, which had been forwarded approximately 110,000 times as of 18 March 2022.
10 Charity Law of the People's Republic of China (promulgated by the Nat'l People's Cong., 16 March 2016, effective 1 September 2016), arts. 3–4.

US–China relations worsened after Trump's ascension to the presidency (Boylan et al., 2021). Despite Trump's anti-LGBTQ policies and rhetoric, the advocacy of sexual minorities' rights was depicted as a US value and, more importantly, a weapon wielded against China.[11] Compared to the earlier decades of economic reform, when the government took up cooperative strategies in dealing with human rights issues, Xi's administration clearly adopted more hostile ones through inciting nationalism, where the US is the non-negotiable Other/enemy.

Therefore, the online trans-exclusionary discourses on Weibo manifest complicated power relations and the reverse of those relations in a specific geopolitical context. The debate over the proper female subject is closely associated with the narrative of national ideology and security.

4 Twitter: Women's safety and the Chinese threat

The trans-exclusionary narratives on Japanese Twitter show similar aspects to the typical TERF narratives. As mentioned above, the most heatedly debated topic on Twitter was in regard to the "proper" female subject. These narratives portrayed trans women as opportunists and potential criminals in women-only spaces. They referred to false scientific evidence to prove that male bodies are ultimately stronger than female bodies, citing women athletes' concerns about Hubbard's participation to depict her as being unwelcomed in women's sports, and even creating conspiracies about her intentionally losing the game to show that trans women do not have physical advantages so that more trans women can compete in women's events.

However, it is worth mentioning that compared to Weibo, where such TERF narratives are engulfed by nationalist discourses, Japanese Twitter users frame their tweets in a more individualistic way. That is not to say that their online discourses are not connected to Japanese nationalism or political conservatives such as the Liberal Democratic Party (LDP). In fact, as I argue in this section, they show a clear connection with online nationalists. By using the term individualistic, I em-

---

11 The ideological opposition between China and the US on sexual minority rights has also been intensified by the promotion of LGBT rights in neighboring areas such as Taiwan, Japan, and Korea, reviving the fault lines between the West and the East during the Cold War. For how China functions as an Other in constructing the progressiveness of Taiwan and Japan through LGBT activism, see Fukunaga (2017).

phasize the way Chinese and Japanese netizens frame their trans-exclusionary arguments in the context of international sports competitions.

Unlike Weibo, where both trans persons and feminists are depicted as external threats, the Japanese tweets posit trans persons as an internal threat to the political right and women's rights. As mentioned above, Japanese trans-exclusionary discourses emphasize the conflict between trans and cis women on an individual level. The references and citations in support of their arguments are often from individual athletes and influencers. For example:

> Later in this video, US weightlifter S. E. Robles responded with a simple "No, thank you," after a few seconds of silence when asked, "It was a historic night competing with Laurel Hubbard, the first transgender player. Please tell us your impressions." What a strong and eloquent response! (@ddslumber, 4 August 2021, 14:34)[12]

Although both the Chinese and Japanese netizens reverse the power relations between cis and trans women, several distinctions are worth addressing. First, by framing the biological female bodies as individual victims, the image of these threatened bodies is more connected to personal life experiences, which makes it easier to incite the precariousness of cis women. It is also crucial to mention that the trans-exclusionary sentiments are often incited by the perceived intrusion or invasion by trans persons into women-only spaces (Fukunaga, 2022, pp. 76–78). However, sociologist Charlotte Jones and queer studies scholar Jen Slater (2020, pp. 162–164) argued that women-only spaces such as women's toilets are built on the protectionist assumption that violence toward women would only be perpetrated by biological men.[13]

However, by stating that the Chinese online discourses are affected by nationalistic political campaigns, I do not mean to deny the individualistic aspect of the debate over women's victimhood. In East Asian trans-exclusionary politics, the construction and patrolling of the boundary of so-called "women-only spaces" are very important strategies, in which the images of female bodies threatened by male violence serve as an inevitable presumption. As Fukunaga (2020) has argued, the trans-exclusionary narratives in South Korea gained momentum through

---

12 Unless otherwise indicated, all Japanese-language tweets have been translated into English by the author. This tweet had been retweeted 465 times as of 4 March 2022.
13 According to a report by the US Department of Justice (2022, p. 11), in 2021, 77.4 % of the offenders in violent crimes were male, 17.6 % were female, and 5.1 % were both male and female. However, given the fact that in most cultures, aggression is considered part of masculinity and sometimes even praised, the low proportion of female offenders is insufficient evidence for claiming that women are less violent than men.

the support of younger generations of feminists refusing to align with the previous generation who endeavored to form alliances with sexual minorities. These younger generations were mobilized by the reports of sexual assaults and femicides, such as the femicide incident in Japan on 6 August 2021, during the Tokyo 2020 Games, when a passenger on the Odakyu train line intentionally targeted women who "looked happy" ("Kachigumi no onna," 2021). Similarly, on 14 June 2022, a group of gangsters attacked three women at midnight in a restaurant in Tang Shan City, China (Gan, 2022). The incident was recorded on CCTV and uploaded online, which shocked many people. After this incident, Weibo became a place to press the government to provide details about the victims and punish the perpetrators harshly, as well as to establish "women-only online spaces" (*chún nǚ kōng jiān*). This stimulated a huge change in online transphobia in China, as daily sexual assaults on women were clearly recorded and disseminated, which would result in a reframing of women's victimhood as an individual or group experience.

Second, unlike the Chinese netizens who quickly link the threatened female bodies to national pride against the ideological West, the Japanese netizens tend to link them to domestic political debates. The most retweeted content in table 2 manifests this framing. Another example is below:

> The Olympics ex-chief Mori has long been calling for the recruitment of excellent women but resigned for being a sexist. Conversely, the IOC who let a trans woman with a man's body compete against women is in fact the real sexist. We can't compare discrimination against transgenders and against women. (@kotamama, 3 August 2021, 12:30)[14]

This excerpt manifests three key characteristics of Japanese online right-wingers, as identified by Nagayoshi's (2019) quantitative survey: (1) they are highly motivated to participate in conservative politics (e.g., elections and lobbying events) and support the LDP; (2) they tend to obey traditional authoritarians and attack social minorities; and (3) they uphold traditional family values. The hostility in the tweet is directed at the IOC, which is framed as the hypocritical global liberalist elite protecting minorities at the expense of cis women's rights. Having resigned under local and international pressure after his sexist remark about women in meetings, Mori continued to make sexist remarks, such as stating that one staffer at a party hosted by LDP lawmaker Kawamura Takeo was "too old to call a woman" ("Disgraced Ex-Olympics Chief," 2021). Yet he is depicted in the tweet as a gender equality lobbyist compared to the IOC, which allows trans women to compete. Further-

---

14 This tweet had been retweeted 67 times and liked 235 times as of 4 March 2022.

more, given the fact that Mori was the LDP candidate elected as the Japanese prime minister in 2000, it is clear that this tweet supports the LDP.

Resembling the TERF coalition with conservative politicians and churches, the Japanese online transphobia is manifested through depicting cis women as individual victims and conservative (especially LDP) politicians as saviors and protectors of traditional values. It is also worth mentioning that the target of these LDP supporters' criticisms has changed. According to Fukunaga (2022, pp. 75–76), the gender mainstreaming in Japan from around 2000 faced a backlash from conservative parties and politicians, which targeted women's recruitment, but in 2022 the inclusion of LGBT rights was criticized on the basis of gender identity instead of sexual orientation. In other words, for these conservatives, gays and lesbians are not a big issue, but trans people are.

As this paper has shown, Japanese online right-wingers have appropriated the language of gender equality and mobilized the precariousness of cis women against trans women through an individualistic rhetoric, producing an image of cis women as threatened female bodies being protected by political conservatives. However, it is necessary to mention that these political conservatives have long been sexist and still are.

Putting these narratives in the East Asian geopolitical context allows us to dissect its imbricated implications. As Yamaguchi (2019) concluded, another characteristic of Japanese online right-wingers is their negative attitude toward South Korea and China, which is in fact an example of a broader negative attitude toward diverse minorities. From the data I collected, the trans identity, for online right-wingers, functions as a perfect stage for rationalizing and disseminating these narratives. As evident in the third excerpt in table 2, where misinformation about three Chinese cis women athletes who looked male was disseminated and widely commented upon as evidence for the Chinese Communist Party's cheating strategy to win at the Games by sending trans women to compete in women's games. Associating Chinese cis women athletes with a Chinese Communist Party conspiracy to win the competition and then to the typical TERF narrative that trans athletes have advantages over cis women (table 2) is exactly the embodiment of this complicated narrative. What makes this narrative eye-catching is its combination of Sinophobia – or, to be specific, the fear of communism fighting back – and transphobia, which frames gender-crossing as rule-breaking behavior.

5 Conclusion

This paper examined online trans-exclusionary discourses in Japanese-language tweets and Chinese-language Weibo posts during the Tokyo 2020 Games. It provides an alternative perspective from East Asia on prior research that has indicated how TERF arguments reverse the power relations between trans and cis women, which find an affinity with political and religious conservatives who have always been against gender equality.

While the Japanese and Chinese online trans-exclusionary discourses share some similarities in framing the biological female body as the victim, they frame their arguments differently. The Chinese netizens rationalize their arguments in terms of an ideologically threatened nation, whereas the Japanese users frame their arguments using individualistic language. Furthermore, these discourses indicate that conservatives are appropriating the language of feminism, as they saw a high level of participation from conservatives, that is, online nationalists in China and online right-wingers in Japan. Furthermore, while Chinese nationalists predominantly attacked white leftists for being brainwashed by the contemporary extremes of Western (mainly US) liberalism, the Japanese online right-wingers created three other targets: the Japanese leftist political parties, the global liberals, and the Chinese Communist Party. The power relations between China, the West, and Japan implied in these trans-exclusionary discourses call for an intersectional interrogation into how trans identity and politics, with all the phobias and patchworks of "truth," play a part in shaping and linking gender/sexuality politics to broader East Asian geopolitics.

References

Boylan, B. M., McBeath, J., & Wang, B. (2021). US–China relations: Nationalism, the trade war, and COVID-19. *Fudan Journal of the Humanities and Social Sciences, 14*, 23–40. https://doi.org/10.1007/s40647-020-00302-6.

Disgraced ex-Olympics chief Yoshiro Mori delivers another sexist remark. (2021, May 27). *The Japan Times.* https://www.japantimes.co.jp/news/2021/03/27/national/mori-sexist-remark-women/.

Fang, K., & Rapnikova, M. (2018). Demystifying "little pink": The creation and evolution of a gendered label for nationalistic activists in China. *New Media & Society, 20*(6), 2162–2185. https://doi.org.10.1177/1461444817731923.

Fuentes, A. (2022, May 12). Opinion: Biological science rejects the sex binary, and that's good for humanity. *The Scientist.* https://www.the-scientist.com/news-opinion/biological-science-rejects-the-sex-binary-and-that-s-good-for-humanity-70008.

Fujitaka, K. (2021). Posuto feminizumu toshite no toransu? Senda Yuki "'Onna' no kyōkaisen o hiki naosu" o yomitoku [Trans as postfeminism? Reading Senda Yuki's "Redrawing the boundaries of 'woman'"]. *Jendā kenkyū: Ochanomizu Daigaku jendā kenkyū sentā nenpō, 24*, 171–187.

Fukunaga, G. (2017). "LGBT furendorī na Taiwan" no tanjō [The emergence of an "LGBT-friendly Taiwan"]. In K. Sechiyama (Ed.), *Jendā to sekushuariti de miru Higashi Ajia* [Gender and sexuality in East Asia] (pp. 187–225). Keisō Shobō.

Fukunaga, G. (2022). Feminisuto to hoshu no kimyōna "rentai": Kankoku no toransu haijo gensetsu o chūshin ni [The absurd "solidarity" between feminists and conservatives: On trans-exclusionary discourses in South Korea]. *Jendā shigaku, 18*, 75–85.

Gan, N. (2022, June 14). *"This could happen to any of us": Graphic video of men stomping on a woman's head shake China to the core.* CNN. https://edition.cnn.com/2022/06/13/china/china-tang shan-restaurant-gender-violence-intl-hnk-mic/index.html.

Guo, L. (2018). Tongzhi solidarity under Chinese authoritarian government: A case study of the Beijing LGBT Center. *Komaba Journal of Asian Studies, the University of Tokyo, 14*, 75–105.

Guo, L. (2021). Owaru eizu, kenkōna Chūgoku: China AIDS Walk o jireini Chūgoku ni okeru gei/eizu undō o saikōsuru [End AIDS for a healthy China: Rethinking gay/AIDS activism in China through a case study of the China AIDS Walk]. *Journal of the Women's Studies Association of Japan, 28*, 12–33.

Heggie, V. (2017). *Subjective sex: Science, medicine and sex tests in sports.* Routledge.

Hildebrandt, T. (2013). *Social organizations and the authoritarian state in China.* Cambridge University Press.

Itani, S. (2021). *"Tai'ikukai-kei joshi" no poritikusu: Shintai, jendā, sekushuariti* [The politics of sports girls: Body, gender and sexuality]. Kansai University Press.

"Kachigumi no onnna koroshitaku naru": Odakyū-sen shishō yōgisha ga kyojutsu ["I want to kill all the women in the winners' group": The Odakyu stabbings suspect confesses]. (2021, August 7). *Sankei shinbun.* https://web.archive.org/web/20210808121754/https://www.sankei.com/article/20210807-ABNQ34UNXFO4XLSEN6BXBFF4S4.

Jones, C., & Slater, J. (2020). The toilet debate: Stalling trans possibilities and defending "women's protected spaces." In R. Pearce, S. Erikainen, & B. Vincent (Eds.), *TERF wars: Feminism and the fight for transgender futures* (pp. 4–24). SAGE.

King, G., Pan, J., & Roberts, M. How censorship in China allows government criticism but silences collective expression. *American Political Science Review, 107*(2), 326–343. https://doi.org/10.1017/S0003055413000014.

Korolczuk, E., & Graff, A. (2018). Gender as "ebola from Brussels": The anticolonial frame and the rise of illiberal populism. *Signs: Journal of Women in Culture and Society, 43*(4), 797–821. https://doi.org/10.1086/696691.

Koyama, E. (2006). Whose feminism is it anyway? The unspoken racism of the trans inclusion debate. In S. Stryker & S. Whittle (Eds.), *The transgender studies reader* (pp. 698–705). Routledge.

Laurel Hubbard: First transgender athlete to compete at Olympics. (2021, June 21). BBC News. https://www.bbc.com/news/world-asia-57549653.

Man, out to kill "happy women," nabbed over random Tokyo train attack. (2021, August 7) Kyodo News. https://english.kyodonews.net/news/2021/08/0f907d5a1ae8-10-passengers-stabbed-or-punched-on-tokyo-train-suspect-arrested.html.

McCurry, J. (2021, February 4). Tokyo 2020 chief pressed to resign after saying women talked too much at meetings. *The Guardian.* https://www.theguardian.com/sport/2021/feb/04/tokyo-2020-chief-pressed-to-resign-after-saying-women-talked-too-much-at-meetings.

Moore, M. (2019, January 24). *Gender ideology? Up yours!* https://chican3ry.medium.com/gender-ideology-up-yours-470575a5311a.

Nagayoshi, K. (2019). Netto uyoku to wa dareka? Netto uyoku no kiteiyōin [Who are the internet right-wingers: Defining factors]. In N. Higuchi (Ed.), *Netto uyoku to wa nanika* [What is an internet right-winger?]. Seikyūsha.

Oi, M. (2021, June 12). *Tokyo Olympics: Why people are afraid to show support for the Games.* BBC News. https://www.bbc.com/news/world-asia-57395010.

Pearce, R., Erikainen, S., & Vincent, B. (2020). TERF wars: An introduction. In R. Pearce, S. Erikainen, & B. Vincent (Eds.), *TERF wars: Feminism and the fight for transgender futures* (pp. 4–24). SAGE.

Rofel, L. (2007). *Desiring China: Experiments in neoliberalism, sexuality, and public culture.* Duke University Press.

Senda, Y. (2020). "Onna" no kyōkaisen o hiki naosu: "Tāfu" o meguru tairitsu o koete [Redrawing the boundaries of "woman": Beyond the "TERF" conflict]. *Gendai shisō: Feminizumu no genzai* [Special issue], March.

Sieg, L. (2021, February 12). *Japan political "village mentality" pierced as Tokyo Olympics Mori set to resign.* Reuters. https://www.reuters.com/lifestyle/sports/japan-political-village-mentality-pierced-tokyo-olympics-mori-set-resign-2021-02-12.

Smith, T. (2021, July 23). *Tokyo Olympics: Transgender Olympian Laurel Hubbard's journey to "just be me."* Stuff. https://www.stuff.co.nz/sport/olympics/nz-olympic-team/125523731/tokyo-olympics-transgender-olympian-laurel-hubbards-journey-to-just-be-me.

StatCounter (2023). *Social media stats in Japan: Mar 2022–Mar 2023.* Last modified March 2023. https://gs.statcounter.com/social-media-stats/all/japan.

Statista. (2022). *Most popular social networks worldwide as of January 2022, ranked by monthly active users.* Retrieved August 1, 2022, from https://www.statista.com/statistics/272014/global-social-networks-ranked-by-number-of-users.

Tokyo train stabbing leaves at least 10 injured as Olympics wind up. (2021, August 7). ABC News. https://www.abc.net.au/news/2021-08-07/japan-stabbing-attack-olympics-tokyo-train-targeted-women/100358186.

US Department of Justice. (2022, September). *Criminal victimization, 2021.* https://bjs.ojp.gov/content/pub/pdf/cv21.pdf.

Wells, A. (2021, August 2). *USA shot-putter Raven Saunders makes "X" gesture in support of oppressed people.* Bleacher Report. https://bleacherreport.com/articles/10009386-usa-shot-putter-raven-saunders-makes-x-gesture-in-support-of-oppressed-people.

Yamaguchi, T. (2019). Netto uyoku to feminizumu [Internet right-wingers and feminism]. In N. Higuchi (Ed.), *Netto uyoku to wa nanika* [What is an internet right-winger?]. Seikyūsha.

Yang, T., & Fang, K. (2021). How dark corners collude: A study on an online Chinese alt-right community. *Information, Communication & Society, 26*(2), 441–458.

Stefan Würrer

Transcending the gendered body? Transphobia and the construction of the self in the writing of Shōno Yoriko

In July 2022, Japanese writer Shōno Yoriko (2022a) declared in a blog post that she would vote for Liberal Democratic Party (LDP) politician Yamatani Eriko in the upcoming upper house election. This came as a surprise to many, as Shōno is considered one of Japan's leading feminist writers, who in the past has publicly supported the Japanese Communist Party (JCP) (Shōno, 2017a, 2017b, 2018, 2019, 2022a), and Yamatani is a right-wing social conservative with a long-standing record of opposing feminist activism and gender equality legislation (A. Shimizu, 2022, p. 381). Why this sudden declaration of support? And was it really out of character?

In the first section of this paper, I examine this alliance between Shōno and Yamatani in light of the similarities between their trans-exclusionary discourses. Since 2020, Shōno (2020a, 2020b, 2020c, 2020d, 2021, 2022a, 2022b, 2022c, 2022d) has published numerous blog posts and essays, in which, similar to Yamatani, she framed trans[1] women as a potential threat to women's safety, denying them the right to self-identification and bodily autonomy based on a biological essentialist understanding of assigned sex as gender. Shōno, in other words, has come out as a trans-exclusionary radical feminist (TERF).[2] I argue that this transphobic alliance is both part of a global phenomenon and symptomatic of historical problems within Japanese feminism.

In the latter sections of this paper, I revisit Shōno's fiction. I show that despite her recent insistence on biological sex as a natural and inescapable foundation of

---

1 "Trans" refers to people whose gender identity differs from the sex they were assigned at birth. While for some trans people, transitioning – that is, aligning their gender presentation, expression, and/or physical attributes with their gender identity – is essential, not all can or do undergo medical or surgical procedures as part of their transition, or transition at all, for financial, medical, ideological, or other reasons. In addition, I use the term "cross-gender" to refer to instances where gender presentation or expression does not match gender identity or assigned sex more generally.

2 According to Christen Williams (2016), this term started being used in online feminist communities around 2008 to distinguish between feminists who take an exclusionary stance toward trans women and those who do not (p. 254). "Radical" refers to the genealogical connection of this exclusionary stance with certain factions of 1970s radical feminism. While Shōno (2020c) has criticized the use of TERF as derogatory, in this paper I follow Williams' (2016) use of the term to refer to contemporary feminists who are opposed to recognizing trans women as women (p. 255).

gender identity, her novels actually are inundated with characters who are struggling with their assigned sex and gender identity, and attempting to move beyond their gendered body and the gender binary. However, this is not necessarily a contradiction. As I will argue, Shōno's trans-exclusionary writing, as a manifestation of transphobia, similar to misogyny and homophobia, can be understood as the performative process of reestablishing a coherent and fixed female identity through the abjection of trans women as the Other of feminism. Shōno's fictional representation of the female body, which oscillates between identification and rejection, can be read as another facet of this process.

1 Unholy alliances: Trans-exclusionary discourse as symbolic "superglue"

Shōno Yoriko made her literary debut in 1981 with the novel *Gokuraku* (*Paradise*), for which she received literary magazine *Gunzō*'s New Writer Award. She has since accumulated numerous other awards, including the *Noma Prize for New Writers* in 1991 for *Nanimo shitenai* (*Doing Nothing*), the prestigious Akutagawa Prize for *Taimusurippu kombināto* (*Timeslip Complex*) in 1994, and the Itō Sei Award for *Kompīra* (*Kompira*) in 2005, making her one of the most decorated Japanese authors of the Heisei period (1989–2019). Her novels have been lauded for their feminist interrogations of the interplay between neoliberalism, sexism, patriarchy, and cultural representation in postindustrial, post-bubble Japan (e.g. Asano, 2018; Bouterey, 1996; Ebihara, 2012; Kotani, 2002; Naikai, 2006; Nakamura, 1999; Nitta, 2007; Noguchi-Amann, 2005; Noya, 1997; Tierney, 2010). These interrogations tend to be performed from the perspective of a socioeconomically marginalized female "I," whose attempts at opening up utopian pockets of self-affirmation and belonging in hostile environments – often through a dense and fantastic interweaving of embodied experience, memory, dreams, history, and religious and mythological motifs – form the core narrative movement of Shōno's otherwise rather plotless, experimental writing.

Yamatani, conversely, was a prominent figure during the so-called "gender-free" (*jendā furī*) backlash of the early 2000s, which targeted efforts by feminists, educators, and governmental agencies to free education from gender stereotypes as a scheme to destroy the traditional Japanese family through "the total erasure of cultural and biological differences between the sexes" (Yamaguchi, 2014, p. 559; see also A. Shimizu, 2020, pp. 90–92; Yamada, 2022, p. 502). More recently, she was at the center of a group of LDP politicians who opposed their party's plans for an alternative to the Draft Bill on the Elimination of Discrimination based on SOGI

(LGBT Sabetsu Kaishōhōan), which had been submitted by four opposition parties to the Diet in 2016. The LDP rejected the opposition's bill, which asked for the legal protection of LGBT people from human rights violations. Instead, it announced in 2018 that it would submit the Draft Bill to Promote Understanding for LGBT People (LGBT Rikai Zōshin Hōan), which aims only to cultivate acceptance toward LGBT people and a more tolerant society but lacks any concrete sanctions for failures to abide by its vague guidelines (Carland-Ecchavaria, 2022, p. 5).

The opposition of Yamatani and other social conservative LDP politicians to the Draft Bill to Promote Understanding for LGBT People centered on the phrase "discrimination on the basis of sexual orientation or gender identity is unacceptable" (*seiteki shikō ya seijinin o riyū to suru sabetsu wa yurusarenai*).[3] Owing to their concern that it would open the door for "legal action to punish or prohibit any speech deemed 'discriminatory'" (Carland-Ecchavaria, 2022, p. 17; see also Nikaidō, 2021, p. 14), the amended draft that was finally submitted to the Diet in 2023 stated, "there should be no unjust discrimination" (*futōna sabetsu wa atte wa naranai*), thereby implying the existence of "just discrimination" (Matsuoka, 2023a).

Yamatani and other LDP politicians also rejected the term *seijinin* to express the concept of "gender identity" because, as Japanese studies scholar Patrick Carland-Ecchavaria (2022) summarized, "it sought to legitimize transgender identities they deemed 'threats' to women" (p. 17). As noted by activist writer Matsuoka Sōshi (2023a), *seijinin* has long been used in Japanese judiciary and governmental documents to translate "gender identity." However, in recent years it has become a symbolic term that represents a shift from the medicalized and pathologizing understanding of trans people codified in the 2003 Law for the Handling of Gender in the Special Cases of People with Gender Identity Disorder (Seidōitsusei Shōgaisha no Seibetsu no Atsukai no Tokurei ni Kansuru Hō; hereafter "GID Law"), to a focus on the lived experiences, self-identification, and human rights of trans people. This reflects a broader global movement toward depathologization that can be seen, for instance, in the removal of "gender identity disorder" from the World Health Organization's manual of diagnoses in 2020 and the Science Council of Japan's (2020) subsequent recommendation to replace the GID Law with legislation that allows trans people to change their legal gender without having to undergo invasive medical procedures.

It is this shift that moral conservatives such as Yamatani oppose. Their rejection of the term *seijinin* is, in fact, an attempt to exclude all traces of depathologization terminology from official discourse. Under their pressure, the wording in the proposed Law to Promote Understanding for LGBT People has been changed

---

3 Unless otherwise indicated, all translations from Japanese into English in this paper are my own.

to *seidōitsusei* (Matsuoka, 2023b), which mirrors the pathologizing language of the GID Law.[4] The GID Law, as queer and trans studies scholar Yamada Hidenobu (2022) emphasized, was "acceptable for moral conservatives" (p. 502) because it stipulates requirements for the legal change of one's gender that effectively prevent the de facto legal recognition of same-sex marriage and the emergence of "male mothers" and "female fathers" who, through their potential gender ambiguity, could expose the gender binary as the normative fantasy that it is: Trans people need to be diagnosed with "gender identity disorder" by two medical practitioners; are not allowed to be married or to have underage children; and have to undergo expensive gender reassignment surgery and sterilization (see also Norton, 2013, p. 597). The official use of terminology such as *seijinin*, therefore, does not pose a threat to cis women through a sudden increase in self-identified trans women using public bathrooms, as Yamatani wants the public to believe (Ibuki, 2021; "Jimin Yamatani-shi," 2021; Nikaidō, 2021, p. 12; Okuno, 2021); in fact, self-identified trans women have always been using public bathrooms with great caution because of the long history of violence *toward* them (Halberstam, 1998, pp. 20–29; Komiya, 2019, p. 137). What is threatened, rather, is the deterministic and essentialist understanding of assigned sex as gender that lies at the core of Yamatani's conservative worldview.

This worldview is shared by Shōno. Ignoring more than half a century of feminist theory that followed Simone de Beauvoir's *The Second Sex* (1949), Shōno (2022d, p. 7) has rejected the concept of a socially constructed gender identity as unscientific "idealism" (*yuishinron*), in her attempt to exclude trans women from the category of "women." For Shōno, there is no "becoming" in being a woman. You are either born one or you aren't one. Only in the "extremely rare" cases of people suffering from "gender identity disorder" should they be allowed to live as women, given that they fulfill the conditions stipulated by the GID Law (Shōno, 2022b, p. 31). Those assigned male at birth who, for financial, medical, ideological, or other reasons do not undergo gender-affirming surgery but identify and live as women, as well as nonbinary persons, are potentially criminal usurpers of women's spaces (Shōno, 2022b, pp. 33–34). Hence her opposition to the term *seijinin:* it would legitimize their existence, which in turn would threaten the social order of Japan (Shōno, 2022b, p. 37). Comparing the inclusion of the expression *sei-*

---

4 The draft bill has since been amended several times and now uses the transliterated term *jendā aidentitī* for "gender identity." It also states that any efforts made to promote understanding toward LGBT people must consider the comfort (*anshin*) of all citizens based on guidelines the government will provide. This has been criticized as effectively hindering the bill's objective, since any action deemed too radical could be rejected for fear of offending the majority (Matsuoka, 2023b; Satō, 2023).

jinin in the aforementioned draft bill to serving someone a "poisoned bun" (*dokumanjū*), Shōno (2022b) argued that recognizing trans women's rights to self-identification would lead to the disappearance of such concepts as "the female body" or "women's rights," in addition to "women's sports, women's changing rooms, women's toilets and, of course, in the case of Japan, women's baths" (pp. 31–34). She decided to vote for Yamatani, because she was the only politician "who told the truth" about this "erasure of women" (Shōno, 2022a).

Fellow writer Li Kotomi (2022) and literary critic Mizugami Aya (2022) have pointed out the manifold factual errors and inconsistencies in, as well as the discriminatory nature of, Shōno's trans-exclusionary feminist writing. Here, I will further scrutinize Shōno's transphobic views, as well as her alliance with Yamatani, in light of how they point to issues within Japanese feminism and call for a critical re-examination of her fiction.

As queer studies scholar Shimizu Akiko (2022) has pointed out, the framing of trans people and trans-inclusive discourse as a threat to society has become a symbolic "super glue" in recent years. Similar to the threat perceived in so-called "gender ideology," this framing enables broad alliances that unite people across political lines by redirecting their discontent with the socioeconomic and political status quo to what they see as the global libertarian elite's prioritization of peripheral and ultimately dangerous identity politics over local people's material needs (Grzebalska et al., 2017; A. Shimizu, 2022, pp. 384–385). The difference between the anti-gender ideology and trans-exclusionary discourses is that the former has mostly targeted feminists and their agenda, while the latter increasingly includes and is included by feminists. Shōno's transphobic writing and her support of Yamatani, as Shimizu Akiko (2022) argued, is a local variant of this global trend (pp. 386–388).

This global "superglue" dimension is also evident in Shōno's (2022b) conspiracy-theory-like framing of trans depathologization as an international "movement to annihilate women's voices and bodies" (*nyotai josei no zanmetsu undō*) (p. 38), which is supported by the likes of George Soros and forced upon the unknowing "common people" (*shomin*) of Japan (Shōno, 2022d, p. 5). This claim, which has antisemitic undertones (Center for Extremism, 2023; Joaquina, 2021; Joyce, 2021, p. 227; Moore, 2020; Rabinowitz, 2022; Yudelson, 2021), has been circulated among conservatives and TERFs since at least the 2010s (see, e.g., Riddell, 2016). Further, Shōno (2022d) has cited Women's Declaration International, a feminist organization founded by leading TERF Sheila Jeffreys, as one of the main sources of her transphobic arguments (pp. 16–7). She has also openly expressed solidarity with fellow TERF writer J. K. Rowling (Shōno, 2022b, p. 28; 2020c). Both Rowling and Jeffreys have been criticized for their direct and indirect support of far-right conservatives (Burns, 2019; Michaelson, 2018; Urquhart, 2023).

At the same time, the figure of Yamatani connects Shōno's transphobic writing with the heteronormative, cisgenderist discourse that dominated the "gender free" backlash in Japan and facilitated the passing of the GID Law in 2003. Those at the center of the backlash claimed that feminists were out to destroy the traditional Japanese family, and ultimately the nation, by erasing biological differences between the sexes and turning underage girls and boys into homosexuals or "genderless beings" (*chūsei ningen*) (Kazama, 2007, p. 26; Yamada, 2022, p. 502). Preventing the emergence of the latter is what the conditions stipulated for the legal change of one's gender in the GID Law effectively do. It is also the reason for Shōno's support of Yamatani. Importantly, feminist rebuttals dismissed the *chūsei ningen* rhetoric as mere fiction. That is, they negated the existence of trans and nonbinary persons, and effectively excluded them from feminist discourse (Kazama, 2007, pp. 28–31; A. Shimizu, 2007, p. 504; Yamaguchi, 2014, p. 570).

It is in this history of transphobic rhetoric on both sides of the backlash that we find, as Yamada (2022, p. 503) argued, the local roots of the recent trans-exclusionary (feminist) discourse in Japan. In other words, feminist discourse in Japan has been complicit in the exclusion of trans people since at least the early 2000s. Shōno's recent writing is symptomatic of this. It is the consequence of the indifference toward this history by the majority of feminist activists and academics in Japan, who continue to ignore, in Shimizu Akiko's (2020) words, the current attacks on trans people "as peripheral events not worth their passing comments" (p. 102). This historical dimension of Shōno's transphobic writing demonstrates, if anything, that in order for Japanese feminism not to become complicit again with social conservative rhetoric and undermine its long-lasting efforts to interrogate and liberate women from precisely the biologically essentialist notions of gender that are now employed to exclude trans women, it is time to build intersectional alliances and to rethink, as feminist scholar Iino Yuriko (2020) put it, "the strategy adopted in the fight against the backlash" of the early 2000s (p. 88).

2 The ambivalent portrayal of the gendered body in Shōno Yoriko's fiction

This problem of undermining one's own efforts to interrogate gender norms can also be discerned in Shōno's fiction. Her novels are full of ambivalent and ambiguous portrayals of the female body. They feature a number of characters who distance themselves from, reject, and at times transcend, the gendered body or the gender binary. How are we to understand these seemingly non-normative characters in light of Shōno's (2022d, pp. 7, 10; 2022b, pp. 35–36) biological essentialism and transphobia?

As literary scholar Shimizu Yoshinori (2003, pp. 10–12) pointed out, Shōno's novels of the 1980s feature a male third-person protagonist – such as in the above-mentioned *Gokuraku* (1981), as well as *Taisai* (*The Festival*, 1981) and *Kōtei* (*The Emperor*, 1984) – or a gender-ambiguous third-person narrator – such as in *Kaijū* (*The Sea Monster*, 1984) and *Yume no shitai* (*Dreaming of Dead Bodies*, 1990). Only in *Ise-shi, Haruchi* (*Ise City, Haruchi*, 1991) does Shōno begin to use a female first-person narrator, which has since become the dominant modus operandi of her fiction. He argued that the early male protagonists can be understood as Shōno's dis-identification with, or her rejection of, her female gender, which she then gradually overcame during the late 1980s (Y. Shimizu, 2003, pp. 69–70).

This seems to echo Shōno's own understanding of her early work. In a series of conversations with fellow writer Matsu'ura Rieko in 1994, she characterized her use of male protagonists as a kind of cross-gender performance to liberate herself from stereotypical expectations toward women's writing, such as a focus on the female body or portrayals of romantic relationship with men. A male protagonist, she said, allowed her to freely explore more abstract issues (Matsu'ura & Shōno, 1994a, pp. 63–64; 1994b, pp. 123–125). Shōno (2022d, pp. 13–14) reiterated this interpretation over twenty years later in one of her recent trans-related essays, explaining her use of male protagonists in the early 1980s as the result of the double-bind of experiencing discrimination as a woman writer not only when rejecting, but also when complying, with these expectations.

Yet this dis-identification seems unresolved. Shōno's novels after the 1990s repeatedly feature characters who struggle with their gender identity. Moreover, the reason for this struggle might not just be societal gender norms in the context of literature, but the complicated relation with their gendered body. In *Kōtei*, the unnamed male protagonist dresses as a woman when outside of his apartment (Shōno, 1984, pp. 222, 250, 256). More precisely, he dresses in clothes similar to that of an old woman that he supposedly killed and robbed earlier (Würrer, 2019, pp. 112–114). While one could, as Shimizu Yoshinori (2003) did, interpret his cross-dressing as a sign of Shōno's "return" (*fukki*) to her "original" female self (p. 70), which Shōno had to kill off in order to survive as a writer, there remains one issue. Even if we accept Shimizu's biographical reading of the cross-dressing in *Kōtei* as a sign for Shōno's newfound acceptance of her female self, there are *two* bodies: that of the dead woman and that of the male protagonist. It is over his *male* body, that *Kōtei*'s protagonist wears women's clothes. That is, the performance of femininity that Shimizu reads as a sign of her renewed identification as a woman is performed on a male body. What implications does this split have for Shōno's supposed identification as a woman later?

3 *Nanimo shitenai* (1991): Talking bodies and the desire for national belonging

In *Nanimo shitenai* we can find traces of this bodily duality. This novel is set during a period of national holidays following the death of the Shōwa emperor and the subsequent ascension to the throne of the Heisei emperor in 1989. It portrays, as literary scholar Asano Urara (2018) showed, how the process of watching the media spectacle surrounding the enthronement becomes the trigger for a reconnection with Japanese society for the socially withdrawn female protagonist (pp. 191–192). Seeing the enthronement festivities on television, the novel's protagonist, who up until then had retreated from society and lived secluded in her apartment, suddenly feels "the oddly palpable sensation of being a citizen of this country" (Shōno, 2007, p. 156), and the wish to go outside and see for herself what she saw on television, to "thoroughly watch in utmost normalcy the things that ordinary people watch" (*futsū no hito ga futsū ni miru mono o futsūsa o tettei shite mitsukusu*) (Shōno, 2007, pp. 168–169). It incites a renewed interest in the world outside of her apartment, a reconnection that she hopes will lead to her own "total [social] acceptance" (*nanimo kamo ga kōtei sarete shimau*) (Shōno, 2007, p. 168). However, the expression "citizen" (*kokumin*) is rendered not in *kanji* (Chinese characters), but in the phonetic script *katakana* used, among other things, for non-Japanese words, which hints, as Asano (2018) argued, at a simultaneous distancing from this newfound feeling of national belonging (pp. 177–178).

Subsequent events mirror this ambivalence. When boarding a train to visit her parents in the city of Ise, the protagonist realizes that some of the royal family are on the same train in order to participate in the new emperor's first visit to Ise Shrine. She refrains from standing up to catch a glimpse of them and disavows her excitement by emphasizing that in contrast to the other starstruck travelers, she already knew that this train connects via Nagoya to Ise (Shōno, 2007, p. 211). This attempt to differentiate herself fails, however, as soon as she reaches Nagoya, where the excessive police presence at the train station makes her feel like a "powerless commoner" (*muryokuna shōshimin*).

Later that day, when watching the news at her parents' house, she worries about the foreign press not accurately reporting about the historical roots and intricate details of this ceremonial visit (Shōno, 2007, p. 222), a fear she had already shown while watching the enthronement festivities (Shōno, 2007, p. 158). As Asano (2018) emphasized, both this knowledge and fear of the protagonist indicate an interest in, if not an identification with, these events and the royal family (p. 186). Similar to the scene on the train, however, the protagonist immediately adds that what really fascinates her are simply the shoes and clothes of the royals, as if to gloss over and disavow this interest. She does realize that she is "absent-mindedly [*boketa kokoro de*] looking at nothing but fabrics," "despite not knowing the first thing about sewing" (Shōno, 2007, p. 234), but can't help watching. *Nanimo shitenai*'s protagonist continues to be thoroughly, if not always consciously, obsessed with royal events. The novel then follows her back home to Tokyo, where it ends with her realization that she will have to move out of her apartment because the building is being made accessible to students only.

Asano (2018) contrasted the ambivalent obsession of *Nanimo shitenai*'s protagonist with post-WWII discourses on the irrelevance of the Japanese emperor. She argued that whereas these discourses see indifference as the proper reaction of the modern Japanese citizen toward this merely symbolic figure, the protagonist's self-contradictory obsession with the enthronement and the subsequent festivities exposes the limitations of such a view (Asano, 2018, pp. 191–192). Asano did not specify what kind of limitations these are, but if we take into account the reason why this ambivalent reconnection was necessary in the first place, they become clear.

As Asano (2018, pp. 174–175) has pointed out, the protagonist has withdrawn from society because of her mother constantly negating her efforts to become a writer by lambasting her for "doing nothing" – not marrying, not having children, or earning enough money (Shōno, 2007, pp. 149–150, 161–2, 172). Given the protagonist's somewhat sarcastic characterization of her mother as a "proper citizen" (*seijōna shimin*) (Shōno, 2007, p. 160), this rejection is not simply an issue of a complicated mother–daughter relationship but can be understood as representative of the protagonist's experience of Japanese society at large. By extension, her ambivalent reconnection with society via the enthronement festivities can then be read as the manifestation of her desire to belong to, and simultaneously keep a cautious distance from, a society whose continuous rejection has driven her into isolation. If anything, it exposes the display of indifference toward the symbolic emperor as a potential privilege: a rejection possible for those who already feel a certain form of social belonging, which the protagonist lacks because of her outsider status as a young aspiring woman writer.

This gendered aspect of national belonging is further emphasized during a scene on the train from Tokyo to Ise. Having realized that the royal family might be on the same train, the protagonist is suddenly reminded of Mishima Yukio's novel *Kamen no kokuhaku* (*Confessions of a Mask*, 1949), which she had read as a teenager in an anthology of Japanese literature. The association is, of course, not that far-fetched, considering Mishima's nationalistic attempt to overthrow the post-WWII constitution and reinstall the emperor as a living god, which famously ended with his ritual suicide in 1970. While the protagonist of *Nanimo shitenai* mentions Mishima's suicide, the reference to the anthology suggests that Mishima here functions not only as a political figure, but also as a representative of Japanese literature. As if to reject this status, the protagonist goes on to say that Mishima was a writer whom she barely read (Shōno, 2007, 208). There is only one scene in *Kamen no kokuhaku* that she remembers: the beginning. There, the narrator – whom she sees as an alter ego of Mishima (Shōno, 2007, p. 209) – remembers his younger self dressing up as the female magician Shōkyokusai Tenkatsu (1886–1944) (Mishima, 2017, pp. 19–21).[5]

Nanimo shitenai's protagonist compares this scene with her own experience of wearing a petticoat and dressing up as a queen with her female cousins. She concludes that both performances of femininity are rather different and that she found the cross-dressing in *Kamen no kokuhaku* "sickening, cool, and horrifying" (*kimochi waruku kakkoyoku osoroshī*) (Shōno, 2007, p. 209). The reason for them being different, she emphasizes, is not necessarily the gender (*seibetsu*) of the performer. What she finds problematic is not that the narrator of *Kamen no kokuhaku* was a boy and she a girl, but rather the "distance between matter [*busshitsu*] and the human . . . the way I perceive my body [*jibun no nikutai*]" (Shōno, 2007, p. 210). What does she mean by this?

In the eyes of *Nanimo shitenai*'s protagonist, this scene from *Kamen no kokuhaku* is not simply the portrayal of an innocent act of a child playing dress-ups. It is the memory of a man who retrospectively draws focus away from the act of cross-dressing to the peripheral phallic objects with which he armed himself before appearing in front of his family – "a rod-shaped silver flashlight" and an "old-fashioned engraved fountain pen" (Mishima, 2017, p. 29) – in the attempt to disavow his "aversion toward dressing up as a woman" and foreground his masculinity (Shōno, 2007, p. 209). That is, what she finds "sickening ... and horrifying" is that he brings up this episode of cross-dressing only to then fetishistically distance himself from it.[6] Femininity, in other words, is shown as something to be rejected. One feels tempted to agree, given that Mishima (2017, pp. 10–16) not only places this episode right after an almost erotic explanation about the roots of the narrator's fas-

---

5 In fact, it is only through the name Tenkatsu that the reader can discern that the novel in question is *Kamen no kokuhaku*, for the title is not explicitly mentioned in *Nanimo shitenai*.

6 This is an argument similar to that of feminist theoretician Carol-Ann Tyler (2003), who argued that not every performance of cross-dressing necessarily questions or subverts the gender binary. Tyler pointed out that, similar to parody and pastiche, cross-dressing is context dependent and in certain cases simply re-emphasizes the ground – the body – as the "original" onto which the "fake" figure – the cross-gender performance – is added, thus reproducing the idea of non-normative gender expressions as an "inferior" copy. In addition, it can function fetishistically, as it highlights the mastery of the performer who flexibly puts on and off the masquerade as if they were not subject to, but rather exist in the beyond of the gender binary (Tyler, 2003, pp. 94–95).

cination and identification with underclass masculinity and his disgust with cross-dressing women, but also portrays it as a source of feelings of shame and guilt.

If this fetishistic distancing is indeed why she rejects that scene, then the protagonist of *Nanimo shitenai* is arguably trying to point out, via the comparison with her own memory of playing dress-up, that the narrator of *Kamen no kokuhaku* can retrospectively reject femininity, whereas she would like to but cannot. This is suggested by her referring to his cross-gender performance as not just "sickening" and "horrifying," but also "cool" (Shōno, 2007, p. 209). She rejects *and* desires it. But why can't she?

The text does not provide us with a conclusive answer to this question, but two hints hidden elsewhere in the text suggest that the reason might be the aforementioned "distance between matter and the human," her own perception of "her physical body" (Shōno, 2007, p. 210). Thinking about the difficulties she had of fitting into society, she remembers taking a walk one day and being mistaken for an older man (*ojisan*) by elementary school girls, complaining: "I don't know why, but children sometimes perceive me as an older man. My clothes might be a factor, but my physique [*taikei*] clearly is that of a woman!" (Shōno, 2007, p. 137). While her gender expression might be ambiguous and she does only speak of a womanly "physique," not explicitly of a female body (*karada, shintai*), her frustration with being misgendered indicates that she understands herself as a woman and desires to be perceived as such.

This seems to be confirmed by another scene in which she talks about the physical discomfort she feels in her arms because of her allergies (Shōno, 2007, p. 213). Later in the novel she compares this ache to an "evil spirit" (*akurei*) running rampage in her elbow (Shōno, 2007, p. 217). The first time she mentions it, however, she calls this "evil spirit" a "male voice she is hearing from inside her elbow" and jokingly interprets it as the manifestation of her childhood desire to have been a man in her past life (*zensei wa otoko da to iu, kochira no yōji no ganbō*) (Shōno, 2007, p. 145). Her body's voice, so to speak, seems to be at least partially male. However, by framing this ambiguity as a child's dream about a previous life, the protagonist defines her present adult self, including the body that is speaking to her in this scene, as female.

Hence, on the one hand she identifies as a woman and wants to be seen as such, and on the other she desires, as the adjective "cool" suggests, – if not to be male, *not anymore* – a distance from the performance of femininity similar to that in *Kamen no kokuhaku*. However, whereas such a distancing for Mishima does not jeopardize his inclusion in the Japanese literary canon (i.e., the anthology), it is more complicated for her. As she has repeatedly experienced, distance from the performance of femininity, deviating from what society considers feminine, means being rejected as "doing nothing." In that way, *Nanimo shitenai* hints at something similar to Shōno's use of a male protagonist in the early 1980s: the difficulty of carving out an epistemological niche of existence for a female identity beyond societal gender norms.

But the bodily ambiguity remains. While the male body beneath the cross-gender performance in *Kōtei* seems to have transformed into a female one in *Nanimo shitenai*, it still makes itself heard. One might even argue that the protagonist of *Nanimo shitenai* is performing a disavowal similar to that which she accuses the narrator of *Kamen no kokuhaku* of: hinting toward the potential experience of her body as (partially) male, while simultaneously disavowing it as a childhood fantasy of a previous life.

4 The strange temporalities of "gender dysphoria"

In fact, Shōno herself has repeatedly stated that during her childhood and early adolescence she believed herself to be male (Matsu'ura & Shōno, 1994b, p. 177; Shiraishi & Shōno, 2008, p. 191; Shōno, 2008, p. 6). Most recently, in her trans-related essays, she wrote about this experience of "a male soul" (*otoko no tamashi*) trapped in a "female body" (*onna no karada*) (Shōno, 2022d, p. 13) in two different ways.

First, she explains it as a "fiction" (*fikushon*) that she clung to during her youth, because she thought "being a woman in itself is some sort of misfortune [*fugū*]" (Shōno, 2022d, p. 13). She felt it difficult to accept being a woman and to keep a distance from societal expectations about her gender. Thus, she escaped into the fantasy of being a man, using the masculine first-person pronoun *ore* and wearing male clothes (Shōno, 2022d, p. 13). She then suggests that the use of a male protagonist in her early novels can be understood as a literary manifestation of this escapist fantasy (Shōno, 2022d, pp. 13–14).

Later on, however, Shōno (2022b) describes this experience within the context of "gender dysphoria" (*seibetsu iwa*) (p. 37). She argues that the use of the term *seijinin* and the depathologization of trans people that it represents would lead to minors getting unnecessary and invasive gender-affirming medical treatments such as mastectomies. Speaking of "more and more children being sacrificed for the profits of big pharma" (p. 37), Shōno points out that she, too, has "struggled with her gender," but that she "has come to terms with [her] *body* without pursuing medical treatment" (p. 37, emphasis mine). In her eyes, "gender dysphoria during adolescence in most cases resolves itself on its own" (p. 37).

The term "gender dysphoria" is commonly defined as the "psychological distress that results from an incongruence between one's sex assigned at birth and one's gender identity" (American Psychiatric Association, 2022, p. 511) and tends to be used in medical contexts to explain the experience of being trans (Nihon Seishin Shinkei Gakkai Seidōitsusei-shōgai ni Kansuru Iinkai, 2018, pp. 9–10, 19, 21). Shōno's use of this expression and her substitution of "gender" with "body" as the cause of her struggles suggest that what she is describing here might not (just) be a struggle with societal expectations, but (also) stems from the *physical* sensation of her gender identity not matching her assigned sex. Nevertheless, she says she overcame it on her own. Thus, minors need no gender-affirming healthcare.

The common argument by TERFs that gender-affirming healthcare is unnecessary and harmful to minors[7] is reminiscent of homophobic discourses about gay people being a threat to children and the negation of non-normative sexual desires as "just a phase." Moreover, by focusing almost exclusively on mastectomies or gender-affirming surgeries (Shōno, 2022b, pp. 34–36), Shōno reduces trans people's transitioning process to invasive surgical procedures, which in Japan are not available to people under the age of eighteen in the first place (The Japanese Society of Psychiatry and Neurology, 2017; Nihon Seishin Shinkei Gakkai Seidōitsusei-shōgai ni Kansuru Iinkai, 2012, pp. 1262–1263). She also ignores the fact that in Japan hormonal treatment for minors is available over the age of fifteen only with parental consent and after a minimum of one year of medical observation (The Japanese Society of Psychiatry and Neurology, 2017). Besides, several studies have shown that access to gender-affirming healthcare can reduce the risk of suicides for trans and nonbinary youth and should not be dismissed if the well-being of minors is of primary concern (Adams et al., 2017; Allen, 2019; Bustos et al., 2021; Herman et al., 2019; Herman & O'Neill, 2021; Rafferty, 2018, p. 3; Tordoff et al., 2022; Turban et al. 2020).

In addition to these factual inconsistencies, there is another internal contradiction in Shōno's arguments. Though arguing that gender dysphoria resolves itself during adolescence, citing her own experience as proof, she also implies that her novels of the 1980s were in part an attempt to come to terms with precisely what she retrospectively (also) calls "gender dysphoria": her struggle with her gender and body. Born in 1956, Shōno was 25 years old when she published her first novel in 1981, and 35 when she published *Nanimo shitenai*, that is, far beyond adolescence. What should have just been a phase during her youth, according to Shōno's own logic, seems to have continued well into her twenties and thirties, or at least it occupied her thinking to the extent that it repeatedly manifested itself in her writing for years after that. This is further indicated by Shōno (2022d) herself stating that she dealt with the experience of a male soul trapped in a female body,

---

7 The feminist sociologist Senda Yūki (2023) recently made a similar claim.

her "soul's gender" (*kokoro no seibetsu*), also in later novels such as *Suishōnai seido* (*The World Within the Crystal*, 2003) and the aforementioned *Kompīra* (2005) (p. 14).

In *Suishōnai seido* the female protagonist Hieda awakens in a hospital of the all-female nation of Uramizumo, where she seems to have fled to escape the misogyny of her native Nihhon, a dystopian version of Japan. However, she doesn't quite feel at home in Uramizumo either. As I noted elsewhere: "She experiences herself harboring two contradictory minds. . . . one part of her is content with her new life, whereas the other rejects it and urges her to flee" (Würrer, 2022, p. 64). Among the various reasons the text offers for this ambivalent feeling of (non-)belonging, is her potential identification as male (Würrer, 2022, pp. 65–69). "In the worst case" she states, "I might have to say 'I am a man'" (Shōno, 2003, p. 114).

Since in the all-female Uramizumo being a man means being subject to incarceration, enslavement, and state-sanctioned murder (Shōno, 2003, pp. 25, 189–192, 207–232, 248), Hieda "had to hide" her "soul's truth" (Shōno, 2003, p. 114). But, instead of leaving Uramizumo or confronting the authorities, she ultimately buries that part of her:

> Having finished her feminist adaptation of Japanese creation myths, Hieda rewrites it one final time, this time not to justify the existence of a nation but to affirm her male self, "to write 'him' down, this man existing nowhere" (238). Expressing both the desire to become "him" and the impossibility of . . . living as a man in Uramizumo, Hieda writes: "This part of me, him, I place him there, on the shores of the underworld. In death I will become a man . . . [b]ut at that point, I won't be me any longer (248)" (Würrer, 2022, p. 68).

Suishōnai seido, in other words, can be read as an elegy: a burial song the protagonist writes for this part of her, for "him," for her male self.

Kompīra, then, can be understood as the attempt to overcome this split between life and death, female and male. It is also the first-person narrative of a female writer. Unlike *Suishōnai seido*, however, Shōno intentionally foregrounds the autobiographical nature of the narrator–protagonist, giving her the exact same birthday and birth city as herself: March 16, 1956, in Yokkaichi, Mie Prefecture (Shōno, 2010, pp. 9–10). In addition, she experiences continuous difficulties adapting to life in Japanese society. Like Shōno, the protagonist of *Kompīra* believed herself to be male, was treated as such by her family (Shōno, 2010, pp. 75–80), and until adolescence expected that "eventually these breasts would fall off and reveal a magnificent masculine physique" (Shōno, 2010, pp. 185). She started working out and engaged with girls in a courteous manner because she thought that this is what is expected of an "accomplished man" (*deki no ii otoko*) (Shōno, 2010, p. 125). Her body, however, continued to develop into that of a woman, leading the people around her to increasingly treat her according to societal norms about what a woman is supposed to be, which resulted in a fundamental sense of (non) belonging (Shōno, 2010, pp. 185–189)

Kompīra tells this story of (non-)belonging retrospectively. It portrays the process of how the protagonist ultimately came to realize at the age of 47 (Shōno, 2010, pp. 10, 27, 319) that the reason for the difficulties she had accepting her female body and fitting into society was that she was not human, but the "genderless" (*seibetsu wa fumei*) deity Kompīra, who happened to decide "out of an impulse inexplicable even to themselves," to leave behind the bottom of the sea where they had originally resided and take possession of the body of a girl who had died shortly after birth (Shōno, 2010, p. 9). This mirrors the development of Shōno's fiction: from the killing of the old woman in *Kōtei*, via the genderless protagonist of the ocean-themed *Kaijū*, to the female protagonist of *Nanimo shitenai* and her ambivalent desire for social belonging.

Importantly, it is not just the original state of the protagonist that is non-binary. Kompīra happens to reside within a female body, but it is through the process of hearing the voice, and finally merging (*shūgō suru*) with the spirit of a man who was buried as a woman in a tomb near their home, that they complete their self-realization and exclaim: "I am Kompīra! I have become Kompīra!" (Shōno, 2010, p. 334). Almost as a sequel to *Nanimo shitenai,* the protagonist's male self makes itself heard from beyond the grave. But whereas in *Suishōnai seido* it was ceremoniously laid to rest there, in *Kompīra* it is brought back to life.

How should we understand this ongoing fictional struggle with the body and gender, and this seeming affirmation of a nonbinary gender identity in the context of Shōno's trans-exclusionary writing? In Shōno's view (2022b), "gender dysphoria in most cases resolves itself on its own" (p. 37), and those who continue to experience it into their adulthood may be allowed to live as women, if they seek medical treatment (p. 31), but any other trans or non-binary adult is a potential threat to women (pp. 33–34). But doesn't her fiction place her in the periphery of precisely this last category of threat?

Before thinking about this question in the final section of this paper, I would like to take a brief look at another novel by Shōno, *Uramizumo dorei senkyo* (*The Uramizumo Slave Election,* 2018) to demonstrate two things: First, that this struggle with the gendered body continued to be central to Shōno's fiction until shortly before the time she began writing about trans women; and second, that whereas in *Kompīra* – mirroring the arguments in her trans-related essays – the female body is presented as an inescapable destiny (onto which then the transcendence of the gender binary, the merging of the female and male souls is performed), in *Uramizumo dorei senkyo* the transcendence of both the gender binary *and* the gendered body is shown as a utopian ideal.

5 *Uramizumo dorei senkyo* (2018): Utopian transcendence

Uramizumo Dorei Senkyō is the sequel to two of Shōno's earlier novels: *Hyōsube no kuni* (*The Land of Hyōsube*, 2016) and *Suishōnai seido*. It takes its main political agenda from the former, a cautionary tale on the Trans-Pacific Partnership (TPP), which was ratified in Japan in a modified form in March 2018 and, more generally, neoliberal politics and the neoliberal cultural climate in Japan (Shōno, 2018, p. 12). From the latter it takes the setting of the eponymous Uramizumo, a country populated only by women, which has separated from the deeply misogynist society of a dystopian future Japan called Nihhon.

There are two main protagonists: First, the ca. 2000-year-old deity Himemiya (Shōno, 2018, p. 36), who in 2068, the present time of the novel (Shōno, 2018, p. 53), appears in the form of a middle-aged woman in the city of S-kura. She is searching for an arrowhead that she suspects is a clue to her lost husband's whereabouts (Shōno 2018, pp. 30, 83–84). He has disappeared after the people of S-kura decided in a referendum – the eponymous *dorei senkyo* – to join Uramizumo. She believes it to be at what once was the National Museum of Japanese History, which has become the Historical Museum of the Men's Farm Sanctuary: an educational institution dedicated to the history of women and sexual harassment, where alongside historical objects, living examples of sexual harassers and rapists are kept and exhibited, and their sperm extracted for procreation.

The second protagonist, Ichikawa Fusayo, grew up in Nihhon, where women are slaves by birth (Shōno, 2018, p.136). She immigrated to Uramizumo in her twenties and worked her way up to become the chief curator of this museum. At the end of the novel, Himemiya meets Ichikawa there and, with her help, retrieves the lost arrowhead and finds her husband. Himemiya's quest for the lost object is the frame that holds this novel together, which through the polyphonic collage of Himemiya and Ichikawa's alternating narration, and several letters by people from Nihhon and Uramizumo inserted throughout the text, introduces the reader to the history of the two lands.

Nihhon is depicted as a country that – as a result of ratifying the TPP – has turned into a "colony" of global companies where corporate interests have become the ideological foundation of national policy, with everything from water, forests, and rice fields to healthcare, education, and state media completely privatized (Shōno, 2018, p. 30). The people work for a minimal wage, and, with no unions left, die young due to harsh working conditions (Shōno, 2018, pp. 31, 85–86). Foreign workers who are brought into the country under the pretext of "globalization" to increase the workforce face the same fate. Land left behind by dead workers is monetized as storage space for radioactive waste, leading to more deaths (Shōno, 2018, pp. 30–33).

This recalls past and present government projects of privatization such as that of Japan Railways and Japan Post in the early 2000s, or the revisions to the Water Supply Act (Suidōhō) in 2018 that enabled private companies to operate the water supply ("Revisions," 2018). It also brings to mind the government-run Technical Intern Training Program (Ginō Jisshū Seido), which aimed at giving people from developing countries opportunities to acquire skills, but has repeatedly been criticized for the resultant exploitation and abuse of low-skilled workers from overseas (Chaigne, 2022; Iwamoto, 2016; Jozuka, 2018; Nara, 2022; Sieg & Miyazaki, 2019).

Shōno combines this sinister critique of neoliberal politics with a critique of patriarchy. In Nihhon, women are first the property of their fathers and then of their husbands. They can become quasi-citizens upon marriage (Shōno, 2018, p. 140), but nevertheless have to pay back the debt they have accumulated through their very existence, that is, the costs for their birth and upbringing. While domestic work is the duty of a slave, it does nothing toward repaying these debts (Shōno, 2018, p. 153). Nihhon is an absolute patriarchy, where women are the commodified property of men and made responsible for all kinds of social issues, from low birthrates to their own sexual harassment (Shōno, 2018, p. 34).

This hierarchy is explained as the result of men being "enslaved themselves" by global companies, that is, men's internalized denial of their own position as subordinates to global capital (Shōno, 2018, p. 71). Accordingly, discourses on "gender equality" are hijacked by men who pervert them into justifications for mistreating women, arguing that having to wear condoms during sex or being kept from entering women-only cars on trains is "sexual discrimination of men" (Shōno, 2018, p. 43). Feminists are portrayed as conspirators in such polemics. They rush to the aid of men, fighting against this "sexual discrimination," arguing, among other things, that "molesting women on trains" should be legalized in order "to prevent false accusations by women" (Shōno, 2018, p. 112). In other words, Nihhon is a sinister, dystopian extrapolation of political, economic, cultural, and social developments in present-day Japan.

However, the question I want to raise here is: What options does *Uramizumo dorei senkyo* suggest for resistance? That is, what is the utopian alternative to Nihhon? At first glance it seems to be Uramizumo. As Himemiya says, "the only thing that might save [us] is something like this all-female nation, which [we] can really only see in our dreams" (Shōno, 2018, p. 31). But is it really?

As we learn at the end of the novel, in 2086, all but two prefectures of Nihhon have become part of Uramizumo. However, similar to *Suishōnai seido*, Uramizumo is repeatedly referred to as a "police state … where democracy has died" (Shōno,

2018, pp. 22, 58), a fascist totalitarian state where "one gets shot for ridiculing the country" (Shōno, 2018, p. 38; Würrer, 2022, pp. 64–65). The exclusionary violence the country is founded upon, the internment of men in the ghetto-like "farm sanctuary," and the most obvious display of state violence, the ritual killing of men during the annual ostracism (Shōno, 2018, p. 176), are portrayed as reasons for feelings of uneasiness among its people. As Ichikawa remarks, Uramizumo is "quite a dystopian paradise" (Shōno, 2018, p. 188).

This ambivalence is further emphasized by the contrasting voices of women from both lands, praising Uramizumo for providing a home to the maltreated women of Nihhon and also criticizing its exclusionary violence (Shōno, 2018, pp. 196–197, 206–223, 241–242, 243–249). No, it is not an all-female world, not separatism, that *Uramizumo dorei senkyo* suggests as an alternative. Its utopian horizon is the dystopian imagination represented by Himemiya's metafictional border crossing. As narrated by Himemiya:

> To put it in a nutshell, [Nihhon] is a parallel world, where as early as 2016, as originally planned, the TPP was ratified. But now, here, in the present – it is the Japan that is still called Japan, which has begun to gradually resemble this fictitious country. (Shōno, 2018, p. 32)

Himemiya, the main narrative authority, hovers between three worlds, or rather, three levels: (a) extra-diegetic narration ("to put it in a nutshell"); (b) diegesis, that is, the two fictitious worlds ("parallel world"); and (c) the extratextual reality ("the Japan that is still called Japan"). In literary terms, we could call this an example of *metalepsis*, a transgression of the boundaries between narrative levels. Himemiya is always one foot across the border to the reality of present-day Japan, linking the reader with the fictitious Nihhon.

Important to note here is that (1), the "all-female country" is qualified as a "dream"; (2) it is a dystopian dream, and (3) this is first and foremost Himemiya's dream. Thus, what *Uramizumo dorei senkyo* posits as the utopian alternative – "that which might save us" – rather than Uramizumo itself, is the process of dreaming, that is, the juxtapositions of contemporary Japanese society, dystopian Nihhon, and the also rather dystopian "all-female country" of Uramizumo. Himemiya's movement between these three worlds, the dystopian imagination embodied by Himemiya, is what *Uramizumo dorei senkyo* posits as a strategy of resistance.

Given that all three of these worlds take the form of a nation-state, Himemiya's hovering between them without belonging to any one of them fully, similar to Hieda's ambivalent status of (non)belonging in *Suishōnai seido*, could be read as a critique of the nation-state and the gendered mechanisms of exclusion it is founded upon (Würrer, 2022, p.69). That Himemiya's shrine is located in the borderlands between patriarchal Nihhon and the all-female Uramizumo would further suggest such a reading (Shōno, 2018, pp. 251–253).

But, Himemiya, in addition to metafictionally transgressing the borders between the narrative levels of *Uramizumo dorei senkyo*, also seems to transcend the gendered body. For one, Himemiya lacks a physical body. This is suggested by her portrayal as immortal (Shōno, 2018, p. 96), but also when she visits the cafeteria at the Historical Museum of the Men's Farm Sanctuary and states that she can only enjoy food through its smells (Shōno, 2018, p. 105), implying that – while seemingly having some sort of olfactory receptors – she lacks a digestive system and the need for nutrition. Consequently, her gender identity, which generally is given as female, is not defined by a physical body. It is her appearance and behavior that convey the impression of an older woman, but not always: when wandering around the borderlands at the beginning of the novel, she is mistaken for a man by Uramizumo's border patrol and almost shot (Shōno, 2018, p. 22). This is reminiscent of the aforementioned misgendering in *Nanimo shitenai*.

This ambiguity is mirrored at the end of the novel when she is reunited with her husband, for their reunification is portrayed as a fusion, a merging together of female and male. Moreover, Himemiya states that her husband later became the guardian deity of the cross-dressing men that started to appear in the borderlands after most of Nihhon joined Uramizumo, and as for herself: "Similarly, my shrine, at least from the outside, looks like that of a goddess" (Shōno, 2018, p. 253). Lacking further details, we are left to wonder what might lie beneath the surface. Here one might draw a parallel to the cross-gender performance of *Kōtei*'s protagonist.

This transgressive nature of Himemiya both in terms of gender and textual positions becomes more obvious when seen in contrast with *Uramizumo dorei senkyo*'s second protagonist, Ichikawa Fusayo. Unlike Himemiya, she had to experience the full force of misogyny and gender discrimination in Nihhon. Ichikawa is not in the privileged position of being able to freely move between worlds. She saw no other way than to move to Uramizumo, which she sees rather ambivalently as the lesser of two evils. In addition, she has a physical, female body whose aging is repeatedly addressed throughout the novel (Shōno, 2018, pp. 189, 195, 249).

So, on the one hand, we have the figure of a somewhat nonbinary, bodyless deity who upon reuniting with her male half becomes the guardian deity of cross-dressing individuals in the borderlands between Uramizumo and Nihhon. She embodies the metafictional omniscience and border-crossing, that is, the utopian horizon of *Uramizumo dorei senkyō*. On the other hand, there is the diegetic reality of Ichikawa Fusayo, who has an ageing, female body and is unable to float freely between worlds. She is also associated with feminism through her name: except for the very last syllable/character, the spelling is identical with that of Japanese feminist, politician, and leader of the women's suffrage movement, Ichikawa Fusae (1893–1981).

By virtue of Himemiya's metafictional position, Ichikawa Fusayo could be understood to be in part Himemiya. After all, Nihhon and Uramizumo with all its inhabitants are first and foremost Himemiya's narrative. Together they could be read as the manifestation of a desire to transcend or leave behind, not just the gendered nation-state and its exclusionary violence, but also the gendered body and the gender binary exemplified in the figure of Ichikawa Fusayo. At the same time, however, the fact that the gender-ambiguous, bodyless Himemiya inhabits the virtual space of metafiction, besides the fact that Himemiya is a supernatural being, can be said to emphasize the opposite: the difficulty, if not the impossibility, of transcending the gendered body and the gender binary as seen in the diegetic reality of Ichikawa Fusayo. Moreover, Ichikawa Fusayo's name connects her aging, female body with social change in the form of feminism.

6 Transphobia as abjection, or the impossible desire for a stable identity

This ambivalence is a common thread in Shōno's fiction. While many of the protagonists ultimately seem to embrace a female identity, traces remain in the text that complicate such an identification: the male body beneath the cross-gender performance of *Kōtei*'s protagonist; the male voice of the protagonist's elbow and her experience of misgendering in *Nanimo shitenai*; the burial and resuscitation of the male self in *Suishōnai seido* and *Kompira*, respectively; and the juxtaposition of the nonbinary, bodiless deity, Himemiya, with the embodied female character Ichikawa Fusayo in *Uramizumo dorei senkyo*.

At first sight the biological essentialism of Shōno's trans-exclusionary essays might seem to contradict this fictional oscillation between an affirmation of and a distancing from an embodied female identity. However, if we consider transphobia as a form of abjection, then her attempt to exclude trans women from the category of woman can be understood as another facet of this ambivalence.

The transphobic nature of Shōno's recent essays becomes most obvious when she argues that the GID Law should be amended, so that it allows for forcibly changing back the legal gender of trans women who have undergone gender-affirming surgery if they commit a crime; or to make it a prerequisite to test trans women for "misogynist tendencies" (*josei ken'o-tekina keikō*) prior to their gender-affirming surgery and prevent them from undergoing it if they are found to be "hating women" (*josei o nikundeiru*) (Shōno, 2022d, p. 35). This claim is based on the unfounded and fearmongering suspicion that all trans women are potential criminals and not to be trusted. Besides, the measures Shōno is asking for are inhumane and most likely unconstitutional. The policing of thought crimes is prohibited under article 19 of the Japanese Constitution; legally treating trans women differently from trans men would be discrimination based on gender, which is prohibited under article 14; and revoking the legal change of gender in case a trans woman commits a crime arguably constitutes double punishment and, thus, would be in violation of article 31.[8]

As Christopher Shelley (2008) has argued, referencing Julia Kristeva's *Powers of Horror* (1980), such a display of transphobia is not simply the repudiation of a feared object. It has to be understood as abjection, that is, repudiation as an attempt to (re-)establish the boundaries of the self through demarcating and distancing oneself from what is not me (pp. 38–39). Summarizing Kristeva's theory of abjection, Judith Butler (1999) wrote in *Gender Trouble:*

> The "abject" designates that which has been expelled from the body, discharged as excrement, literally rendered "Other." This appears as an expulsion of alien elements, but the alien is effectively established through this expulsion. The construction of the "not-me" as the abject establishes the boundaries of the body which are also the first contours of the subject. (p. 170)

Since what is rejected as "not-me" is always also part of the self, abjection never fully succeeds. The coherence of the self is constantly threatened by the abject. Hence, abjection needs to be repeated, if the self is to maintain its idealized boundaries. Butler (1999) emphasized that this process of abjection, the repulsion of the "not me," underpins the social reproduction of "hegemonic identities":

> As Iris Young has suggested in her use of Kristeva to understand sexism, homophobia, and racism, the repudiation of bodies for their sex, sexuality, and/or color is an "expulsion" followed by a "repulsion" that founds and consolidates culturally hegemonic identities along sex/race/sexuality axes of differentiation. Young's appropriation of Kristeva shows how the operation of repulsion can consolidate "identities" founded on the instituting of the "Other" or a set of Others through exclusion and domination. What constitutes through division the "inner" and "outer" worlds of the subject is a border and boundary tenuously maintained for the purposes of social regulation and control. (p. 170)

Abjection, in other words, is the manifestation of the desire for the impossibility of a coherent and stable identity. It is an ambivalent and precarious process of subjectification, where what was once "me" is transfigured into an external threat and

---

8 I would like to thank attorney Satō Maiko from the Tokyo Taiju Law Office for clarifying this point.

fought off. Only through the fight with this disavowed part of the self can it keep up the porous and vulnerable boundaries of its idealized identity.

As queer theorist Eve K. Sedgwick demonstrated in *Between Men* (1985) and *The Epistemology of the Closet* (1990), homophobia functions in such a way. Heteronormative societies establish the heterosexual man as the norm through instilling fear in the individual. It is consolidated through keeping the boundaries between socially appropriate and inappropriate relationships between men – the border between homosocial and homosexual bonds – "invisible, carefully blurred, always-already-crossed" (Sedgwick, 1985, p. 89), so that "not only must homosexual men be unable to ascertain whether they are to be objects of 'random' homophobic violence, but no man must be able to ascertain that he is not (that his bonds are not) homosexual" (Sedgwick, 1990, pp. 88–89). The "progromlike" "randomness of violence" against homosexual people (Sedgwick, 1985, p. 88) and "the historically shifting, and precisely the arbitrary and self-contradictory, nature of the way *homosexuality* (along with its predecessor terms) has been defined in relation to the rest of the homosocial spectrum" (Sedgwick, 1990, p. 185; emphasis in the original) has resulted in the "blackmailability," a fundamental vulnerability, of not just homosexual men, but all men. Displays of homophobia, thus, are a defense mechanism: a preemptive abjection of homosexual desire to ensure one's always threatened social status as a proper male subject.

But all gender identities are vulnerable and unstable. As Butler (1999) has argued, if coherence and continuity are basic conditions of identity and if having a gender is the prerequisite for social acceptance, then for individuals to become socially "intelligible," they need to present coherent gender identities, that is, "those which in some sense institute and maintain relations of coherence and continuity among sex, gender, sexual practice, and desire" (p. 23). While the very definition of "biological sex" is an ongoing cultural process and there is no universal way in which biological sex translates into social behavior (gender) and desire (sexuality) (Butler, 1999, pp. 10–11), in heteronormative, cis-genderist societies, social recognition hinges on the performative display of continuity between these three dimensions. "Discontinuity" and incoherence" are punished:

> Inasmuch as "identity" is assured through the stabilizing concepts of sex, gender, and sexuality, the very notion of "the person" is called into question by the cultural emergence of those "incoherent" or "discontinuous" gendered beings who appear to be persons but who fail to conform to the gendered norms of cultural intelligibility by which persons are defined. (Butler, 1999, p. 23)

That is, the foundational "flaw" of "discontinuity" and "incoherence", while being at the very heart of any gender identity, is transfigured into gender and sexual "deviants" – the abjection of homosexual people, transgender and nonbinary people, among others – whose social policing then becomes the way through which the normative fantasy, the naturalization of sex as gender is consolidated. When biologist and transgender activist Julia Serano (2016) wrote that "transphobia is first and foremost an expression of one's own insecurity about having to live up to cultural gender ideals" (p. 12), she was describing this projection of "discontinuity" and "incoherence" onto trans people that allows for cis people – despite their own "insecurities" – to remain the norm.

In her critique of trans-exclusionary feminism, Sarah Ahmed (2016) argued that we can understand gender as "places in which we dwell," and gender norms as the walls that surround them (p. 32). Some feel "more at home than others . . . walls that are experienced as hard and tangible by some do not even exist for others" (Ahmed, 2016, p. 32). Cis women and trans women may share some of the rooms; others are accessible only to cis people. But while we might not share the experience of being in a certain room, or being hindered by a certain wall – perceived as "incoherent" or "discontinuous" different than others – we share the experience of being put into these rooms, and the need to, as Ahmed (2016) put it, "chip away at those walls" (p. 32), if we want to tear down not just a few walls, but the whole structure, that is, the binary gender norms and the oppression they create. Transphobia is the rejection of this potential for intersectional alliances and radical change in favor of pushing trans women into the darkest corner of this structure, effectively reproducing, reinforcing the walls of essentialism that surround both cis and trans women.

7 Conclusion

Through her trans-related essays, Shōno does precisely that. Whatever the ambivalent and ambiguous portrayal of gender in her novels signifies – a struggle with societal norms, gender dysphoria, or both – they demonstrate the restrictive nature of essentialist and binary gender norms. Even if we understand Shōno's fiction not as an *ongoing* struggle with her gender and body, with what it means to have a gendered body that transgresses binary norms, but, as Shimizu Yoshinori and Shōno herself have suggested, an affirmation of her identity as woman – and I hope to have shown that her texts allow for doubt about such a teleological reading – this does not foreclose, as Ahmed emphasized, solidarity with trans women. Similar to the framing of the male voice in *Nanimo shitenai* as a child's dream of a previous life, or the burial of Hieda's male self in *Suishōnai seido*, however, Shōno opted for exclusion, for framing trans women as a threat to women as such, for locking them away in the darkest, smallest room in the back of the giant normative structure that is the gender binary. This ultimately bespeaks both the desire for and the impossibility of a stable, normative female identity.

Shōno's repudiation of trans women as potential criminals seems like an attempt to rid herself of the "incoherence" and "discontinuity" that lies at the core of her fiction and threatens such an identity from within, by construing it as an external threat to her and other "proper" women. The boundary-defying ambiguity and ambivalence of the gendered body in her fiction could have had the potential to inspire radical feminist interrogations of the gender binary and biological essentialism. With her recent essays, however, Shōno, pushes herself, and the interpretation, of her fiction back into the confines of precisely these norms.

References

Adams, N., Hitomi, M., & Moody, C. (2017). Varied reports of adult transgender suicidality: Synthesizing and describing the peer-reviewed and gray literature. *Transgender Health, 2*(1), 60–75. https://doi.org/10.1089/trgh.2016.0036.

Ahmed, S. (2016). An affinity of hammers. *Transgender Studies Quarterly, 3*(1–2), 22–34.

Allen, L. (2019). *Well-being and suicidality among transgender youth after gender-affirming medical interventions* [Unpublished doctoral dissertation]. University of Missouri-Kansas.

American Psychiatric Association. (2022). *Diagnostical and statistical manual of mental disorders* (5th ed.). American Psychiatric Association.

Asano, U. (2018). Shōno Yoriko "Nanimo shitenai" ron: "Chūtō hanpa" no rikigaku" [On Shōno Yoriko's "Doing nothing": The dynamics of "not this nor that"]. In H. Tsuboi (Ed.), *Baburu to ushinawareta 20-nen: Hontō ni "sengo" wa owatta no ka?* [The bubble and the lost 20 years: Is the "post-war" period really over?] (pp. 165–194). Rinsen Shoten.

Bouterey, S. (1996). Shōno Yoriko "Nōnai no tatakai": "Ise-shi, Haruchi" kara "Taiyō no Miko" made [Shōno Yoriko's "Mental battles": From "Ise City, Haruchi" to "The Shrine Maiden of the Sun"]. *Seijō bungei, 155*, 112–122.

Burns, K. (2019, September 5). *The rise of anti-trans "radical" feminists, explained.* Vox. https://www.vox.com/identities/2019/9/5/20840101/terfs-radical-feminists-gender-critical.

Bustos, V. P., Bustos, S. S., Mascaro, A., Del Corral, G., Forte, A. J., Ciudad, P., Kim, E. A., Langstein, H. N., & Manrique, O. J. (2021). Regret after gender-affirmation surgery: A systematic review and meta-analysis of prevalence. *Plastic and Reconstructive Surgery – Global Open, 9*(3), Article 3477. https://doi.org/10.1097/GOX.0000000000003477.

Butler, J. (1999). *Gender trouble: Feminism and the subversion of identity.* Routledge. (Original work published 1990)

Carland-Echavarria, P. (2022). We do not live to be productive: LGBT activism and the politics of productivity in contemporary Japan. *The Asia-Pacific Journal 20*(2), Article 5669. https://apjjf.org/2022/2/Carland.html.

Center for Extremism. (2023). *Antisemitism & anti-LGBTQ+ hate converge in extremist and conspiratorial beliefs.* Anti-Defamation League. https://www.adl.org/resources/blog/antisemitism-anti-lgbtq-hate-converge-extremist-and-conspiratorial-beliefs.

Chaigne, T. (2022, April 15). *Unbearable hours, threats of being fired: The abuse of migrant interns in Japan.* France 24. https://observers.france24.com/en/asia-pacific/20220419-unbearable-hours-threats-of-being-fired-the-abuse-of-migrant-interns-in-japan.

Ebihara Akiko. (2012). *Naze otoko wa Shōno Yoriko o osorerunoka* [Why do men fear Shōno Yoriko?]. Shunpūsha.

Grzebalska, W., Kováts E., & Pető. (2017, January 13). *Gender as symbolic glue: How "gender" became an umbrella term for the rejection of the (neo)liberal order.* Political Critique. https://political critique.org/long-read/2017/gender-as-symbolic-glue-how-gender-became-an-umbrella-term-for-the-rejection-of-the-neoliberal-order.

Ibuki, S. (2021, May 31). *"Inochi o mamoru hōritsu o tsukutte kudasai": Jimintō gi'in no sabetsu hatsugen, ima tōjishatachi ga tsutaetai omoi* ["Please create laws that protect lives": What those affected think of the discriminatory remarks made by members of the Liberal Democratic Party]. Buzzfeed. https://www.buzzfeed.com/jp/saoriibuki/ldp-lgbt-protest.

Iino, Y. (2020). Feminizumu wa bakkurasshu to no tatakai no naka de saiyō shita mizukara no "senryaku" o minaosu jiki ni kiteiru" [It is time for feminists to rethink their strategy adopted in the fight against the backlash]. *Etosetora, 4,* 85–88.

Iwamoto, K. (2016, August 18). Abuses rampant in foreign trainee program, Japan labor ministry finds. *Nikkei Asia.* https://asia.nikkei.com/Economy/Abuses-rampant-in-foreign-trainee-program-Japan-labor-ministry-finds.

Jimin Yamatani-shi "bakageta koto okiteiru": Sei jinin meguri [LDP's Yamatani speaking of "ridiculous developments" regarding gender identity]. (2021, May 19). *Asahi shinbun.* https://www.asahi.com/articles/ASP5M52GTP5MUTFK004.html.

Jozuka, E. (2018, December 7). *Japan needs immigrants, but do immigrants need Japan?* CNN. https://edition.cnn.com/2018/12/06/asia/japan-immigration-bill-foreign-workers/index.html.

Kotani, M. (2002). Space, body, and aliens in Japanese women's science fiction. *Science Fiction Studies, 29*(3), 397–417.

Halberstam, J. (1998). *Female masculinities.* Duke University Press.

Herman, J. L., Brown, T. N. T., & Haas, A. P. (2019). *Suicide thoughts and attempts among transgender adults: Findings from the 2015 US transgender survey.* The Williams Institute.

Herman, J. L., & O'Neill K. (2021). *Suicide risk and prevention for transgender people: Summary of research findings.* UCLA School of Law Williams Institute. https://williamsinstitute.law.ucla.edu/wp-content/uploads/Trans-Suicide-Summary-Sep-2021.pdf.

The Japanese Society of Psychiatry and Neurology. (2017, May 20). *"Sei dōitsusei shōgai ni kansuru shindan to chiryō no gaidorain" (dai-yon han): Ichibu kaitei no oshirase* [Notice of a partial revision of the *Guidelines for the diagnosis and treatment of gender dysphoria* (4th ed.)]. https://www.jspn.or.jp/modules/advocacy/index.php?content_id=32.

Joaquina. (2021, January 2). *Transphobia and antisemitism.* The social review. https://www.thesocialre view.co.uk/2021/01/02/transphobia-and-antisemitism.

Joyce, H. (2021). *Trans: Gender identity and the new battle for women's rights.* Oneworld Publications.

Kazama, T. (2007). "Chūsei ningen" to wa dare ka? Seiteki mainoritī e no "fobia" o fumaeta teikō e [Who are those "genderless people"? Toward a resistance that's aware of the phobia against sexual minorities]. *Joseigaku, 15,* 23–33.

Komiya, T. (2019). "Feminizumu no naka no toransu haijo" [Trans exclusion within feminism]. *Waseda Bungaku 10*(21), Winter, 132–142.

Li, K. [Lǐ, Q.] (2022). Sabetsu ni katan shinai tame no intānetto riterashī [Internet literacy to avoid contributing to discrimination]. *Shimōnu, 6,* 110–121.

Matsuoka, S. (2023a, May 11). *LGBT hōan "ōkiku kōtai": Shūseian no mondaiten o kaisetsu* [The LGBT draft bill: "A big step backward" – The problems of the revised draft]. Yahoo Japan. https://news.yahoo.co.jp/byline/matsuokasoshi/20230511-00349138.

Matsuoka, S. (2023b, June 6). *Mohaya "LGBT rikai yokusei hō": Yotō to ishin no saishūseian ga shūin naikaku iinkai de kaketsu* [This is actually an "LGBT understanding suppression bill": The House of Representatives Cabinet Committee passes the amended bill of the LDP and the Japan Innovation Party]. Yahoo Japan. https://news.yahoo.co.jp/byline/matsuokasoshi/20230610-00353187.

Matsu'ura, R. & Shōno, Y. (1994a, April 28). "Dankon shugi" o koete! [Moving beyond "phallocentrism"!]. *Sapio, 6*(7), 62–68.

Matsu'ura, R., & Shōno, Y. (1994b). *O-karuto o-dokumi teishoku* [Cultist, poisonous delicacies]. Kawade Bunko.

Michaelson, J. (2018, April 23). *Radical feminists and conservative Christians team up against transgender people.* Daily Beast. https://www.thedailybeast.com/radical-feminists-and-con servative-christians-team-up-against-transgender-people.

Mishima, Y. (2017). *Kamen no kokuhaku* [Confessions of a mask]. Shinchōsha Bunko. (Original work published 1949)

Mizugami, A. (2022). Tatta hitori, watashi dake no heya de [Just me, in my own room]. *Bungei,* Spring, 410–419.

Moore, M. (2020, August 5). *J. K. Rowling, "Gender ideology" and antisemitism: Getting to grips with the fuzzy coalition of scapegoating.* Medium. https://chican3ry.medium.com/jk-rowling-gender-ideol ogy-and-antisemitism-7dd043bad37b.

Naikai, K. (2006). Tekusuto ni okeru kurosu jendā pafōmansu (2): Shōno Yoriko "Kompīra" o chūshin ni [Cross-gender performances in literary texts (2): Shōno Yoriko's "Kompira"]. *Frontiers of Gender Studies, 5,* 386–392.

Nakamura, M. (1999). Tatakau sekushuariti: Shōno no resutoresu wārudo. *Bungakukai, 44*(1), 108–114.

Nara, R. (2022, July 26). *Focus: Abuse of foreign trainees continues under technical internship.* Kyodo News. https://english.kyodonews.net/news/2022/07/c5e9af8e7f16-focus-abuse-of-foreign-train ees-continues-under-technical-internship-program.html.

Nihon Seishin Shinkei Gakkai Seidōitsusei-shōgai ni Kansuru Iinkai. (2012). Seidōitsusei shōgai ni kansuru shindan to chiryō no gaidorain [Guidelines for the diagnosis and treatment of gender dysphoria]. *Seishin shinkeigaku zasshi, 114*(11), 1250–1266.

Nihon Seishin Shinkei Gakkai Seidōitsusei-shōgai ni Kansuru Iinkai. (2018). *Seidōitsusei shōgai ni kansuru shindan to chiryō no gaidorain (dai-yon han)* [Guidelines for the diagnosis and treatment of gender dysphoria, 4th ed.]. The Japanese Society of Psychiatry and Neurology. https://www. jspn.or.jp/uploads/uploads/files/activity/gid_guideline_no4_20180120.pdf.

Nikaidō, Y. (2021). "Korewa sensō dewanai": LGBT rikai zōshin hōan miokuri ["This is not a war": The Law to Promote Understanding for LGBT People]. *Sekai, 947,* 10–1.

Nitta, K. (2007). Uramizumo ga kokka de aru koto no kyōkun [The meaning of Uramizumo being a state]. *Gendai shisō, 35*(4), 169–177.

Noguchi-Amann, K. (2005). Japan wahrnehmen. Zum Zusammenhang zwischen Sprache und Wirklichkeitskonzeption in Shono Yorikos Erzählungen [Perceiving Japan: On the connections between language and concepts of reality in Shōno Yoriko's prose]. In R. Domenig, S. Formanek, & W. Manzenreiter (Ed.), *Über Japan denken: Japan überdenken* [Thinking about Japan: Rethinking Japan] (pp. 303–322). LIT Verlag.

Norton, L. (2013). Neutering the transgendered: Human rights and Japan's law no. 111. In S. Stryker & A. Z. Aizura (Eds.), *The transgender studies reader 2* (pp. 591–603). Routledge.

Noya, F. (1997). Shōno Yoriko ron: Majikku to riarizumu no hazama de [An analysis of Shōno Yoriko: In between magic and realism]. *Bungakukai*, *51*(6), 270–280.

Okuno, A. (2021, May 21). Yamatani Eriko-shi no LGBT sabetsu hatsugen wa "muchi": "Akiraka na gorin kenshō ihan" tekkai motome shomei mo [Yamatani Eriko's discriminatory remarks about LGBT people criticized as "ignorance" and "a clear violation of the Olympic Charter": Demands for a retraction and a petition]. *Tōkyō shinbun*. https://www.tokyo-np.co.jp/article/105806.

Rabinowitz, A. (2022, February 25). *Fears of creeping transhumanism give space for overt conspiracism in gender critical communities.* The Skeptic. https://www.skeptic.org.uk/2022/02/fears-of-creeping-transhumanism-give-space-for-overt-conspiracism-in-gender-critical-communities.

Revisions that allow private firms to run water supply services draw mixed reviews. (2018, December 7). *The Mainichi.* https://mainichi.jp/english/articles/20181207/p2a/00m/0na/023000c.

Riddell, K. (2016, August 11). George Soros: The money behind the transgender movement. *The Washington Times.* https://www.washingtontimes.com/news/2016/aug/11/george-soros-the-money-behind-the-transgender-move.

Satō, T. (2023, June 13). *LGBT "sabetsu" zōshinhō ni NO: Puraido parēdo sura, dekinakunaru kiki. "Konna hō o tōsu kuni wa, hontō ni saitei desu"* [No to the Law for LGBT discrimination: Even pride parades are now at risk. "A country that passes such a law is truly despicable"]. HuffPost News. https://www.huffingtonpost.jp/entry/story_jp_6487b4b5e4b048eb9110f7bb.

Science Council of Japan. (2020). *Teigen "Sei-teki mainoriti no kenri hoshō o mezashite (II): Toransujendā no songen o hoshō suru tame no hōseibi ni mukete" no pointo* [The essential points of our recommendation "Toward ensuring the rights of sexual minorities (part II). Toward legal measures to guarantee the dignity of transgender individuals]. https://www.scj.go.jp/ja/info/kohyo/kohyo-24-t297-4-abstract.html.

Sedgwick, E. K. (1985). *Between men: English literature and male homosocial desire.* Columbia University Press.

Sedgwick, E. K. (1990). *The epistemology of the closet.* University of California Press.

Senda, Y. (2023, June 6). *LGBT hōan no mō hitotsu no shōten: Gakkō kara iryō ni okurareru kodomotachi* [Another focus of the LGBT draft: Schools sending children to medical care]. Yahoo Japan. https://news.yahoo.co.jp/byline/matsuokasoshi/20230511-00349138.

Serano, J. (2016). *Whipping girl. A transsexual woman on sexism and the scapegoating of femininity.* Basic Books.

Shelley, C. (2008). *Transpeople. Repudiation, trauma, healing.* University of Toronto Press.

Shimizu, A. (2007). Scandalous equivocation: A note on the politics of queer self-naming. *Inter-Asia Cultural Studies*, *8*(4), 503–516.

Shimizu, A. (2020). "Imported" feminism and "Indigenous" queerness: From backlash to transphobic feminism in transnational Japanese context. *Ochanomizu University Journal of Gender Studies*, *23*, 89–104.

Shimizu, A. (2022). Sūpāgurū ni yoru itten kyōto: Han-jendā undō to toransujendā haijo [Single-issue alliances via superglue: The anti-gender movement and the exclusion of transgender people] [Commentary]. In S. Faye, *Toransujendā mondai* [The transgender issue] (Y. Takai, Trans.) (pp. 381–389). Meiseki Shoten.

Shimizu, Y. (2003). *Shōno Yoriko: Kokū no senshi* [Shōno Yoriko: Warrior of the void]. Kawadeshobō Shinsha.

Shiraishi, Y., & Shōno Y. (2008). Gokushi kara ōkiku furikaette yomu "Dainihhon" sanbusaku [Taking an extensive look back at the *Dainihhon* triology from the perspective of the ultrapersonal]. *Ronza, 157,* 184–199.

Shōno, Y. (2001). Kōtei [The emperor]. In Y. Shōno, *Shōno Yoriko shoki sakuhin-shū* [Shōno Yoriko's early novels] (pp.113–258). Kōdansha Bungei Bunko. (Original work published 1984)

Shōno, Y. (2007). Nanimo shitenai. In Y. Shōno, *Shōno Yoriko sankan shōsetsu-shū* [Shōno Yoriko's triple crown novels] (pp. 135–244). Kawade Bunko. (Original work published 1991)

Shōno, Y. (2008, March 16). Shōno Yoriko intabyū [An interview with Shōno Yoriko]. *Kyōto Daigaku shinbun,* 5–7.

Shōno, Y. (2018). *Uramizumo dorei senkyo* [The Uramizumo slave election]. Kawade Shobō Shinsha.

Shōno, Y. (2019, July 21). *Kinkyō gohōkoku_2019 nen 07 gatsu 21 nichi (nichi)* [Status update_21 July 2019 (Sunday)]. *Shōno Yoriko shiryōshitsu* [Resources on Shōno Yoriko]. https://restless.adrgm.com/text/kinkyo20190721.html.

Shōno, Y. (2020a, September 24). Ohenji kimashita jidōteki ni shōmetsu suru kinkyō hōkoku [I got an answer; this status update will delete itself]. *Shōno Yoriko shiryōshitsu* [Resources on Shōno Yoriko]. https://restless.adrgm.com/text/kinkyo202009.html.

Shōno, Y. (2020b). "Daidokorona nō de? Died corona no day [With a kitchenesque brain? Died corona no day]." Kawade Shobō Henshūbu (Ed.), *Shisō toshite no "Shingata korona uirusu-ka"* [COVID-19 as a new way of thinking] (pp. 89–100). Kawade Shobō Shinsha.

Shōno, Y. (2020c, October 18). Kyōsantō no kenkai [The Communist Party's viewpoint]. Female Liberation Japan. https://femalelibjp.org/nf/?p=225.

Shōno, Y. (2020d, November 7). *FLJ dokusha no mina-sama e* [To the readers of FLJ]. Female Liberation Japan. https://femalelibjp.org/nf/?p=333.

Shōno, Y. (2021, October 20). *Gobusatashite orimasu. (Shōno Yoriko-san yori)* [It's been a while. (From Shōno Yoriko)]. Female Liberation Japan. https://femalelibjp.org/nf/?p=621.

Shōno, Y. (2022a, July 16). *Ogenki desuka mata shite mo, ... (2)* [How are you? Here we go again... (2)]. Female Liberation Japan. https://femalelibjp.org/nf/?p=815.

Shōno, Y. (2022b). Josei bungaku wa hakkin bungaku nanoka? [Is women's literature forbidden literature?]. In Y. Shōno, *Shōno Yoriko hakkin shōsetsu-shū* [A collection of Shōno Yoriko's banned novels] (pp. 25–38). Kawade Shobō Shinsha.

Shōno, Y. (2022c, January 22). *Kaidai futatsu, essei to shōsetsu ni tsuite dai-ikkai* [Two analyses, about an essay and a novel, part 1] Female Liberation Japan. https://femalelibjp.org/nf/?p=660.

Shōno, Y. (2022d). Hakkin sakka ni natta riyū?: Kenpō nijū-ichi jō ni nottori genkō hō ni shitagai, josei no seizon to hyōgen no jiyū no kiki o uttaeta kara [Why did I become a banned author? Because I brought to attention women's right to live and the crisis of free speech in accordance with article 21 of the constitution]. In Y. Shōno, *Shōno Yoriko hakkin shōsetsu-shū* [A collection of Shōno Yoriko's banned novels] (pp. 1–19). Kawade Shobō Shinsha.

Sieg, L., & Miyazaki, A. (2019, March 20). Vietnamese blue-collar workers in Japan seen facing risks as labor system opens up. *The Japan Times.* https://www.japantimes.co.jp/news/2019/03/20/national/social-issues/vietnamese-blue-collar-workers-japan-seen-facing-risks-labor-system-opens.

Tierney, R. (2010). *Japanese literature as world literature: Visceral engagement in the writings of Tawada Yoko and Shono Yoriko* [Unpublished doctoral dissertation], University of Iowa.

Tordoff, D., Wanta, J. W, Collin, A., Stepney, C., Inwards-Breland, D. J., & Ahrens, K. (2022). Mental health outcomes in transgender and nonbinary youths receiving gender-affirming care. *JAMA Network Open, 5*(2): e220978. https://doi.org/10.1001/jamanetworkopen.2022.0978.

Turban, J. L., King, D., Carswell, J. M., & Keuroghlian, A. S. (2020). Pubertal suppression for transgender youth and risk of suicidal ideation. *Pediatrics 145*(2), 68–76. https://doi.org/10.1542/peds.2019-1725.

Tyler, C. (2003). *Female impersonation*. Routledge.

Urquhart, E. (2023, March 25). *J. K. Rowling tweets support for activist embroiled in Nazi controversy*. Assigned. https://www.assignedmedia.org/breaking-news/j-k-rowling-tweets-support-for-activist-embroiled-in-nazi-controversy.

Williams, C. (2016). Radical inclusion. Recounting the trans inclusive history of radical feminism. *Transgender Studies Quarterly, 3*(1–2), 254–258.

Würrer, S. [Vyūra, S.] (2019). *"Watashi wa watashi de wa nai" to wa dare ni ieru kotoka? Hiteisei hihan toshite Shōno Yoriko "Kōtei" o yomu"* [Who is able to say "I am not me"? Reading Shōno Yoriko's *The emperor* as a critique of negativity]. In Chūō Daigaku Jinbungaku Kenkyūjo (Ed.), *Yomukoto no kuia: Zoku ai no gihō* [The queerness of reading: Practices of love, part 2] (pp. 101–131). Chūō Daigaku Shuppanbu.

Würrer, S. (2022). A short history of ambivalence toward the feminist utopia in Japanese science fiction. *Science Fiction Studies, 49*(1), 53–80. https://doi.org/10.1353/sfs.2022.0005.

Yamada, H. (2022). GID as an acceptable minority; or, the alliance between moral conservatives and "gender critical" feminists in Japan. *Transgender Studies Quarterly, 9*(3), 501–506. https://doi.org/10.1215/23289252-9836162.

Yamaguchi, T. (2014). "Gender free" feminism in Japan: A story of mainstreaming and backlash. *Feminist Studies, 40*(4), 541–72.

Yudelson, L. (2021, September 29). "Are you Jewish?" Assault in Teaneck brings up questions of hatred and propaganda. *Jewish Standard*. https://jewishstandard.timesofisrael.com/are-you-jewish.

Yutaka Kubo

Feeling the friction: Reworking Japanese film studies/criticism from a queer lens

From 29 September 2020 to 15 January 2021, I curated an exhibition titled, *Inside/ Out: LGBTQ+ Representation in Film and Television*, at Tsubouchi Memorial Theatre Museum at Waseda University in Tokyo. It traced how the Japanese film and television industry, from 1945 to early 2020, had depicted the lived experiences of lesbian, gay, bisexual, and trans people, as well as scenes that could potentially invite viewers to interpret as queer intimacy. Following the recent worldwide movement in museum curation to excavate LGBTQ+ memories in collections (Sullivan & Middleton, 2019), this exhibition attempted to challenge how museum and archival curations have narrated the history of mainstream Japanese cinema and television without sufficient attention to the presence of LGBTQ+ individuals in Japanese visual cultures (Kubo, 2020c, pp. 6–7). To this end, it displayed the museum's collection of scripts, stills, posters, movie pamphlets, film festival programs, lesbian and gay magazines, and manga that showed visitors a limited but rich history of cinema and television in Japan from a queer lens, a critical perspective that questions the power dynamics that normalize heterosexuality (Kikuchi et al., 2019, p. 5).

The exhibition designed the welcome board as a space where visitors could leave their responses to the exhibition content on Post-it notes. Many visitors had dialogues through those Post-it notes, resonating with a shared understanding and attitude with respect to the current state of LGBTQ+ representations in Japanese cinema and television. Some seemed excited about the recent increase in the number of film and television productions with gay male characters; some expressed disappointment at the severe imbalance in representation. What struck me the most was that visitors shared how LGBTQ+ representations in visual media have mattered to their experiences of survival and loss as members of LGBTQ+ communities in contemporary Japanese society, encouraging each other to keep on living no matter what.

Standing in front of this board, one nonbinary teenage visitor expressed how they "felt relieved to be assured that it is okay to live as [they are], though [they] had not felt this way for a long time until [they] had stepped into this exhibition and had seen lots of content that [they] had not known before." Hearing this voice as the curator of this exhibition, responsible for researching and organizing its content and editing the catalogue, I felt relieved that the exhibition might have saved someone's life. It also highlighted how much access to various LGBTQ+ representations in visual media matters to the survival of sexual and gender minorities whose everyday lives are filled with heteronormative images and expectations.

In preparing the exhibition, I found the literature, both in Japanese and English, on the history and reception of queer films in Japan since the 1960s indispensable (see, e. g., Grossman, 2000; Ishihara, 1996; Izumo, 2002, 2005).[1] Some individual essays on film anthologies in Japanese offered a lesbian/gay/queer reading of Japanese films in the twentieth century (i. e., Mizoguchi, 2005; Shinjō, 2010).[2] However, the more I researched, the more I realized that there was a severe lack of academic research and film criticism that explored cinematic expressions in the Japanese film industry regarding the sexualities and gender identities of people in the past who had been rendered abnormal or strange, and marginalized by the heteronormative expectations of Japanese society.[3] Although queer cinema studies has developed significantly worldwide since the early 1990s, there are still no comprehensive accounts of numerous practices in filmmaking, film criticism, and film reception in Japan from a queer lens.

How successful, then, have Japanese film studies and film criticism been in narrating and preserving the histories of Japanese queer cinema? Despite a surge in the literature from the late 1990s to the early 2000s, it seems that the mainstream discourses since the late 2000s have not yet developed sufficient ways to systematically analyze LGBTQ+ representations in Japanese cinema of the past and the present. In order to answer this question, I examine two aspects in this paper. First, I will trace the development of LGBTQ+ representations in Japanese cinema from the 1990s gay boom to the 2010s LGBT boom, paying attention to similarities and differences between them in terms of the commodification and marketing of homosexuality, while also investigating the meaningful contributions of independent filmmakers in terms of family, aging, disability, and authenticity. Second, I will demonstrate how film studies and film criticism in Japan have struggled to incorporate a queer perspective into research and criticism, arguing that changes for the better have started to emerge though some issues remain to be solved. Overall, my aim in this paper is to expand the scope of film studies and

---

1 While it is not easy to define queer cinema, for the purposes of this paper I adopt one of the three definitions suggested by Ronald Gregg and Amy Villarejo (2021) in *The Oxford Handbook of Queer Cinema:* "a body of narrative, documentary, and experimental work previously collated under the rubric of homosexual or lesbian, gay, bisexual, and trans (LGBT) cinema" (p. xi). This emphasizes the existence of Japanese films that depict the experiences of LGBTQ+ individuals, many of which have been overlooked in film studies in Japan.
2 Most recently, individual pieces have appeared in handbooks of Japanese cinema in English (Kanno, 2020, 2021b) and journals both in Japanese and English (i. e., Jo, 2021; Katō, 2021).
3 However, see, most recently, Kanno (2021a).

film criticism in Japan from a queer lens to trace the history of Japanese queer cinema, record the contemporary state of film practice and reception of LGBTQ+ representations, and envision a hopeful future for more diverse and inclusive films.

1 Moving from the gay boom to the LGBT boom

1.1 The gay boom and the 2000s

A prominent phenomenon in Japanese popular culture during the first half of the 1990s was the so-called gay boom. The boom was already budding by the end of the year 1990 (Hirano 1994, p. 23), but the February 1991 issue of the women's lifestyle magazine *CREA* with its 46-page feature article "Gei runessansu '91" (Gay Renaissance '91) was a notable example that inaugurated the boom and spurred Japanese popular culture, including the moving-image industry on commodifying and marketing male homosexuality in film and television (Hall, 2000, p. 41). For instance, two films from 1992, Matsuoka Jōji's *Kira kira hikaru* (*Twinkle*) and Nakajima Takehiro's *Okoge*, introduced a gay couple as protagonists trying to form a family with a heterosexual woman. While heterosexual filmmakers directed most gay films throughout the 1990s, openly gay independent filmmakers Ōki Hiroyuki and Hashiguchi Ryōsuke also emerged in the same era. Although representations of lesbian relationships and female intimacy had been present in both mainstream and independent Japanese cinema at least since the early 1950s,[4] including films such as Masumura Yasuzō's *Manji* (1964), Yazaki Hitoshi's *Kazetachi no gogo* (*Afternoon Breezes*, 1980), and Nakahara Shun's *Sakura no sono* (*The Cherry Orchard*, 1990), the gay boom mostly visualized gay male experiences and did not provide enough spaces for "films by lesbians, images, narratives, and themes of lesbians, or films for lesbians" (Kanno, 2015, p. 206).[5]

The 1990s Japanese film industry continued to invest in images and stories of gay men more than those of other sexual and gender minorities even after the gay boom. However, the early 2000s saw a growing interest in same-sex relationships between women in their late teens to early 30s within Japanese independent cinema: Shindō Kaze's *Love/Juice* (2000), Kazama Shiori's *Kasei no kanon* (*Mars*

---

4 There may possibly be queer films from the 1930s, as illustrated by Kawate Jirō's *Fukujusō* (*A Pheasant's Eye*, 1935), which was based on a story from Yoshiya Nobuko's *Hana monogatari* (*Flower Tales*, 1916–1924), a series of tales about romantic friendships between girls.

5 Unless otherwise indicated, all translations from Japanese in this paper are the author's own.

Canon, 2001), and Andō Hiroshi's *Blue* (2002), to name a few. *Mars Canon* tells of a fragile romance between two women in their early 30s, Kinuko and Sei, who depend on each other emotionally. Their relationship is filled with both pain and warmth, resisting social pressures to end their relationship. Japanese lesbian films tend to have a tragic, painful, and suffocating ending, but *Mars Canon* ends with the hope that this relationship will continue even beyond the narrative and that these women might succeed in leading a life together; its movie pamphlet even shows a glimpse of their life after the film.

Why did this suggestion of two women aging together matter in the early 2000s? Sociologist Ogura Yasutsugu (2009) has argued that issues of aging were gaining attention within the LGBTQ+ community in the early 2000s (pp. 168–170). An important sociologist in the development of gay studies and queer studies in Japan, Kawaguchi Kazuya (2003), noted that LGBTQ+ persons who survived through the 1980s AIDS panic might have started to wonder how they would spend their midlife and older years outside the traditional marital and family system (p. 76). It was an inevitable social consequence because in 2007 Japan was known to be heading toward a super-aging society, of which LGBTQ+ persons would no doubt be a part. Just as *Twinkle* had already offered the possibility of an alternative family unit in 1992 as another platform for aging, some Japanese queer films from the early to mid-2000s, including *Mars Canon*, began to share a similar interest. To give a few examples, Hamano Sachi's *Yurisai* (*Lily Festival*, 2001), Hashiguchi Ryōsuke's *Hasshu!* (*Hush!*, 2001), Takashi Toshiko's *Shukufuku* (*Blessed*, 2001), and Inudō Isshin's *Mezon do Himiko* (*La Maison de Himiko*, or *House of Himiko*, 2005) offered insights into the concerns, anxieties, fears, loneliness, celebrations, and excitement of getting old outside the conventional way. While these films dealt with issues of aging from different perspectives, they shared an interest in showing how LGBTQ+ persons would cope with their desires and anxieties in exploring life options for the remainder of their lives.

1.2 The LGBT boom

According to sociologist Ishida Hitoshi (2019), there has been a so-called LGBT boom in Japan since around 2012 (pp. 12–13). While the budding and spread of this boom may parallel the timing of sociopolitical movements toward equal rights for sexual and gender minorities in Japan throughout the 2010s and onward, the LGBT boom itself has been strongly associated with financial profits and business opportunities for various corporations, for it was inaugurated by business magazines that paid attention to the potential of pink money, such as *Shūkan daiamondo* (*Diamond Weekly*) and *Shūkan Tōyō keizai* (*Weekly Toyo Keizai*). It did not have an immediate impact on the mainstream moving-image industry, unlike the gay boom in its early stages. Nevertheless, LGBTQ+ characters never really disappeared from Japanese cinema, not only because arthouse theaters and film festivals since the 1980s have functioned as platforms to accommodate LGBTQ+-themed independent films such as Hamano Sachi's *Yuriko, dasuvidāniya* (*Yoshiko & Yuriko*, 2011), but also because such mainstream films as Okita Shūichi's *Yokomichi Yonosuke* (*A Story of Yonosuke*, 2012), Yamada Yōji's *Chiisai ouchi* (*The Little House*, 2014), and Ishikawa Jun'ichi's *Eipuriru fūruzu* (*April Fools*, 2015) included gay and (possibly) lesbian characters.

The influence of the LGBT boom on the Japanese film industry became most evident after the wards of Shibuya and Setagaya implemented a same-sex partnership system in 2015. One of the most significant changes that started to appear within the mainstream cinemas in 2016 was that the production committees (*seisaku iinkai*) of big-budget films began to cast actors who were already very popular among the public for playing a gay man or trans woman. The most notable example was Lee Sang-il's *Ikari* (*Rage*, 2016), based on Yoshida Shūichi's 2014 mystery novel of the same name. The narrative moves around three different arcs in different Japanese locations. One of the arcs narrates an erotic encounter between two gay men in their early 30s, Yuma (Tsumabuki Satoshi) and Naoto (Ayano Gō), which results in a tragic separation. While Ayano had previously played a gay character in *A Story of Yonosuke*, it was the first time for Tsumabuki to play such a role. Much of the promotional media focused on the pair's preparations for their roles, which required a brief sex scene and almost full nudity, making it seem as though gay sex was the only important aspect of the storyline.

If a film makes more than one billion yen at the box office, it is considered a commercial hit in Japan. The all-star-packed film *Rage* earned 1.6 billion yen at the box office, which had a commercial and marketing impact on mainstream film production because casting famous actors in the roles of gay, lesbian, and trans women characters gradually became a trend to garner audiences. But, most importantly, just like the gay boom that was later criticized for its commodification of male homosexuality (Vincent et al., 1997), the LGBT boom also encouraged the mainstream film industry to invest in casting popular actors for gay roles rather than in developing a variety of stories in which lesbians, bisexual women and men, trans women and men, nonbinary persons, and other sexual and gender minorities take central or supporting roles.

It was in 2018, after the budding of the LGBT boom, that LGBTQ+ characters proliferated on film and TV. There were six TV series, including three by the public broadcaster NHK (e. g., *Joshiteki seikatsu*, or *Life As a Girl*), and at least 15 films, ranging from mainstream and independent narrative films to experimental films and documentaries. Even though lesbians, an intersex person, a trans woman, and a genderfluid person also appeared on screens in 2018, stories about gay men still occupied the majority of the works.[6] The enormously popular TV series *Ossanzu rabu* (*Ossan's Love*) was one such work that centered on a male–male romance. A feature-length film *Ossan's Love: LOVE or DEAD?*, directed by Rūto Tōichirō in 2019, further depicted the life of the two central male characters who had become a couple at the end of the TV series. As an example of typecasting, Hayashi Kento, who had played a gay high school student in Miike Takashi's *Aku no kyōten* (*Lesson of the Evil*, 2012) and a young gay salaryman in Kusano Shōgo's *Nigakute amai* (*Bitter Sweet*, 2016), played Maki, the only central character to disclose his sexual orientation, who exposes the hardships of living as a gay man in Japan.

Manga scholar Fujimoto Yukari (2019) evaluated the TV series *Ossan's Love* as having "succeeded in dismantling every aspect of the public's common understanding [*jōshiki*] about love while presenting possible problems expected even after overcoming discrimination [against gay men]" (pp. 146–147). While I concur to a certain extent, the film adaptation failed to further explore and develop this idea to offer an image of a society that cares about LGBTQ+ persons' political uncertainty regarding equal rights. Instead, the film's trailer hinted that new "possibly gay" characters might interfere in the gay relationship that had been built by the central characters. In the film, however, it turns out that the new characters are heterosexual. This is an example of a queer-baiting strategy that implies, as Judith Fathallah (2015) explained, "a queer relationship between two characters, and then emphatically den[ies] and laugh[s] off the possibility" (p. 491). Therefore, the film adaptation reflected a strong sense of exploitation and commodification of a same-sex romance (Kubo 2020b, p. 23). Nonetheless, it earned 2.65 billion yen at the box office, making it the highest-grossing LGBTQ+-themed film in Japan as of December 2022.

It is highly likely that the success of the *Ossan's Love* franchise motivated the mainstream film industry to produce more works with gay characters in the late 2010s, as it now invests a larger budget, better-known actors, and broader promo-

---

6 Films released in 2018 included: Imai Mika's *Niji-iro no asa ga kuru made* (*Until Rainbow Dawn*); Imamura Ayako's *11-sai no kimi e: Ironna katachi ga suki* (*To 11 Year Old You: Various Kinds of Love*); Nakagawa Shun's *Karankoe no hana* (*Kalanchoe*); Watanabe Seigo's *Seibetsu ga, nai! Intāsekkusu mangaka no kuia na hibi* (*No Gender!: The Queer Life of an Intersex Manga Artist*); Masuda Genki's *Watashi wa watashi: Over the Rainbow* (*I Am What I Am: Over the Rainbow*); Minorikawa Osamu's *Kāsan ga donna ni boku o kirai demo* (*No Matter How Much My Mom Hates Me*); Igashi Aya's *Makkana hoshi* (*A Crimson Star*); Takeda Tomokazu's *Watashi no ibasho: Shin sekai monogatari* (*Where I Belong*); Yukisada Isao's *Ribāzu ejji* (*River's Edge*); Nakamura Takuro's *Seihokusei* (*West North West*); Tanimoto Kaori's *Hana wa sakuka* (*Does the Flower Bloom?*); Furukawa Ayaka's *Freedom*, and Kimura Ryō's *KISS*, as well as *21-seiki no onnanoko* (*21st Century Girl*), which was planned and produced by Yamato Yuki with 15 other directors.

tion campaigns to ensure the commercial success of what may be considered "blockbuster Japanese gay films." Since 2019, the mainstream Japanese film industry has constantly produced a body of gay films such as Ōtomo Keishi's *Eiri* (*Beneath the Shadow*, 2020), Yukisada Isao's *Kyūso wa chīzu no yume o miru* (*The Cornered Mouse Dreams of Cheese*, 2020), Nakae Kazuhito's *Kinō nani tabeta?* (*What Did You Eat Yesterday?*, 2021), and Kazama Hiroki's *Cherī mahō! 30-sai made dōteidato mahōtsukai ni narerurashii* (*Cherry Magic! Thirty Years of Virginity Can Make You a Wizard?!: The Movie*, 2022). Their box office success varied depending on the popularity of the novel or manga on which they were based and the timing of their release during the COVID-19 pandemic, but *What Did You Eat Yesterday?* managed to earn 1.39 billion yen.

While it remains necessary to maintain a critical view of the way the LGBT boom commodifies male homosexuality and targets pink money, it is also important to look at the shifts that the LGBT boom appears to have triggered in the film and television industry and their sponsors. For example, the LGBT boom has more than ever before highlighted the subtle audience demography attracted to LGBTQ+ representations, which was most likely founded during the gay boom and continued to grow through the 2000s and 2010s. This development was impossible without the rise and decline of VHS/DVD/Blu-ray rental services, the digitization of film distribution, and the spread of social media, all making access to LGBTQ+ representations much easier than it had been in the twentieth century (Kubo, 2020c). It is true that independent filmmakers tend to struggle to find reliable funding sources compared to mainstream productions, but the growth of this particular audience demography seems to have contributed to a shift in the financial investment in works on LGBTQ+ themes that may challenge stereotypes and imbalances in representation. For example, Tamada Shin'ya's *Sobakasu* (*Freckles*), a 2022 film about an aromantic woman, was financed by grants from the Agency for Cultural Affairs, suggesting that the government sees value in supporting a queer film in order to diversify the scope of its support for Japanese cinema.

Despite these changes in audience and investment, struggles for wider and longer distribution in cinemas across Japan remain, especially for films with LBTQ+ characters and lesser-known actors, and by lesser-known directors. For instance, a 2021 lesbian film called *Haruhara-san no uta* (*Haruhara-san's Recorder*) by Kyōshi Sugita, who had only directed two feature-length films before, first opened in a small number of arthouse theaters. Luckily, it managed to gradually expand its distribution after gaining critical success at international film festivals and positive reviews on social media. While this film managed to reach a wider audience, Japanese films with LBTQ+ characters released at arthouse theaters tend to be missed by many audiences interested in LGBTQ+ representation in general, for two reasons. One reason is the lack of access to arthouse theaters that show films with LBTQ+ characters, and the other is the lack of clear information in promotions about the presence of LBTQ+ characters in new films. By the time viewers learn about them, the films in question already have limited availability. The imbalance in distribution between films with gay characters and those with other LGBTQ+ characters is serious. However, video-on-demand (VOD) services such as Netflix, Amazon Prime, U-Next, and Gaga00Lala now function as platforms to distribute both mainstream and independent LGBTQ+ films, enabling access to some of the 2018 films listed previously, as well as Fukada Kōji's *Yokogao* (*A Girl Missing*, 2019), Shiota Akihiko's *Sayonara kuchibiru* (*Farewell Song*, 2019), Yazaki Hitoshi's *Sakura* (2020), Hiroki Ryūichi's *Kanojo* (*Ride or Die*, 2021), Hamaguchi Ryūsuke's *Gūzen to sōzō* (*Wheel of Fortune and Fantasy*, 2021), and Nakagawa Ryū-tarō's *Yagate umi e to todoku* (*One Day, You Will Reach the Sea*, 2022). In addition, Normal Screen, an independent film screening project, provides access to LGBTQ+ films that are rarely available on VOD services. Access to such platforms and screening events is not without problems of economic disparities among viewers, but at the moment, they are one solution to the problem of distribution.

2 Independent cinema: Family, aging, disability, and authenticity

The mainstream Japanese film industry once operated under the studio system, which sustained the structure of film production, marketing and promotion, distribution, and the training of filmmakers, actors, and other essential members of film production, until this system collapsed entirely in the 1980s. Major film companies such as Shōchiku, Tōhō, Tōei, and Nikkatsu still focus primarily on distributing films mostly to cinema complex theaters and managing copyrights. Those films are often produced under the aforementioned production committee, which con sists of the film and other companies that share profits depending on the percentage they invest in the production budget. The advantage of the production committee is its financial capability that allows wider options for exploring story ideas, securing adaptation rights, and casting actors and production staff. However, at the same time, to ensure profits, some decisions, for example on which actor to cast to play a trans woman, must be made in favor of the companies that have invested a larger percentage.[7]

---

7 Open access to documentation from these production committees in future would facilitate further research on their influence on LGBTQ+ representations.

While independent films occasionally operate with a production committee for its financial and distribution advantages, most of them are made outside the release schedule of mainstream commercial films. They have made enormous contributions to Japanese queer cinema. In what follows, I will discuss how independent films have portrayed the experiences of LGBTQ+ persons dealing with issues of family, youth and old age, disabilities, and authenticity with a degree of attention and understanding that the mainstream film industry during the LGBT boom has not shown.

Explorations and visions of the family outside traditional images have appeared in Japanese queer cinema since at least the 1980s. Hashiguchi's *Hush!*, for instance, attempts to queer the standards of the family unit by seeking the possibility of a gay couple and a cis heterosexual woman, all in their early 30s, having a baby together (Kawaguchi, 2003). Almost 20 years after *Hush!*, screenwriter Asada Atsushi explored this idea in a more realistic way with detailed attention to family law in *his* (2020), directed by Imaizumi Rikiya, which dramatizes a court dispute between a gay/bisexual man and his ex-wife over parental rights for their child. Asada is not accusing the parents of failing in their marriage but focuses on bringing the issue of discriminatory consciousness within the law against LGBTQ+ persons and single mothers into the open. Set in the relatively rural town of Shirakawa, *his* ends with a somewhat optimistic solution whereby the man and his same-sex partner, whose relationship eventually becomes open in the community, and the ex-wife, who remains in Tokyo, try to seek a better relationship so that they can raise their child together.

While most of these Japanese queer films center the view of adults who wish to explore the chance to have a family and raise children, Tsukikawa Shō's *Satō-ke no chōshoku, Suzuki-ke no yūshoku* (*Sato Family Breakfast, Suzuki Family Dinner*, or *Breakfast and Dinner*, 2013) focuses on the perspectives of Takumi and Sora, a teenage boy and girl who are raised by same-sex couples. Screened at the 2013 Taiwan International Queer Film Festival, this film depicts the process of Takumi and Sora dispelling ill feelings against their uncertainty not only about their relationship with their parents but also about their own (sexual) identity. Raised by lesbian parents, Takumi starts to wonder who his father may be and asks his uncle about it. His uncle turns out to be the sperm donor, and it is suggested that he may be gay. Learning about his birth causes Takumi to question his sexual orientation and distance himself from his parents, who had not shared anything about his father. His rebellion is dissolved after his sexual exploration with Sora, who has also had unsettling feelings about her relationship with her parents – a gay man and a bisexual man. The film offers an insight into one example of the tremendous efforts sexual minorities in Japan have been making to acquire a family and how children raised by same-sex parents balance what society thinks is normal and abnormal in terms of family and parenthood.

Mainstream teen films focus on "young heterosexuality" and often involves "a romance plot" (Driscoll, 2011, p. 2). LGBTQ+ youths, who are likely to be struggling with their own sexual orientation and/or gender identity, may be able to find their own experiences in independent films. For example, Kusano Shōgo's *Kanojo ga sukina mono wa* (*What She Likes*, 2021) centers on a gay teen protagonist, Jun, who is oscillating between his (sexual) desires and gay identity and his wish to lead a "normal" life like his heterosexual friends. It depicts his struggles of finding a gay role model successfully exploring a life outside a heteronormative life course. Nishihara Takashi's *Starting Over* (2014) and Nakagawa's *Kalanchoe* also trace the struggles of LGBTQ+ youths in being different in terms of their sexual orientation, and Oda Manabu's *Saimon & Tada Takashi* (*Simon & Tada Takashi*, 2017) warmly depicts a gay teenager's bittersweet first love. Although access to these independent films can be difficult at times depending on where one lives and one's access to VOD subscription services, it is crucial that independent filmmakers continue to produce stories about the everyday experiences of LGBTQ+ youths for younger audiences.

The family theme prevails in queer films because it is closely associated with the anxiety of planning a life course outside the heteronormative family system as one ages. The interest in issues of aging shown by Japanese queer films from the early to mid-2000s seems to have decreased during the LGBT boom, but the question of how and with whom LGBTQ+ persons would spend their later life continued to be pondered. For example, in Take Masaharu's queer road movie *EDEN* (2012), based on Funado Yoichi's short story "Natsu no uzu" (Whirls of Summer, 2001), the gay 42-year-old protagonist Miro finds his friend Noripī, who had been suffering from a heart problem after her sex reassignment surgery, dead in his apartment. Miro and his colleagues/friends mourn Noripī's passing. To their surprise, her body, which her family refused to receive, is returned to Eden, the gay bar where they all work. Spurred not only by anger and disappointment toward her family, but most importantly by their love and affection for Noripī, they take her body home to Chiba. While some may argue that *EDEN* does not subvert the ideals of family, what lies at the core of this film is the caring relationship among gay and trans persons who look after each other when they are older and lonely. *EDEN* offers a vision for a small community bonded by mutual support outside the heteronormative, patriarchal system.

While narrative films have helped to extend the imagination of aging outside the heteronormative family system, documentary films have offered a glimpse into more realistic details of aged LGBTQ+ persons. For instance, Takeda Tomokazu's (2018) *Watashi no ibasho: Shin sekai monogatari* (*Where I Belong*), follows the life of Nishimoto Noboru, an older male who identified as a woman with a feminine manner and was beloved as "Hiroko-mama" (Mama Hiroko). Hiroko-mama once ran an okonomiyaki eatery called Senryō near the Tsutenkaku Tower in Osaka, which she had started at the age of 40 after having worked in a bar for years. After being diagnosed with cancer, Hiroko-mama decides to visit her hometown of Kagoshima for the first time in 52 years, having left at around the age of 15 for Osaka during the mass employment (*shūdan shūshoku*) nationwide, when postwar Japan was in its early stages of rapid economic growth. Teenage labor forces were valued as golden eggs, especially in the manufacturing industry in which Hiroko-mama was hired as a child worker. The camera follows Hiroko-mama's journey back to Kagoshima, as she reflects on her adolescence and the years that have since passed. Although her life might have been filled with laughter and affection from her customers at Senryo, this rare documentary about an older queer person succeeds in capturing the loneliness that may be peculiar to LGBTQ+ persons who are not yet afforded equal rights and protection in Japan. At the time of filming in 2007, Hiroko-mama was 63 years old; she passed away in 2019 after years of fighting cancer.

While Takeda's *Where I Belong* and other documentary films such as Toda Hikaru's *Ai to hō* (*Of Love and Law*, 2017), Graham Kolbeins's *Queer Japan* (2019), and Asanuma Tomoya's *I Am Here: Watashitachi wa tomo ni ikiteiru* (*I Am Here: We Are Here Together*, 2020) tend to evoke a sense of authenticity through the visualization of actual LGBTQ+ persons, how could narrative films reflect the authentic experiences of LGBTQ+ persons? One of the ongoing discussions regarding representations of LGBTQ+ persons in popular culture is how to provide actors of LGBTQ+ and other socially marginalized communities equal opportunities for performance, including for auditions. While I do not neglect any possibility of non-LGBTQ+ actors succeeding in playing LGBTQ+ characters in inviting and thoughtful ways, it is crucial not to overlook the unique authenticity that only those with lived experience can convey. Some independent films produced outside the mainstream filmmaking system have proven the power of this authenticity. *Niji-iro no asa ga kuru made* (*Until Rainbow Dawn*, 2018), directed by Imai Mika, a deaf and nonbinary filmmaker, depicts the experiences of those positioned as a double minority. The central characters, Hana and Ayumi, who form a lesbian relationship, are played by deaf actors Nagai Eri and Kobayashi Haruka. This casting decision made it possible for Imai and her production team to narrate the film through sign language. The film's spatial setting is also essential. Set in a town in Gunma Prefecture, the film is concerned with how Hana and Ayumi develop their relationship within a closed deaf community that is not necessarily LGBTQ+-friendly. According to an interview with Imai, the deaf communities in each prefecture across Japan tend to be so small that rumors can quickly spread (Kubo, 2020a). Therefore,

Hana and Ayumi visit an LGBTQ+ event for deaf people held in Tokyo to avoid unnecessary conflicts in their hometown. Meeting with other deaf sexual and gender minorities at the event helps to shake off Hana's anxiety in seeking a life with Ayumi.

Another queer film that has proven the power of authenticity is *Katasode no sakana* (*The Fish With One Sleeve*, 2021) by Shōji Tsuyoshi. Based on a poem by Fuzuki Yumi, this film portrays Hikari, a trans woman who believes her self is not as perfect as she wishes it to be. However, after a reunion with her high school classmates, Hikari learns to move on with more confidence in her self. What is unique about *The Fish With One Sleeve* as an independent trans film is its transparent casting process that called trans women actors to an audition for the role of Hikari, for which a fashion model and actor Ishizuka Yū was chosen. This was the first casting process of its kind in Japan, countering the approach of two recent mainstream trans films, Ogigami Naoko's *Karera ga honki de amutoki wa* (*Close-knit*, 2017) and Uchida Eiji's *Middonaito suwan* (*Midnight Swan*, 2020), both of which cast a cis male actor to play the central role of a trans woman. Although *Midnight Swan* did cast a trans woman to play a supporting trans role, these films did not overcome the issues surrounding the labor opportunities for trans actors, such as "a deficiency in stories," "imbalance in casting," "a lack of evaluation standards," and "wage gap" (Suzuki, 2020, p. 28). As a new attempt to address these issues, *The Fish With One Sleeve* received critical acclaim both domestically and internationally.

What can independent filmmakers bring to the landscape of Japanese queer cinema? Independent films tend to subvert the stereotypes often seen in mainstream queer films and question the sugar-coated stories that tend to exclude minority groups within the LGBTQ+ community, causing the imbalance in representation. What independent and mainstream queer films in Japan seem to have in common, though, is that they rarely depict the lives of LGBTQ+ persons in the past, unlike an increase in queer films produced in other countries that try to excavate LGBTQ+ memories of actual people who were known as queer in films such as *Tove* (Zaida Bergroth, 2020) and *Benediction* (Terence Davies, 2021). The obsession with the present in contemporary Japanese queer films may imply the filmmakers' wish to document what is happening now rather than films such as *Carol* (Todd Haynes, 2015) and *Portrait of a Lady on Fire* (Céline Sciamma, 2019), which depict what could have happened in the past.

When film archivist Vito Russo published *The Celluloid Closet: Homosexuality in the Movies* in 1981, looking back on the past of Hollywood films was a critical approach to thinking about the present in which the mainstream film industry was not offering enough LGBTQ+ representations. It was the result of much-needed efforts to fight homophobia in the film industry. In the case of the Japanese film industry, at least since the 2010s, both mainstream and independent films have been producing queer films more than ever, focusing on issues that LGBTQ+ persons face today. While it is important to examine changes that the LGBT boom brought to the Japanese film industry's attitude toward LGBTQ+ representations, we must also not forget that the current proliferation of queer films in Japan could also be the result of filmmakers and film audiences fighting homophobia in the twentieth century. I argue that it is a task of Japanese film studies and film criticism to examine the past of Japanese cinema through a queer lens while also paying attention to the present. But how can it succeed?

3 Queering Japanese film studies/film criticism

Film history is never complete because there is always the presence of people whose voices and stories are silenced and overlooked in mainstream discourses. The history of Japanese queer cinema is not an exception. For instance, the recently published *Nihon eiga sakuhin daijiten (Comprehensive Encyclopedia of Japanese Cinema)* (Yamane, 2021) maps Japanese cinema history from 1908 to 2018, covering more than 1,300 directors and 19,500 works in total. Although it includes some filmmakers, such as Kinoshita Keisuke, Donald Richie, and the aforementioned Kazama, Hashiguchi, Hamano, and Ōki, who have made queer films, it does not provide sufficient details about the development of Japanese queer cinema. What can Japanese film studies or practices of film criticism do to fill this absence?

Japanese film studies have long dismissed the need to excavate the presence of LGBTQ+ persons and their contributions. While film critics Yodogawa Nagaharu, Mizuno Haruo, Osugi (Sugiura Takaaki), and Masuda Takamitsu are well known to be gay, their contributions have been entirely overlooked and understudied in the heterosexist discipline of Japanese film studies. In her review of *The Oxford Handbook of Japanese Cinema* (2014), film scholar Kanno Yūka (2017) pointed out how "Japanese cinema and Japanese film studies have been dominated by men" (p. 108), adding that scholarly discourses on cinema from perspectives of gender, feminism, and sexuality have been virtually overlooked in Japan (p. 109). Kanno's criticism of a lack of studies on women filmmakers in Japan and of attention to representations outside the heteronormative ideology also applies to the roundtable discussion on the future of Japanese cinema and Japanese film studies, featured in Kurosawa et al.'s (2011) *Nihon eiga wa doko made ikuka? (Where Will Japanese Cinema Reach?)*, the last installment of the eight-book series *Nihon eiga wa ikiteiru (Japanese Cinema Is Alive)*. Although the fourth installment of this series, *Sukurīn no naka no tasha (The Other Within the Screen)*, had included an article offering a possible way of writing about Japanese queer cinema (Shinjō,

2010), none of the seven scholars at the all-male roundtable presented on the need to bring in a queer lens to Japanese film studies. In addition, the *Research Guide to Japanese Film Studies* (Nornes & Gerow, 2009), which continues to be one of the most detailed, valuable resources for scholars and students engaged in studies of Japanese cinema, industry, market, and other aspects, also lacks insight into how to conduct research on Japanese queer cinema, even in its Japanese translation (see Nornes & Gerow, 2016). One possible interpretation of this absence is that the heteronormative and phallocentric discourses in Japanese film studies have hindered a "queer intrusion into film studies [that] not only brought new themes but also the effect of reconsidering the convention and norm within the discipline, including epistemology and methodology," seen primarily in the US (Kanno, 2021a, p. 4).

Academic conferences on film studies and media studies have functioned as platforms for sharing the possibilities of "queer intrusion" (Kanno, 2021a, p. 4) into Japanese film studies. For instance, the annual conferences of the Society for Cinema and Media Studies, which supports LGBTQ+ members through the Queer and Trans Caucus, often include presentations on queering Japanese films. They tend to focus on experimental and independent filmmaking in the 1960s, such as Matsumoto Toshio's *Bara no sōretsu* (*The Funeral Parade of Roses*, 1969), which is one of the few Japanese queer films mentioned in Schoonover and Galt's (2016) *Queer Cinema in the World.* It suggests that studies on Japanese queer cinema have not developed as much as those in other countries and are therefore still narrow and limited in scope. There have also been some presentations from a queer lens at academic conferences on film studies and media studies in Japan since the 2010s, but the total number remains low. The academic space is dominated by heteronormative tension that continues to make early-career scholars and graduate students hesitant to conduct research from a queer lens.

While Japanese film studies struggles to incorporate a queer lens, commercial practices of film criticism have contributed to introducing ways to understand the body of both domestic and imported queer films. Film critic Kodama Mizuki, for example, represents a new generation of such film critics who show empathy and intimacy toward queer films and queer filmmakers (see, e.g., Kodama 2021, 2022a, 2022b). Kodama's writing reminds contemporary readers of the work of film critic Ishihara Ikuko, who led queer film criticism in Japan from the 1980s until her premature death in the early 2000s (see, e.g., Ishihara 2000a, 2000b). The realm of commercial film criticism in Japan operates under the heteronormative system. However, Kodama's contributions in film magazines such as *Kinema junpō* and *Eiga geijutsu* and on various other platforms such as movie pamphlets and websites always offer delicate yet powerful analyses that help readers and viewers explore cinematic complexities. Kodama finds the joy, pain, celebration, and sorrow of queerness woven into films such as *Sakura* and *Haruhara san's Recorder* in a way that attests to her queer sensibility, which is rare in today's commercial film criticism in Japan.

There are at least two trends in the critiques of queer films in Japan today. First, some tend to fall into a binary trap of evaluating a work only between good and imperfect representations of LGBTQ+ characters. It is crucial to reexamine the necessity of certain stereotypes accumulated historically through media; filmmakers and the film industry must also unlearn the conventional ways of presenting LGBTQ+ characters on the screen. However, this trend may cause an inevitable conflict in discussing the representations of LGBTQ+ characters: it may fail to recognize the danger of creating a new list of conventions that may only praise one-sided portrayals of LGBTQ+ characters and end up excluding anything that does not fit into the narrow scope of "good" representations. Just as B. Ruby Rich coined the term "New Queer Cinema" in a 1992 essay to value a new wave of queer films that demonstrated a counter-approach to the body of apologetic gay films of the 1980s, film criticism in Japan also needs a revolutionary perspective that picks up voices silenced and overlooked by critics who only see the sugar-coated surface of visibility.

The other trend is universalizing the experiences of LGBTQ+ persons in comparison with those of non-LGBTQ+ persons, which may demonstrate similarities between the majority and minority to help viewers and society become more accepting of the presence and lives of LGBTQ+ persons in the flesh. For instance, in writing about the TV version of *What Did You Eat Yesterday?*, which centers on the everyday meals of a gay couple, Shiro and Kenji, journalist Jibu Renge (2021) argued that "this TV drama is simply universally important beyond sexual orientation" (p. 220). It may be true that this series makes the viewers realize that there is no difference in the manner and joy of having meals together with someone important and intimate.

However, universalizing may erase the complexities and differences that LGBTQ+ persons experience in the everyday lives. The producer of the film adaptation of *What Did You Eat Yesterday?*, Seto Mariko (2021), also falls for the trap of universalizing the experiences of the gay couple in their 50s by emphasizing that "everything they experience can be measured up as our own experiences" (p. 5). Yet is it really so? One of the central issues dealt with in its manga, television, and film adaptations is how the gay couple must maintain their health by eating healthy foods because the law does not acknowledge their relationship. Universalizing this work fails to understand how this series is about survival as members of the LGBTQ+ community who still face countless difficulties in contemporary Japan.

4 Conclusion

LGBTQ+ representations significantly matter to the lives of LGBTQ+ persons who are eager to find images upon which they may be able to reflect on their own lived experience. Since the 1990s gay boom, the Japanese film industry, both mainstream and independent, has offered various images and stories of LGBTQ+ persons, despite the imbalance in representation and accessibility that remains to be resolved. Japanese film studies and film criticism have now entered a new phase in which a new generation of film scholars and critics are not only actively revisiting works from the past from a queer lens but also finding meaning and value in contemporary works that may contribute to bringing positive changes to the lives of LGBTQ+ persons.

These collective efforts from multilayered approaches may fill the absence of inclusive research and writing on the development of Japanese queer cinema and queer visual cultures, including film festivals and screenings of imported queer films at arthouse theaters. However, such collective efforts appear to be difficult given the current distance between people inside and outside the academic system, which is also not free from the issue of inequality in labor and wage. Although it should be not required, writing about queer cinema sometimes forces those involved to disclose their gender identity and/or sexual orientation. Such expectations of revelation, or coming out, will continue to be a burden for those who write about queer cinema.

How will Japanese film studies and film criticism from a queer lens develop in response to the growing body of Japanese queer films and imported queer films? Even though it seems that the visualization of LGBTQ+ characters has advanced since the 2010s, the imbalance in representation and accessibility continues to linger, blurring the issue of who has the power to decide whose stories are to be told. Moreover, during the LGBT boom, Japanese queer films targeting mainstream audiences have tended to oversimplify the peculiarities of LGBTQ+ experiences, which may erase the complexities of queer politics. Simplicity is an effective strategy often employed in documentary filmmaking to reach out to a broader audience. However, as the protagonist Jun from *What She Likes* says – "I do not want to make the world simple by ignoring the complexities" – Japanese film studies and film criticism, as well as filmmakers and the film industry, must not look away from a queer perspective. In the process of looking back on history, standing still to examine the present, and looking forward to seeing the future of Japanese queer cinema, we must not miss the moments of erasure but rather navigate the friction of the complexities.

References

Driscoll, C. (2011). *Teen film: A critical introduction*. Berg.

Fathallah, J. (2015). Moriarty's ghosts: Or the queer disruption of the BBC's *Sherlock*. *Television & New Media*, *16*(5), 490–500. https://doi.org/10.1177/1527476414543528.

Fujimoto, Y. (2019). "Ossanzu rabu" to iu bunkiten [*Ossan's Love* as a turning point]. In J. Welker (Ed.), *BL ga hiraku tobira: Henyō suru Ajia no sekushuariti to jendā* [BL opening doors: Sexuality and gender transfigured in Asia] (pp. 141–150). Seidosha.

Gregg, R., & Villarejo, A. (2021). Introduction. In R. Gregg & A. Villarejo (Eds.), *The Oxford handbook of queer cinema* (pp. xi–xv). Oxford University Press.

Grossman, A. (Ed.). (2000). *Queer Asian cinema: Shadows in the shade*. Harrington Park Press.

Hall, J. M. (2000). Japan's progressive sex: Male homosexuality, national competition, and the cinema. In A. Grossman (Ed.), *Queer Asian cinema: Shadows in the shade* (pp. 31–82). Harrington Park Press.

Hirano, H. (1994). *Anchi heterosekushizumu* [Anti-heterosexism]. Pandora.

Horvat, A. (2021). *Screening queer memory: LGBTQ pasts in contemporary film and television*. Bloomsbury.

Ishida, H. (2019). *Hajimete manabu LGBT: Kiso kara torendo made* [First lessons about LGBT: From basics to trends]. Natsumesha.

Ishihara, I. (1996). *Za toransu sekushuaru mūbīzu: Sumire iro no eigasai* [The trans sexual movies]. Film Art sha.

Ishihara, I. (2000a). *Īsuto Ajia eiga no bi* [The beauty of East Asian cinema]. Hōga Shoten.

Ishihara, I. (2000b). *Eiga o tōshite ikoku e* [To foreign countries through cinema]. Hōga Shoten.

Izumo, M. (2002). *Chanbara quīn* [Chambara queen]. Pandora.

Izumo, M. (Ed.) (2005). *Niji no kanata ni: Rezubian, gei, kuia eiga o yomu* [Over the rainbow: Reading lesbian, gay, and queer films]. Pandora.

Jibu, R. (2021). *Jendā de miru hitto dorama: Kankoku, Amerika, Ōshū, Nihon* [Analyzing successful TV drama series through gender: South Korea, US, Europe, and Japan]. Kōbunsha.

Jo, G. [Xú, Y.]. (2021). Bosei gensō to rezubian kansei: "Banka" to "Onna de arukoto" ni okeru Kuga Yoshiko [Maternal fantasy and lesbian sensibility: Yoshiko Kuga in Banka and Onna de arukoto]. *Eiga kenkyū*, *15*, 4–26.

Kanno, Y. (2015). Kuia LGBT eigasai shiron [Essay on the queer LGBT film festival]. *Gendai shisō*, *43*(16), 202–209.

Kanno, Y. (2017). Review of the book *The Oxford handbook of Japanese cinema*, by Daisuke Miyao, ed. *Eizōgaku*, *97*, 106–110.

Kanno, Y. (2020). Queer resonance: The stardom of Miwa Akihiro. In H. Fujiki & A. Phillips (Eds.), *The Japanese cinema book* (pp. 179–191). Bloomsbury.

Kanno, Y. (2021a). Kuia to shinema o meguru shikō to jissen [Thinking and practice on queerness and cinema]. In Y. Kanno (Ed.), *Kuia shinema stadīzu* [Queer cinema studies] (pp. 1–12). Kōyō Shobō.

Kanno, Y. (2021b). When Marnie was there: Female friendship film and the genealogy of queer girls' culture. In J. Bernardi & S. T. Ogawa (Eds.), *Routledge handbook of Japanese cinema* (pp. 68–80). Routledge.

Katō, K. (2021). A man with whom men fall in love: Homosociality and effeminophobia in the Abashiri bangaichi series. *Japanese Studies*, *41*(1), 59–71. https://doi.org/10.1080/10371397.2020.1851178.

Kawaguchi, K. (2003). *Kuia studīzu* [Queer studies]. Iwanami Shoten.

Kikuchi, N., Horie, Y., & Iino, Y. (2019). Joshō: Kuia sutadīzu to wa nanika [Preface: What is queer studies?]. In N. Kikuchi, Y. Horie, & Y. Iino (Eds.), *Kuia sutadīzu o hiraku: Aidentiti, komyuniti, supēsu* [Exploring queer studies: Identity, community, space] (pp.1–14). Kōyō Shobō.

Kodama, M. (2021). Dakishime au no ni, dareka no shōnin wa iranai [We don't need approval to love each other]. In *Kanojo ga sukina mono wa* [What she likes] [pamphlet] (pp. 25–26).

Kodama, M. (2022a). Kono uta wa watashi o kizu tsuke nai [This song will not hurt me]. In *Haruhara-san no uta* [Haruhara-san's recorder] [pamphlet] (pp. 40–43).

Kodama, M. (2022b). Yukidoke ni oitsukarenai hayasa de [Before the snow melts]. In *Yunhi e* [Yunhui-ege/Moonlit winter] [pamphlet] (pp. 25–26).

Kubo, Y. (2020a, December). *Imai Mika kantoku ni eiga seisaku no katei o kiku: Dare no tame ni tsukuru no ka – "Niji-iro no asa ga kuru made" jōeikai* [Interview with director Imai Mika at the screening of *Until rainbow dawn*]. Waseda University Tsubouchi Memorial Theatre Museum event report. http://www.waseda.jp/enpaku/ex/11629.

Kubo, Y. (2020b, August). Nihon eiga ni okeru dansei dōseiai hyōshō no kako genzai mirai [The past, present, and future of gay male representations in Japanese cinema]. *Kinema junpō, 1846*, 21–24.

Kubo, Y. (2020c). Tenrankai shushi [The purpose of the exhibition]. In Y. Kubo (Ed.), *Inside/out: LGBTQ + to eizō bunka* [Inside/out: LGBTQ+ representations in film and television] (pp. 6–7). Tsubouchi Memorial Theatre Museum.

Kurosawa, K., Yomota, I., Yoshimi, S., & Lee, B. (Eds.). (2010). *Sukurīn no naka no tasha* [The Other within the screen]. Iwanami Shoten.

Kurosawa, K., Yomota, I., Yoshimi, S., & Lee, B. (Eds.) (2011). *Nihon eiga wa doko made ikuka* [Where will Japanese cinema reach?]. Iwanami Shoten.

Mizoguchi, A. (2005). "Suna no onna" saidoku: Rezubian rīdingu no aratana kanōsei [Rereading *The woman in the dunes*: A new lesbian reading]. In N. Nisihjima (Ed.), *Eizō hyōgen no orutanatibu: 1960 nendai no itsudatsu to sōzō* [Alternatives of cinematic expressions: Deviation and creation in the 1960s] (pp. 246–274). Shinwasha.

Nornes, M., & Gerow, A. (2009). *Research guide to Japanese film studies*. University of Michigan Press. https://doi.org/10.3998/mpub.9340103.

Nornes, M., & Gerow, A. (2016). *Nihon eiga kenkyū e no gaidobukku* [Research guide to Japanese film studies] (M. Dougase, Trans.). Yumani Shobō. (Original work published 2009)

Ogura, Y. (2009). Gei no eijingu to iu fīrudo no toikake: Ikikata o jikken shiau kyōdōsei e [Questioning gay aging in the field: Toward exploring life choices as a community]. In O. Seki & T. Shida (Eds.), *Chōhatsu suru sekushuariti* [Provoking sexuality] (pp. 168–191). Shinseisha.

Rich, B. R. (1992). The new queer cinema. *Sight & Sound, 2*(5), 30–34.

Russo, V. (1981). *The celluloid closet: Homosexuality in the movies*. Harper & Row.

Schoonover, K., & Galt, R. (2016). *Queer cinema in the world*. Duke University Press.

Seto, M. (2021). Production note. In *Kinō nani tabeta?* [What did you eat yesterday?] [pamphlet] (pp. 5–6).

Shinjō, I. (2010). Nihon kuia eigaron josetsu: Ōshima Nagisa "Senjō no merī kurisumasu" o kōgen to shite [An introduction to Japanese queer cinema: An analysis of Nagisa Oshima's *Merry Christmas Mr. Lawrence*]. In K. Kurosawa, I. Yomota, S. Yoshimi, & B. Lee (Eds.), *Sukurīn no naka no tasha* [The Other within the screen] (pp. 113–139). Iwanami Shoten.

Sullivan, N., & Middleton, C. (2019). *Queering the museum*. Routledge.

Suzuki, M. (2020, September). "Toransu yaku wa toransu no haiyū ni" to iu shuchō ō dō kangaeruka? [Examining the claim: "Trans roles should be offered to trans actors"]. *Kinema junpō, 1849*, 28–29.

Vincent, K., Kazama, T., & Kawaguchi, K. (1997). *Gei sutadīzu* [Gay studies]. Seidosha.

Yamane, S. (Ed.). (2021). *Nihon eiga sakuhin daijiten* [Comprehensive encyclopedia of Japanese cinema]. Sanseidō.

Contributors

Genya Fukunaga is an associate professor in the Diversity & Inclusion Department at the College of Arts and Sciences, University of Tokyo. He also teaches feminism and queer studies at several other universities in Japan. He obtained his PhD from the University of Tokyo in 2022, with his thesis titled *Sexual Politics in Post–Cold War East Asia: From the Perspective of Taiwan and Korea*. His areas of expertise include gender and sexuality studies, sociology, and area studies (East Asia), and his primary research interests lie in the intersection of (post-)colonialism, the Cold War regime, and gender/sexual politics in East Asia.

Guo Lifu is a researcher and PhD candidate in area studies at the University of Tokyo, as well as a part-time lecturer at several universities in Japan. He holds a master's degree in global studies from the University of Tokyo, where his research focused on feminism and queer studies, post-colonial studies, and area studies. His primary research interests lie in exploring Chinese local queer politics and theory. His groundbreaking research on the determinative effect of an imagined Western ideological and political threat on sexual politics in modern China has been published in several prominent journals.

Saori Kamano received her PhD in sociology at Stanford University and is a senior researcher at the National Institute of Population and Social Security Research, Japan. Her research interests are in families, sexualities, and gender. She has done research on same-sex couples, such as housework division and the experiences of "lesbian" couples in the Japanese context. Taking a queer demography approach, her recent academic endeavors include exploring various ways to capture respondents' sexual orientation, gender identity, and partnership/family statuses in population-based surveys and to examine how they are related to people's well-being, life chances, ideas, and attitudes.

Kazuyoshi Kawasaka is principal investigator of the Deutsche Forschungsgemeinschaft (DFG)-funded project "Sexual Diversity and Human Rights in 21st Century Japan: LGBTQ+ Activisms and Resistance from a Transnational Perspective" at the Institute for Modern Japanese studies at Heinrich Heine University Düsseldorf, Germany. He received his DPhil in Gender Studies (Humanities) at the University of Sussex in 2016. His research focuses on nationalism and queer politics in Japan, the globalisation of LGBTQ+ politics, and transnational anti-gender/LGBTQ+ movements.

Diana Khor received her MA and PhD in Sociology from Stanford University, and BSocSc and MPhil in Sociology at the University of Hong Kong. Her early research focused on gender, including feminist grassroots activism in Japan, the construction of knowledge in women's/gender studies, and gender research in sociology. In recent years, she has conducted research in the field of sexuality and is currently the principal investigator of a project on same-sex partnerships and kin relations in Hong Kong and Japan. Through her research and writing, she is committed to engaging with, while at the same time decentering, the universalized knowledge of gender and sexuality produced in the context of "the West," and developing theories and concepts based on Asian experiences.

Yutaka Kubo is associate professor of film studies at Kanazawa University. He received his PhD from Kyoto University in 2017. His research focuses on reworking the histories of Japanese cinema from a queer perspective. He is the author of *Yūyakegumo no kanata ni: Kinoshita Keisuke to kuia na* *kansei* (*Over the Sunset: Kinoshita Keisuke and Queer Sensibility*, 2022) and the curator of the exhibition *Inside/Out: LGBTQ+ Representation in Film and Television* (2019) for the Tsubouchi Memorial Theatre Museum at Waseda University. He is currently working on the project "Kuia eiga ni miru shokushū-kan: Beikoku no LGBT eigasai puroguramu ni kansuru kenkyū" (Foodways in Queer Cinema: LGBT Film Festival Programs in Focus) for which he receives funding from the Japan Society for the Promotion of Science (JSPS) Kakenhi grant.

Hiroyuki Taniguchi is professor of law at Aoyama Gakuin University. His work focuses on international human rights laws on LGBTQ issues and the comparative study of laws and policies on same-sex relationships, legal gender alteration, and discrimination based on sexual orientation, gender identity and expression, and sex characteristics. He is also a member of the Science Council of Japan. He earned his PhD from Chūō University in 2005. His latest book *Seiteki mainoriti to kokusai jinken hō: Yōroppa jinken jōyaku kara kangaeru* (*Sexual and Gender Minorities and International Human Rights Law: Jurisprudence of the European Convention on Human Rights*, 2022), was awarded the Ikuo Onaka Award, one of Japan's most prestigious academic awards for family law.

Stefan Würrer is assistant professor in the Faculty of Humanities at Musashi University, Tokyo, and research fellow at the Center for Gender Studies at International Christian University. He studied Japanese studies, comparative literature, interdisciplinary cultural studies, queer studies and Japanese literature at the University of Vienna, Hōsei University, and the University of Tokyo. His research focuses on feminist and queer readings of modern and contemporary Japanese literature. Recent publications include the chapter "Onna dōshi no kizuna o mirai ni tsunagu, ushiromuki no nosutarujikku na manazashi: Miyagi Futoshi 'Ikuyo' ni okeru kuia yūtopianizumu" (A Nostalgic Gaze Backward that Connects Two Women's Bond to the Future: Queer Utopianism in Miyagi Futoshi's "Ikuyo") in *Miyagi Futoshi: Monogatari o tsumugu* (*Miyagi Futoshi: Weaving Stories*, 2023) and "A Short History of Ambivalence Toward the Feminist Utopia in Japanese Science Fiction," published in *Science Fiction Studies* in 2022.

Azusa Yamashita is assistant professor at the Office for the Promotion of Gender Equality, Hirosaki University, Japan. She received her MA in human rights from Curtin University, Australia, and has worked with sexual and gender minority communities since 2005. In 2011 she founded the Iwate Rainbow Network, a grassroots LGBTIQ+ group in Iwate Prefecture, Japan, and served on the board of the International Lesbian, Gay, Bisexual, Trans and Intersex Association (ILGA) from 2012 to 2014. Her field of expertise is international human rights law with a focus on sexual orientation, gender identity/expression and sex characteristics. She received the Grants-in-Aid for Scientific Research from the Japan Society for the Promotion of Science (2018–2022, 2023–2027) for her research projects on sexual and gender minorities during disasters.

Index

www.ingramcontent.com/pod-product-compliance
Lightning Source LLC
Chambersburg PA
CBHW022315280326
41932CB00010B/1111